Table of Contents

SECTION

I

SECTION

II

SECTION

III

THE MULTIDIMENSIONAL MODEL OF
PREJUDICE PREVENTION AND REDUCTION   *145*

SECTION

IV

CASE EXAMPLES OF THERAPY FOR PREJUDICE   *175*

COUNSELING FOR PREJUDICE PREVENTION AND REDUCTION

10 9 8 7 6 5 4 3 2 1

American Counseling Association
5999 Stevenson Avenue
Alexandria, VA 22304

Director of Acquisitions
Carolyn Baker

Director of Publishing Systems
Michael Comlish

Copyeditor
Wendy Lieberman

Library of Congress Cataloging-in-Publication Data
Sandhu, Daya Singh, 1943–
    Counseling for prejudice prevention and reduction / by Daya Singh
Sandhu, Cheryl Blalock Aspy.
        p.   cm.
    Includes bibliographical references (p.   ) and index.
    ISBN 1-55620-164-8 (alk. paper)
        1. Prejudices—United States.   2. Racism—United States—
Psychological aspects.   3. Ethnic relations—Psychological aspects.
4. United States—Race relations—Psychological aspects.   5. United
States—Ethnic relations—Psychological aspects.   6. Cross-cultural
counseling—United States.   I. Aspy, Cheryl B.   II. Title.
BF575.P9S34   1997
303.3'85—DC21   96-49703
                                                                                    CIP

COUNSELING FOR PREJUDICE PREVENTION AND REDUCTION

Daya Singh Sandhu
Cheryl Blalock Aspy

ACA
AMERICAN
COUNSELING
ASSOCIATION

SECTION

V

Acknowledgments

Every project carries within it the potential to become either a labor of love or a possessing demon. The assistance of the following people made this project (almost always) a labor of love. We would like to extend our deepest appreciation to these individuals for their contributions in helping to complete this project:

- To LaVonne Wolf, for her typing and editing of the manuscript;
- To Jay Garrett, graduate assistant and doctoral student, for his help in completing the bibliography;
- To Craig Ziegler, doctoral student, for his help with statistical analysis in the development of scales included in this book;
- To Dr. Eugene Russell, for his suggestions for improving the manuscript;

- To our colleagues in our respective departments for their support and encouragement;
- To our families for their love, patience, and encouragement;
- To our editor, Carolyn Baker, for her insightful contribution to the improvement of this manuscript;
- To Dr. Courtland Lee, for his willingness to write the Foreword for this edition;
- To Dr. Paul Pedersen, for his comprehensive and integrative Prologue;
- To our reviewers, Dr. Frederick D. Harper at Howard University and Dr. Roger Herring, at the University of Arkansas–Little Rock, whose comments and suggestions significantly improved this work; and
- A special thanks to Dr. David Aspy, without whose creative contribution this project could not have become a reality.

We would like to dedicate this book to our spouses,
Ushi and David,
for their encouragement and patience.

About the Authors

Daya Singh Sandhu, Ed.D., NCC, NCCC, NCSC, is an associate professor and chairperson in the Department of Educational and Counseling Psychology at the University of Louisville. He received his B.A., B.T., and M.A. (English) degrees from Punjab University, India. After moving to the United States in 1969, he received his M.Ed. from Delta State University, Specialist in English degree from the University of Mississippi, and Doctor of Counselor Education from Mississippi State University. He has more than 30 years experience in education, both at the secondary and the university levels. He taught English, mathematics, physics, and chemistry in India. In the United States he taught English for 11 years in public schools and also served as a high school guidance counselor and agency testing coordinator for 7 years with the Choctaw Agency, Bureau of Indian Affairs Schools, in Philadelphia, Mississippi. Since 1989, he has taught graduate courses in counselor education and counseling psychology at Nicholls State University and the University of Louisville.

Dr. Sandhu has a special interest in school counseling, multicultural counseling, neurolinguistic programming, and the role of spirituality in counseling and psychotherapy. Previously he has published two books, *Numerical Problems in Physics* and *A Practical Guide to Classroom Observations: A Multidimensional Approach*. He has also published more than 50 articles in state, national, and international journals. His first book was in Punjabi poetry, *Satranghi Pingh*. Dr. Sandhu is also an experienced presenter and professional workshops trainer. He has made more than 100 presentations at the international, state, and local levels. His presentations have focused on a wide variety of subjects that can be broadly classified under school counseling and multicultural counseling.

Dr. Sandhu has served on various committees of the American Counseling Association, such as the Human Rights Committee, the Interprofessional and International Collaboration Committee, and the AMCD Award Committee. Currently, he is a member of the Executive Board of the Council for the Accreditation of Counseling and Related Educational Programs (CACREP). He has also served as a member of several editorial boards including *The Journal of Multicultural Counseling and Development, Journal of Humanistic Education and Development, The School Counselor, Journal of Accelerative Learning and Teaching,* and *The Journal of Counseling & Development*.

Cheryl Blalock Aspy, Ph.D., M.Ed., B.S., received B.S. and M.Ed. degrees from Texas Woman's University and a Ph.D. in Measurement, Statistics, and Evaluation from the University of Maryland. Since 1981 she has focused her energies on researching the human technologies that will contribute to a better society.

During the 1980s, she and her husband David Aspy were co-directors of the Carkhuff Institute of Human Technology, where they studied and encouraged the development of effective teaching and counseling models to increase thinking and productivity in classrooms, counseling settings, and organizations.

In 1987, she became the research director at the Department of Family and Community Medicine at the University of Louisville, where she authored proposals that were awarded over $1,000,000 in funding. Her research focus was the exploration of the components of an effective doctor-patient relationship. She also participated in the development of a fellowship for physicians in Humanism in Medicine, the only one of its kind in the United States.

Dr. Aspy is the author or coauthor of three books on education, nearly 30 articles, and numerous book chapters and monographs. She has presented over 50 national and international workshops and seminars on a variety of skill development topics.

Currently, Dr. Aspy is an associate professor of research in the Department of Family and Preventive Medicine at the University of Oklahoma, where she teaches Behavioral Medicine to residents training to become family physicians. Her current research focuses on the effects of the doctor-patient relationship on patient outcomes, especially in managed care environments.

Preface

This book is about prejudice. Since that term is ambiguous, the authors want to make it clear that they selected the definition posed by Gordon Allport (1954), who said that prejudice is "thinking ill of others without sufficient warrant" (p. 7). This position was supported by Kleg (1993), who defined prejudice as "a readiness to act stemming from a negative feeling, often predicated upon a fixed over-generalization or totally false belief and directed toward a group or individual members of that group" (p. 114). This meaning was chosen because it describes the type of prejudice that is most commonly believed to be harmful to human beings. Kleg (1993) further stated, "Prejudice generally has negative connotations in the area of race and ethnic relations" (p. 114). We address prejudice as an intergroup phenomenon and leave for others the concept of intragroup prejudice.

The purpose of this book is to help counselors reduce prejudice in their clients and to address client problems that are related to prejudice. Unfortunately, prejudice is one of those conditions that probably will never be totally eradicated. It can only be reduced and hopefully restrained. There is a rich body of literature that deals with rehabilitation from the effects of prejudice, but there is a relative paucity of writing that focuses on reduction of prejudice (Ponterotto & Pedersen, 1993). Thus, this text is addressed primarily to that task.

Pettigrew and associates (Pettigrew et al., Fredrickson, Knobel, Glaser, & Veda, 1982) described prejudice and discrimination against specific groups as "major strands in the history of the American people" (p. 88). They also identified another strand in American history as the use of law to combat prejudice and its effects. These authors observed, "The history of this effort is closely entwined with the history of the largest racially defined minority group in the United States: Blacks" (Pettigrew et al., 1982, p. 88). However, they qualified the statement by saying, "Because the attack on discrimination emphasized the equality of races, laws designed to keep down Chinese and Japanese fell before it along with those designed to keep down Blacks" (Pettigrew et al., 1982, p. 90).

Pettigrew et al. (1982) described five major periods in the effort to reduce prejudice: pre-Civil War, Civil War and reconstruction, from the end of reconstruction to the New Deal, the new deal and World War II, and the 1970s and beyond discrimination. They provided a vivid description of the events in the late 1960s:

> In the middle and late 1960s, as Blacks rioted in cities in the United States, as Mexican Americans and Puerto Ricans became politically active, as American Indians for the first time entered the arenas of national politics, and as White ethnic groups also became more assertive—both in reaction to Black political action, and to foster aims of their own, such as establishing the legitimacy of the maintenance of their cultures and languages—the American polity seemed to be engaged in a massive effort finally to put problems of racial and ethnic discrimination behind it. (Pettigrew et al., 1982, p. 119)

A book on this topic is timely. The O. J. Simpson double murder trial has concluded, and the nation stands on the threshold of the Oklahoma City bombing trial. Both of these travails are widely viewed as prejudice-based events. Certainly, they have stirred powerful emotions that tend to divide citizen from citizen and exacerbate biases that many hoped had been extinguished. Those dormant attitudes and beliefs have been restored, and they threaten the very foundations of the always-tenuous civilization that is the best hope of humankind to attain its noblest qualities.

One week after the O. J. Simpson trial, *Newsweek* (Whitaker, 1995) gave the following response to the situation:

> The reaction to the Simpson verdict did indeed show that Blacks and Whites don't understand each other; they argued, and proved that Martin Luther King's vision of a harmonious, colorblind society is nowhere in sight. So rather than spend so much energy and money trying to promote integration, perhaps both Blacks and Whites should focus on strengthening imperiled institutions in the Black community. For example, The Reverend Rivers argues that instead of spending $40 million a year on busing, Boston should pour that money into predominantly Black, inner-city schools. "Maybe it's time that the traditional liberal assumptions about race be completely rethought," he says. "What does equality mean?" (p. 23)

These high-profile incidents have reinforced the notion that prejudice is still a virile pathogen (Delaney, 1980; Skillings & Dobbins, 1991; Welsing, 1970) that perpetually resides within individuals and society. Periodically, it emerges in the form of crises that force us to expend vast resources to arrest it. When these lessons fade we relax our efforts, and the pathology returns to create another crisis. It would be wiser to maintain a steady course of reduction. Thus, counselors should be proactive in their prejudice-reducing efforts.

Section I of this book is devoted to a discussion of prejudice. Theories of the nature of prejudice are presented in Chapter 1. The final chapter of this section (Chapter 2) is devoted to a review of the status of prejudice in the United States today. The facts presented in this chapter are somewhat discouraging, considering our previous efforts to reduce prejudice. But it is important to know the size of the problem we face so that we can amass the resources we will need to make a difference for the future.

Section II addresses counseling styles and prejudice. A fundamental concept of psychology is that human perception is idiosyncratic. People choose what they see. Perhaps it is more accurate to say that people see what they can afford to see. Thus, it is critical to understand the lens through which individuals make their observations. Specifically, when discussing counselors' views of prejudice, it is important to clarify their theoretical orientations, because prejudice differs slightly from each position.

Counselors have many theoretical orientations. Corey (1991) identified three categories under which he felt most of the contemporary systems fall but listed and described nine approaches. Patterson (1986) listed 15 theoretical orientations in his text. Other writers have described hundreds of models. Therefore, it is both fitting and accurate to assert that the field of counseling includes considerable theoretical diversity.

Because there are many counseling points of view from which to perceive prejudice, the authors have chosen to discuss it from nine counseling orientations that seem to adequately reflect the diversity in the field. The selections were made after reviewing the literature and identifying counseling modes that presented effective procedures for reducing prejudice. These models include: (a) Adlerian, (b) psychoanalytic, (c) existential, (d) gestalt, (e) human resource development, (f) invitational, (g) person centered, (h) behavioral, and (i) trait and factor. We introduce these models with a section on the theoretical formulations of Abraham Maslow as a paradigm for discussing prejudice formation.

Each discussion presents the definition, assumptions, assessment procedures, goals, and therapy procedures for counseling. Additionally, each chapter dealing with a specific orientation closes with a case study that illustrates how a counselor using that approach might work with a client presenting prejudice-related problems. We also provide examples of representative therapeutic dialogues for each model.

Section III of this text introduces a new model of prejudice prevention and reduction: the Multidimensional Model of Prejudice Prevention and Reduction. This model is delineated, and counseling applications are presented. It is representative of multimodal therapy that depends in large part on the pragmatic application of counseling theory and techniques.

Section IV contains two case illustrations of prejudice related to race and sexual orientation bias. Three counseling techniques are illustrated and applied to these two cases. Each technique is representative of one of the three main counseling categories: psychodynamic, cognitive/behavioral, and experiential/relationship. The three models selected to illustrate the categories are Adlerian, Rational Emotive, and Human Resource Development, respectively.

Section V contains 15 instruments for measuring various forms of prejudice. Each instrument is presented in its entirety along with scoring instructions and reliability and validity data, when available.

References for all cited material are provided in alphabetical order. They are followed by an appendix containing an annotated bibliography and a glossary.

This book is about prejudice, which is herein defined as "thinking ill of others without sufficient warrant." Both objective and subjective data indicate that the harmful effects of prejudice ought to be opposed and that reduction is a preferred mode for counselors' contribution to that effort. This position does not denigrate rehabilitation but rather complements it as armamentarium in a noble war.

Reduction of prejudice must address both its personal and social origins, and a successful effort entails an acknowledgment of the diversity within counseling. Thus, we have discussed the topic from nine different points of view to illustrate the multiplicity of approaches offered by counseling professionals. The extensive variety of counseling procedures is appropriate in light of the range of situations presented by clients.

Preventive counseling services are appropriate for both potential victims as well as perpetrators of prejudice. They are intended to redirect and/or eliminate the cycle of prejudice, which originates in unresolved personality conflicts and/or lessons learned from society that later are activated by situations that render them reasonable.

The effort to prevent prejudice is justified by the prevalence of its deleterious effects. It reduces both possible alternatives and deserved opportunities for victims in addition to causing immeasurable pain. In this perspective, an all-out program for reduction is more than reasonable.

The cultural prominence of prejudice is described by Geoseffi (1993) in the following statement:

> Prejudice in all its manifestations—xenophobia, ethnocentrism, sexism, androcentrism, genocidal politics and militarism, environmental and social racism, cruel colonization and cultural destruction, crimes of cultural exclusiveness and expansionism, imperialism, ethnic wars and hatred of each other—is still the major focus of our literature, our history-making events, and our nightly news. (p. xlix)

In this light, the reduction of prejudice should rightfully be elevated to the highest priority on the national agenda, and adequate resources should be allocated to that effort. It is both a moral and a practical imperative. This text is dedicated to that purpose.

DAYA SINGH SANDHU
CHERYL BLALOCK ASPY
1997

Foreword

This book has come along at a critical time in the history of the United States. Within the last several years, we have witnessed a disturbing backlash to gains in civil rights and progress in intergroup communication. This is symptomatic of a growing climate of intolerance that seems to pervade the 1990s. An atmosphere has developed throughout the country in which differences are not accepted, but rather feared. Such fear is perpetuated by ignorance about ethnic, gender, class, religious, sexual orientation, and other cultural differences. This ignorance has lead to increasing misinformation, prejudicial assumptions, and gross generalizations that have resulted in the breakdown of communication across cultural boundaries.

Furthermore, in reflecting on this climate of intolerance, it seems that the political process often mirrors and reinforces this trend. A number of politicians at the local, state, and national level have exploited this climate and promoted an ideology based on fear and ignorance. Their goal seems to be garnering votes based on emotions rather than logic. Political success, therefore, has often been based upon fostering societal reaction to fear and prejudice.

Taking all of this into consideration, three prominent questions emerge. First, is this the way that American society wants to start the 21st century? Second, where does the counseling profession fit into this discussion? Third, what can individual professional counselors do to address this pervasive climate?

With this landmark book, Sandhu and Aspy provide important answers to these questions. This book will assist counselors in being a part of the solution in addressing the climate of intolerance in the United States. The purpose of the book is to help counselors reduce prejudice. In this respect it is a significant work. The authors provide counselors with a conceptual framwork for practice that challenges intolerance from a developmental/preventive perspective. Regardless of one's theoretical orientation, the book provides both practical direction as well as a degree of inspiration for reducing prejudice through counseling interventions.

This is not yet another book on multicultural counseling theory and practice. Rather, it focuses on how the counseling profession can help to make multiculturalism and diversity work as positive societal concepts. As such, the authors take all counseling theory and practice into the increasingly important realm of social activism. As counselors we must not only focus on intrapsychic issues, but on the pressing social issues that impact the lives of our clients as well. This book will force the reader to consider whether his or her theoretical foundation, skills repertoire, and overall professional orientation are adequate for addressing the serious challenges of intolerance at both the individual and societal levels. I hope this book will lay the groundwork for a new type of counseling professional, one who is committed to both individual and societal change.

COURTLAND C. LEE
University of Virginia

Prologue

This book is directed toward the prevention or at least reduction of prejudice through counseling. Not only are the authors ambitious; they are optimistic. They draw attention to the "upside" of cultural differences, which enhance our identities and teach us the meanings of life. They are unwilling to let counseling be overtaken by pessimists who hide their pessimism behind their own "objective detachment." For a long time now pessimism has been the fashion, particularly among those who perceive cultural differences as inconvenient or unimportant. Many good reasons for being pessimistic have existed, considering the many examples of hurtful prejudice in our sociopolitical context. Much less empirical and rational evidence supports optimism, but still that optimism exists.

The authors are systematic in building their theoretical foundation, suggesting alternatives to prejudice and then providing measures for evaluation.

In their first two chapters, the authors do not trivialize the powerful negative influence of prejudice in society generally and in counseling particularly. Most of the literature in this field attempts to describe prejudice. Precious little of the literature is focused on preventing or reducing it.

The next 10 chapters discuss prejudice in the context of each major psychological theory, demonstrating the variety of ways in which prejudice influences the counseling process. Each of the nine major theories are discussed according to Abraham Maslow's view of prejudice. The next 2 chapters present a Multidimensional Model of Prejudice Prevention and Reduction, based on the multimodal therapy model, which integrates and adapts to each theory and cultural context. They go beyond criticism by offering an alternative to continued or enhanced prejudice in counseling. The next 4 chapters present and discuss case illustrations of prejudice by race and gender from the Adlerian, rational emotive, and human resource development theoretical perspectives. The last section of the book presents 15 measures of prejudice for counselors to measure the extent of prejudice in a great variety of counseling settings.

The heart of this book is in the Multidimensional Model of Prejudice Prevention and Reduction, in Chapter 13. It shares many advantages of multimodal therapy in its purposive eclecticism, and emphasis on proactive rather than the typically reactive approaches to prejudice through counseling. It suggests that counselors become "players" rather than spectators and demonstrate the courage of their convictions when confronting prejudice. This advocacy is what makes the book special and unique. It provides refreshing idealism that is needed in the published literature about counseling. The factors of social norms, political pressure, and individual personalities combine to construct prejudice, and prejudice can only be reduced by changing the context in which it flourishes. As active change agents, counselors can influence that context and reduce the predisposing factors favoring prejudice. These predisposing factors are identified in detail along with suggestions for changing individuals, influencing social norms, and managing political power through alternatives to prejudice.

In their attempt to protect their objectivity, counselors have frequently been reluctant to "get involved" as advocates, advisors and/or change agents. However, data shows clients cannot often afford the luxury of detachment and have more practical or immediate needs. This book is valuable as part of the new, more active and less passive, more optimistic and less pessimistic, more practical and less abstract literature about the role of contemporary counseling.

PAUL PEDERSEN
The University of Alabama at Birmingham

INTRODUCTION

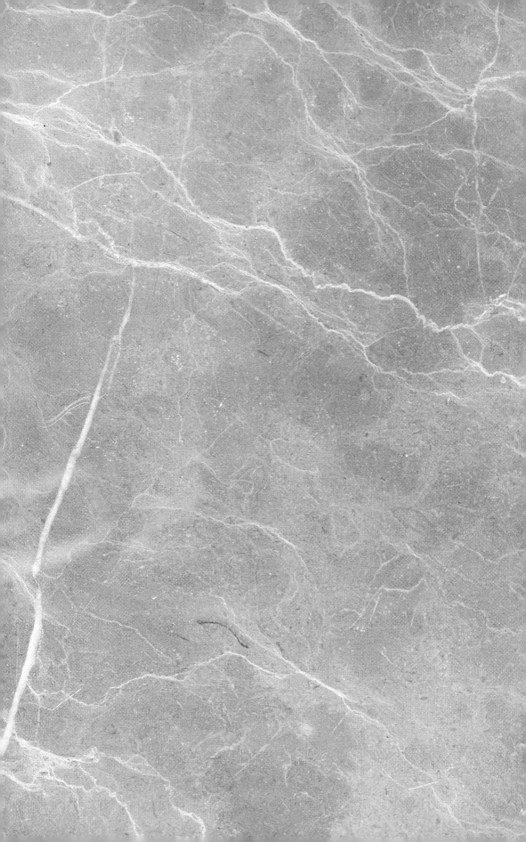

Introduction

Allport (1954) defined *prejudice* as "thinking ill of others without sufficient warrant" (p. 7). While "thinking ill of others" may seem a trivial problem, prejudice as manifested in action and behavior is a stain on the social fabric of the United States. DuBois (1903), in *The Souls of Black Folk*, announced that the "problem of the twentieth century is the problem of the color line—the relation of the darker to the lighter races of men in Asia and Africa, in America, and the islands of the sea" (p.54). This prediction was to be affirmed repeatedly in national and international events from the beginning to the end of the 1900s.

Although prejudice is more broadly conceived than any of the "isms" that it effects, ultimately the behaviors that target specific groups and individuals and result in their loss of freedom must be preempted. Such a restriction in individual rights becomes the enemy of all those who believe that this country was founded on the presumption that freedom is the paramount value in our culture.

We often live with a conflict between our stated values and those we practice. Myrdal (1944) suggested that many majority citizens of the U.S. experience an internal moral conflict between their commitment to the general egalitarian tenets of the "American creed" and their more specific prejudices. Myrdal said:

> The American Dilemma . . . is the ever-raging conflict between, on the one hand the valuations preserved on the general plane which we shall call the American Creed, where the American thinks, talks, and acts under the influence of high national and Christian precepts, and on the other hand, the valuations on specific planes of individual and group living, where personal and local interest; economic, social and sexual jealousies; considerations of community prestige and conformity; group prejudice against particular persons or types of people; and all sorts of miscellaneous wants, impulses, and habits dominate his outlook. (p. xxi)

Prejudice is a prerequisite for racism that allows public figures to insult various groups in very public displays. The following five examples are representative of our racism-embedded culture.

- Shortly before the 1988 Superbowl, Jimmy "the Greek" Snyder was dismissed by CBS Sports for a putatively racist explanation to a television reporter of why a disproportionately large number of NFL players were Black. He offered two major reasons for Blacks' dominance in the sport: first, that they were hungrier for success, and second that by nature they were better athletes because of the size of their thigh muscles. Snyder ascribed the latter difference to selective breeding by slave owners in the antebellum South (Cohen, 1988, p. A15).
- Earnest Hollings, a five-term senator from South Carolina claimed he was just joking when confronted by an outraged NAACP Board Chairman William F. Gibson. He was quoted as saying, "Everybody likes to go to Geneva. I used to do it for the Law of the Sea conferences and you'd find these potentates from down in Africa, you know, rather than eating each other, they'd just come up and get a good square meal in Geneva" ("NAACP chair outraged," 1988).

- Andy Rooney of *60 Minutes* was suspended for 3 months by CBS for the following comment: "I've believed all along that most people are born with equal intelligence, but Blacks have watered down their genes because the less intelligent ones are the ones that have the most children. They drop out of school early, do drugs, and get pregnant" ("CBS suspends," 1990).
- Rutgers University President Francis L. Lawrence indicated that disadvantaged students' genetic hereditary background contributes to Black applicants' lower Scholastic Aptitude Test (SAT) averages.
- State Senator Warren E. Barry described President Bill Clinton's proposal to allow gays and lesbians in the military as "fags in the foxhole" ("Racist jokes," 1993, p. 6).

The notion that racism flows in only one direction, though, is also false. In 1990, Leonard Jeffries (City College of New York) promulgated a theory that all human beings are divided into only two categories: "ice people" (Whites) and "sun people" (Blacks). The descendants of ice people are materialistic, selfish, and violent, while those descended from sun people are nonviolent, cooperative, and spiritual. Professor Jeffries maintained that Blacks are biologically superior to Whites because they have more melanin, and melanin regulates intellect and health (Calabrisi, 1994).

These examples are important in that the public outcry against the documented behavior supports, at least in our public lives, the expectation that equality, opportunity, and respect are available to anyone regardless of race, color, or creed. However, there is much evidence to support the notion that this public expectation does not extend to private individuals and groups. Thibodaux (1992) recognized that the ideal of all people, regardless of superficial differences, living together in prosperity and harmony requires mutual respect. However, in the politically correct (PC) environment on college campuses, Thibodaux (1992) suggested that it is the "politically incorrect" individuals such as conservatives and fundamentalist Christians who are mistreated. He characterized the PC crowd as having no respect for others, rejecting them and vilifying them as well.

Our failings in this regard cannot be attributed to the "state of nature" in which we exist. Holt (1992) observed, "Nature is a symphony of diversity, and therein lies its magnificence. It is interesting that we have noticed this and taken advantage of it in every living system with the exception of our own. Human beings have interpreted differences as symbols to fear" (p. ix). Until we can truly appreciate the strength and uniquely held knowledge among diverse peoples, we will continue to stratify our society with meaningless and nonproductive groupings.

Herrnstein and Murray (1994) hypothesized that race and class differences are largely genetic in nature and are therefore essentially immutable. They concluded their book *The Bell Curve* with the following statements: "All of these good things are available now to those who are smart enough or rich enough. . . . It is time for America once again to try living with inequality" (p. 551).

However, Gould (1994) dismissed their arguments as merely an attempt to support the cutting of social programs for personal financial gain. He viewed their arguments that beneficiaries are unable to make use of these programs because of genetic cognitive limits (expressed as low IQ) as providing a socially acceptable excuse for personal ungenerosity.

As early as 1968, Dr. Martin Luther King remarked that racism had poisoned the soul of White America. He had earlier characterized racism in this way: "The problem is deep. It is gigantic in extent and chaotic in detail" (King, 1968). These observations have been difficult for the American majority to encompass primarily because it is far easier to acknowledge racism in the fringe groups like the Ku Klux Klan than in the church-goers on Sunday. However, many have noted that 11:00 A.M. to noon on Sunday morning is the most segregated hour of the week.

By 1976, after the Civil Rights act of 1964 and numerous changes in our social institutions, Katz (1976) concluded that racism was still one of our greatest domestic problems, sometimes described as a social disease of epidemic proportions. She also pointed out that other social problems such as drug addiction had unified, national efforts to counteract their negative effects, but there was no massive funding for projects designed to eliminate racism in children and adults. Perhaps that is why after 25 years of effort, the question remains whether we have truly improved the situation.

Skillings and Dobbins (1991) have posited that throughout the social fabric of our society is an embedded thread of racism that is infecting the whole culture. They said, "We further suggest that racism is a disease that is often unwillingly and unwittingly hosted by members of the dominant American culture. The disease damages both the host and the target individuals, as well as their families and communities" (p. 206).

In fact, if West (1993b) is correct, it may be our cultural conservatism that is the disease, and racism may be the symptom. He gave this description of the current social situation in the United States:

> In White America, cultural conservatism takes the form of chronic racism, sexism, and homophobia. . . . In Black America, cultural conservatism takes the form of an inchoate xenophobia (e.g., against Whites, Jews, and Asians), systemic sexism, and homophobia. (p. 27)

We may have succeeded in reaching the moon, but we are still failing to reach the minds of men and women. We remain tolerant of racism in many ways even though it clearly cannot be distinguished from abuse. Like child abuse, we have been sweeping it under the rug. However, to risk exposure and force debate is to admit that we face a double-edged sword. Psychologically, both the oppressors and the oppressed suffer: The former from guilt, shame, and remorse; the latter from anger, despair and thoughts of revenge. In fact, oppressors practice prejudice as a temporary antidote to those negative feelings. Fear has in large part perpetuated our lack of development in this dimension of human interaction. Allport (1954) stated:

> Civilized men [and women] have gained notable mastery over energy, matter, and inanimate nature generally, and are rapidly learning to control physical suffering and premature death. But by contrast, we appear to be living in the Stone Age so far as our handling of human relationships is concerned. (p. xiii)

Prejudice and Bigotry Defined

The most common definition of prejudice used in academic circles is the one previously cited by Gordon Allport in his classic *The Nature of Prejudice* (1954) that states that prejudice is "thinking ill of others without sufficient warrant" (p. 7). However, another treatise on prejudice is W. E. B. Du Bois's *The Souls of Black Folk* (1903). Silence in regard to this text may speak volumes in regard to prejudice against its author. Many times, saying not much is saying too much. Gaines and Reed (1994) have recognized this intent: "It comes as no surprise, then, that when European American social psychologists are asked to identify the preeminent treatise on prejudice, they are likely to point to Allport's *The Nature of Prejudice*, not Du Bois's *The Souls of Black Folk*" (p. xx).

In some quarters it is has been argued that people are genetically predisposed toward prejudicial behavior. Works such as *The Bell Curve* by Herrnstein and Murray (1994) have postulated a genetic basis for all human behavior. Extensions of this view contend that all human brains are wired to notice and emphasize differences such as color and size and that they innately construct cognitive categories along those lines. Thus, authors with this point of view assert that people are preprogrammed to act prejudicially. Even if this is true, there also is evidence that human beings are capable of cognitively redirecting many of their biologically based behavioral tendencies. Indeed, a large portion of the treatment for alcoholism stems from that premise.

Some physical differences have been noted across racial groups; however, problems arise when they are used to show relationships with other human faculties of mind. Cohen (1988) surmised that the reason Jimmy "the Greek" Snyder was dismissed by CBS for attributing the success of Black football players to genetic physical differences was that many people fear that once physical differences beetween the races are recognized, then intellectual and psychological differences will be also. Cohen was quick to point out that intellectual differences among the races do not exist, but physical ones do.

Geoseffi (1993) declared that there were no biological foundations for prejudice because all so-called races of humankind whether Jewish, German, African, European, or Asian stemmed from the same genetic pool, which he thought to have originated in the heart of Africa over 250,000 years ago. This idea of common origins disallows separation into we and they, ingroup and outgroup. If this is truth, then we must find other sources to blame for our prejudice.

Bigotry is a form of prejudice. It describes the intolerance of one who cannot or refuses to accept others who are different in appearance, belief, or some other trait that conflicts with the person's own strongly held beliefs. The term *bigot* might be useful to describe those people who are members of the extremist groups such as the White Aryans. Kleg (1993) said, "Their hatreds for other racial and ethnic groups are manifest in their beliefs about these groups. Quite often the bigoted zealot's stereotype of a select group includes a combination of hate and fear, which brings us to the problem of xenophobia" (p. 153).

Pettigrew (1973) recognized two types of bigots, depending on the source of the attitude. Authoritarian bigots result from the authoritarian personality syndrome, which is characterized by general submission to those in power and aggression toward those who are viewed as lower in status. The second type of bigot is the conforming bigot. These individuals reflect the opinions of those who are important to them. If these people are prejudiced, then these attitudes are adopted by the conformers.

Pettigrew estimated that in the United States, one fifth of the population is tolerant of all others, one fifth is authoritative and bigoted, and the remaining three fifths are conforming bigots. He suggested that the task of reducing racism is not so much that of curing bigots as removing the institutional racism that supports the three fifths of the population who are conforming.

Dynamics of Prejudice

Prejudicial behavior can be conceptualized as the end result of three conditions that converge at a point. First, the predispositions toward prejudice are embedded in both personal characteristics such as prejudicial attitudes and in societal biases such as ethnocentrism. The source of these predispositions will be discussed later. However, interventions might be targeted to prevent the formation of predispositions as well to reduce or limit their effect.

Second, the predispositions are activated by events that seem to make prejudice an appropriate, rewarding response. For example, when we enter a competitive situation, our body chemistry prepares us for action, and we begin to make very rapid discriminations about who is on our side and who is not. If we have learned that a certain group is our enemy, then we automatically identify its members as adversaries.

Third, people often act prejudicially because they are afraid. In this sense, prejudice can be a fear response.

Geoseffi (1993) commented about the basic dynamics of prejudice. She thought that self-hatred was at its core and that the basis of prejudice was the process of projecting onto others what we believe is lacking in ourselves. She said, "Prejudice is a worldwide phenomenon and the dynamics of every instance of it—throughout human history—are analogous" (p. xvii).

An alternative notion is that prejudice may be self-pity projected onto a target group. This condition may also be associated with a need for self-glorification. That is, individuals may focus their "bad" characteristics onto others such that "poor me" becomes "poor you." This separation of the other then provides the opportunity to show the other as lesser and thus glorify or aggrandize the self.

The Effects of Prejudice

Perpetrators of prejudice reduce their alternatives by eliminating possible choices. For instance, a medical school admissions committee shrinks its candidate pool when it omits applicants from a specific group. Likewise, prejudiced businesspersons diminish their potential earnings by *a priori* elimination of possible customers.

Victims of prejudice are deprived of a portion of the range of opportunities they deserve. When a candidate who is qualified for a position is eliminated from consideration because of a selection committee's bias, that person's opportunities for fulfillment are reduced unfairly. Slaves deserved freedom and were deprived of it because of the color of their skin. Many women have deserved professional promotions that have been denied because they were female. For many years, those using wheelchairs were denied access to buildings because ramps were not required and were not available.

Prejudice reduces the possibilities of both perpetrator and victim. It is as if individual items in a distribution are systematically excluded, and the variability is thereby diminished. In short, prejudice often ensures that a situation can never actualize its full potential because all of its elements are not available. We understand it vividly when we see an athletic coach exclude players for economic, racial, religious, gender, or sexual preference reasons. The team's potential is reduced accordingly.

The statistics of prejudice do not address or express the human pain it causes. It is one thing to speak of fewer alternatives and lost opportunities as abstractions, but it is quite another to experience them. In that sense, the human pain produced by prejudice is immeasurable, and eliminating it should be a top priority for the entire human race (Carter, 1994).

Kistner, Metzler, Gatlin, and Risi (1993) studied the effects of race and gender on children's relations. Their results were supportive of previous research that found that children in the racial minority in their classrooms received fewer positive nominations. These findings were more explicit for girls in that they received more negative nominations from classmates when they were racial minorities in their classrooms. These findings showed that effects of racism were related to gender and that minority girls were at risk for rejection. They stated:

> Concerns for academic competence rather than social
> acceptance were the impetus for racial integration of schools,
> but competence in these two domains is not mutually
> exclusive. Children who are rejected by peers are less likely
> to complete school and are at risk for other undesirable
> outcomes. (Kistner et al., 1993, p. 451)

Children learning to understand and accept differences among various racial and ethnic groups tend to actively engage one another to test their assumptions. When this process is allowed to be constructive, the results will be good. However, instances of racial and ethnic prejudice cannot be tolerated if we are to create a society where there is equality for all (Lynch, 1991).

Even when racism is subtle, its effects can be devastating because of perceived discrimination, negative stereotypes, ostracism practices, pessimism due to limited opportunities, and cultural alienation. Sandhu, Portes, and McPhee (1996) have contended that coexistence of ethnic minority groups remains a very real, painful experience. They have developed the Cultural Adaptation Pain Scale to assess the degree of psychological distress people experience in day-to-day social interactions, confrontations, and even collaborations with diverse peoples in a multicultural society like the United States.

Although racism in its most benign form is problem enough, it is also clear that these prejudices may result in violent behavior. Kleg (1993) stated, "Nevertheless, attitudes by their nature provide the basis for social action, and those attitudes of ethnic and racial prejudice form the wellspring from which violence flows" (p. 13).

Allport (1954) suggested that many people who are committed to the American creed have deliberately rejected prejudiced beliefs but continue to respond to Blacks and other outgroups in a prejudiced or intolerant manner (and they are often unaware). Any deliberate act of discrimination against any other human is a most insidious kind of injustice. It wounds the spirit and dehumanizes the individual. From this wellspring, revolution is born. Rosa Parks became the mother of the civil rights movement by her unwillingness to accept the injustice of the required seating pattern on public transportation.

Long after laws have been changed, the effects of racism remain, deeply seated in the emotions. Allport (1954) observed, "Defeated intellectually, prejudice lingers emotionally" (p. 28).

Pettigrew (1987) provided a graphic illustration of this phenomenon:

> "Many Southerners have confessed to me, for instance, that even though in their minds they no longer feel prejudice toward Blacks, they still feel squeamish when they shake hands with a Black. These feelings are left over from what they learned in families as children" (p. 20).

Chapter Summary

In this introduction, we have outlined the problem of prejudice in our country today. Even though the past 30 years have seen mountains of legislation and implementation of diverse programs, prejudice remains much as it was defined originally by Allport (1954): "thinking ill of others without sufficient warrant" (p. 7). What has changed is the societal awareness of "acceptable" behavior regarding prejudice. Thus, in our public lives, we may behave as if we are less prejudiced even though our attitudes have not changed. In some ways, this is a more intractable problem, since subtle prejudice is not as easily addressed as the more public variety.

This notwithstanding, prejudice has also displayed itself in acts of violence in recent times in our schools, neighborhoods, and even churches. The Ku Klux Klan remains active, and neo-Nazi or private militia groups are active in most of the United States today. Thus, we live in a time when prejudice remains a threat to the fabric of our society, and it will require skills and energy to overcome its negative direction. It is our hope that through counseling and teaching, we can create a new society that truly reflects the American dream that all individuals have an equal right to pursue happiness, regardless of race, color, gender, sexual orientation, or creed.

CHAPTER

1

The Nature and Theories of Prejudice

Allport (1979) described prejudice as "a feeling, favorable or unfavorable, toward a person or thing, prior to, or not based on actual experience" (p. 6). This definition implies that prejudice could have both positive and negative valence. However, in common usage today, prejudice or any of its behavioral forms (e.g., racism, sexism, ageism) carry a negative connotation. The key point in defining prejudice is that it is a strong positive or negative attitude without objective verification. It develops as a process of structuring experience and behavior to reinforce the practice of either positive or negative prejudice.

One of the first questions that must be addressed regarding prejudice is the source from which it derives. Many theories are available for explanation and are grouped according to the originating source: individual or social. In the following paragraphs, we will present various theories and discuss prejudice in its operationalized forms as ageism, elitism, ethnocentrism, nationalism/regionalism, racism, and sexism. These sections are definitional and are intended to provide an overview of the problem of prejudice as it is manifested in our culture. Additionally, we address prejudice against gay men, lesbians, and bisexual persons.

Finally, we present a new paradigm of prejudice that springs from a culture of finite resources in which competition for society's rewards is keen. This increase in competition may provide new energy to prejudice to effectively eliminate whole groups from the process.

Individual Sources

Unresolved Personality Conflicts

Katz (1976) proposed that prejudice was the likely result of unresolved personality conflicts. Willie, Kramer, and Brown (1973) believed that early developmental experience greatly influenced personality development. They described personality as containing both immature and mature aspects as well as controlling and surrendering aspects. They believed that behavior was a result of the dominating aspects at any given time. To the degree that immature and controlling aspects are dominant, an individual might behave in a prejudicial manner.

Conflicts within the personality may also result in prejudicial behavior due to projection of personal inadequacies and inferiorities onto other groups or individuals within those groups. The position that projection is a source of prejudice is supported by writers such as Ashmore and del Boca (1976), Bettelhiem and Janowitz (1964), and Levine and Campbell (1972).

Incomplete Racial or Ethnic Identity

Ponterotto and Pedersen (1993) maintained that "race appreciation is a lifelong developmental process that begins with a healthy sense of one's own racial/ethnic identity" (p. 39). This includes an awareness and appreciation of one's racial/ethnic history. When one does not acquire this healthy sense of self, then the stage is set for the development of negative prejudice toward other racial groups who may be viewed as oppressors and potential threats to one's own safety and security.

Flawed Cognitive Processes

Kleg (1993) identified dysfunctional cognitive processes as an individual source of prejudice. That is, one may seek only a simple explanation of others' behaviors and thus misinterpret behavior that is in fact quite complex and perhaps not prejudiced. The question should arise regarding the societal forces that support this type cf cognitive process. Educational techniques, entertainment media, sports, and popular literature may all contribute to simplistic cognitive functioning.

Katz (1976) supported the notion of prejudice resulting from simple cognitive structures. He described individuals with this type of cognition as likely to make extreme judgments based on external influences. He also believed that they had low resistance to frustration and a high degree of conformity. Goldman (1995) held that prejudice is a kind of emotional learning. He said, "Later in life you may want to change your prejudice, but it is far easier to change your intellectual beliefs than your deep feelings" (p. 157).

Categorical thinking is a characteristic of simple cognitive structures. Tajfel (1969) described research in which categorization of objects into separate groups resulted in exaggerated differences between groups. He suggested that the mere defining of ingroups and outgroups may cause a favoritism of the ingroup and rejection or discrimination against the outgroup.

Personality inadequacies and cognitive limitations are interrelated. Mackie and Hamilton (1993) asserted, "Cognition produces affect which in turn dictates subsequent cognitive processing" (p. 9). Williams and Giles (1992) also supported self-serving identity needs abetted by cognitive shortcuts as one reason why people act in prejudicial ways.

Allport (1958) summarized the relationship between prejudice and cognition by stating, "It is characteristic of the prejudiced mentality that it forms in all areas of experience categories that are monopolistic, undifferentiated, two-valued, and rigid" (p. 172). The need to find simple solutions for complex problems is an extension of this notion. The energy required to think in systems rather than in unidimensional relationships is significant; for many it is overwhelming such that well-meaning individuals find themselves accepting the status quo rather than attempting to find meaningful solutions for social problems.

Social Sources

Group Competition

Many social scientists have concluded that social and economic competition can breed conflict and prejudice. Negative stereo-typing, prejudice, and discrimination clearly increase whenever competition for limited resources increases (Shepherd & Penna, 1991). Unfortunately, many in the United States today attribute our economic success directly to competition that they see as a significant human motivator and therefore acceptable for application to children's education as well as sports involvement. However, others have shown that defining new goals of mutual benefit will encourage children to cooperate and does not diminish achievement but enhances it (Johnson & Johnson, 1994).

Group Frustration

Katz (1976) suggested that frustration heightens as a result of relative deprivation in which expectations remain unsatisfied. Then, aggression toward others is amplified, causing people to strike out against the perceived cause of their frustration. When the true source of frustration is not easily identified, the frustrated individuals or groups may direct their aggression toward a more visible, vulnerable, and socially sanctioned target. Immigrants and other minorities have long been the recipients of displaced aggression and xenophobic behavior (Shepherd & Penna, 1991).

Social Distance

Kleg (1993) reported a high correlation between average social distance and average types of social contacts. He held that this correlation may indicate not only a tendency to limit the number of different types of social contacts with those they dislike, but with those about whom they know little or nothing as well.

Allport (1979) also recognized this phenomenon. He stated, "With plenty of people at hand to choose from, why create for ourselves the trouble adjusting to new languages, new foods, new cultures, or to people of a different educational level?" (p. 17). In our culture, which increasingly offers more and more information, we may find this phenomenon on the rise. With so much input through television, movies, and the Internet, when we do connect with other human beings, we may find that the "trouble" with associating with individuals different from ourselves is too discouraging to overcome.

Belief Congruence

Rokeach, Smith, and Evans (1960) formulated a theory of belief congruence to explain the underlying causes of prejudice as the dissimilarity in cultural values, attitudes, and beliefs among various groups. Naturally, people belonging to outgroups who do not share the same beliefs are more susceptible to prejudice and discrimination than are people within the same ingroups with similar belief systems.

Several empirical studies have supported the hypothesis that belief similarities could override racial and ethnic differences (Rokeach & Mezei, 1966; Smith, Williams, & Willis, 1967). However, Triandis (1961) has vehemently argued that in the case of intimate relationships, such as dating or marriages, belief similarities become less important than racial and ethnic similarities.

Cognitive Categorizations

Taylor (1969) proposed that cognitive categorization of people into discrete groups plays an important role in the development and perpetuation of prejudice through stereotyping. Persons classified into one special group tend to exaggerate similarities with the members of their own group and dissimilarities with members of outgroups. The major weakness of this theory is that stereotyping cannot adequately explain all of the predisposition of humans toward prejudice.

Social Identity

This theory proposes that prejudice and discrimination are related to the self-esteem needs of a given ethnic group to enhance its positive social identity. In a society in which all ethnic or racial groups are not equally valued, competition for social standing requires superiority over other groups. For this reason, ethnocentrism plays a dominant role in promoting ingroup favoritism as well as outgroup hostilities. Most studies are supportive of this theory (Brewer & Kramer, 1985), but it may be too early to make definitive conclusions at this time. It is possible that this phenomenon is related to the process of racial identity development (Hardiman, 1982; Helms, 1984; Ponterotto, 1988), or as Ponterotto (1991) suggested, it may be rapid demographic changes (an increasing White minority) interacting with stages of identity development that result in greater conflicts between ingroups and outgroups.

Franklin (1975) argued that our founding fathers were to blame for setting the stage for all succeeding generations to be prejudiced against Blacks by betraying the ideals of freedom. He said the act of denying them personhood allowed future generations to "apologize, compromise, and temporize on those principles" (p. 10).

The sense of the foregoing statements is that prejudice is a belief that others are inferior and deserve to be maltreated for that inferiority. This belief is latent until it is activated by circumstances that empower it. Then, the prejudice is translated into action. Within that concept, the various "isms" of prejudice are represented by the general paradigm shown in Figure 1.1.

The New Paradigm of Prejudice

The superiority-driven model of prejudice presented in Figure 1.1 is considered the "old" model. The new prejudice paradigm is fear driven, as shown in Figure 1.2

This new paradigm is the product of a societal paradox pointed out in *American Dilemma* by Gunnar Myrdal (1944). The American system is composed of two apparently contradictory

FIGURE 1.1

Prejudice Paradigm

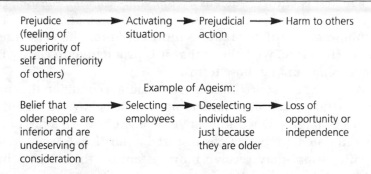

premises: (a) the ideal of equality and (b) the practice of competition, which is sometimes translated into the colloquialism "root hog or die." Thus, society's moral force and its economic force are in opposition. Myrdal's proposition lays the foundation for the conclusion that prejudice in the United States of America is basically a rationalizing process for justifying unprincipled tactics in the struggle over control of and access to the immense power of the American system. That is, if one group can convince itself that another group is inferior, then it is justified in excluding them from decision-making positions. This rationalization often includes the notion that the exclusionary practices are patriotic because they protect the strength of the American system from being undermined by inferior groups.

FIGURE 1.2

Fear-Driven Prejudice Paradigm

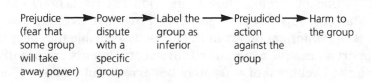

Definition of Terms

One of the problems in discussing prejudice is the multiple terms by which it is known, such as *ageism, anti-Semitism, classism, ethnocentrism, nationalism, racism, regionalism, sexism,* and others. The ensuing dialogue often produces more confusion than enlightenment. Therefore, we believe that it is productive to clarify the relationships among those terms.

We believe that prejudice is an attitudinal condition that may (or may not) result in innumerable specific behavioral manifestations or targets. Once a negative behavior toward a target has been initiated, prejudice has resulted in an "ism." Some of the specific "isms" may receive more attention than others but, although there are differences among them, they all share a common quality: they are harmful to human beings. Reid observed, "A review of the social-psychological literature reveals many similarities between the processes of racism and sexism" (Tobach & Rosoff, p. 115).

The foregoing stance runs counter to the thinking of those who religiously categorize various types of prejudice. These advocates tend toward a myopic posture that limits their awareness to a segment of the general problem area. They adopt a neodenominationalistic approach and often compete for resources rather than sharing them productively. The paradox is that in many cases, proponents of antiprejudice efforts are themselves prejudiced against advocates for other antiprejudice organizations. Thus, one of the essentials is to avoid internecineism within the antiprejudice community.

Although prejudice exists toward specific behavioral targets, there are also specific processes by which negative attitudes may be characterized. McGuire (1969) has shown that attitudes can be described by their several components: (a) affective ("gut" feelings), (b) cognitive (beliefs and information), and (c) conative (behavioral intentions). Thus, an individual's gut reaction to a specific target group may be negative, but cognitive override may be invoked if information about the group is available that does not support a negative action. If all three components are negative, then the likelihood of a negative behavior is much more likely.

Having established the position that prejudice is a generic condition, it is helpful to discuss some of its behavioral manifestations. That is, what is the nature of prejudice that results consistently in the targeting of specific groups for negative treatment?

Ageism

In the United States today, we worship the culture of youth. Friedan (1993) wrote, "The dread of age has become so ingrained in our consciousness that even those who study or report on age seem to seek only the fountain of youth" (p. 49). This attitude has been supported in part by our focus on the elderly in the media using negative stereotypes. Friedan stated:

> In studies over the past 20 years, young people, middle-aged people, doctors, occupational therapists, nurses, institutionalized older persons, and even gerontologists saw older people as childlike, mentally incompetent, unattractive, lonely, dependent, and powerless. (Friedan, 1993, p. 50)

This focus on the elderly as less than competent and a burden on society influences the way we value their contributions and ultimately their right to live. In recent years the "right to die" movement has increased among the terminally ill. Aggressive treatment at the end of life has certainly been questioned in medical circles, and most hospitals are diligent about securing a signed statement about technological intervention in the event of a life crisis. Although Governor Richard Lamm of Colorado was highly criticized for his statement regarding the duty of the elderly to die so that resources could be used by the young, many agreed with him. Friedan (1993) further described the situation of the older generation:

> Depression should not be surprising in any person suddenly stripped of power, of job or earnings, of a sense of productivity and purpose; in any person who suffers the increasing isolation and "sense of no-goodness" that results from others' avoidance of the old. (p. 61)

Ageism may be as subtle as speaking slowly and in childlike language to elderly persons or as obvious as forced retirement or refusal to hire. Regardless, the force of prejudice creates an environment that is at best unsupportive and at worst destructive of the life force of elderly persons.

Classism and Elitism

Adler (1995) wrote, "The common thread (the new fault lines running through American society) is class." The notion that we can identify individuals who are "superior" based on an agreed-upon classification is not new. For many years, the color of one's skin and other physical characteristics provided a means for easy classification. However, in reality there are only two classes (of course on a continuum): the oppressed and the oppressor, the powerful and the powerless, or the haves and have nots. There may be little that can be done against the biological makeup of ethnic groups, but much can be done to eliminate the differences created by our own political and economic systems.

Allport (1954) addressed the need for status and discriminated between social status that is ascribed, as it is for the British royalty, and that which is achieved by a person or family. Within any society it may be easy to determine the hierarchy, but knowledge alone would not be sufficient for the development of prejudice. However, Allport (1954) also described social class as "cultural invitations to prejudice" (p. 322).

Lind (1995) criticized the privileged class severely. He accused members of this class of arranging society for their convenience and then consuming a larger share than warranted of the national wealth. To add insult to injury, he also indicted them for using this wealth to increase the barriers between them and those they would describe as inferior. In the process, the privileged class made themselves independent of the industrial cities as well as the schools, public transportation, and medical care. This lack of investment in our cities by those most financially able to make a difference will leave an environment incapable of sustaining healthy human functioning.

Adler (1995) described an epochal event in the sociology of the United States, which he termed the birth of the overclass. He said:

> Designating them "the overclass" is not just another way for journalists to package the squeal of the skewered bourgeoisie.

> When "the poor" became the "the underclass" it meant no
> longer thinking of them as just "a lot of people without
> money," but as the inheritors of a "culture of poverty." (p. 33)

As the differences between the classes increase, the widen-
ing gulf allows the overclass to increasingly justify their advantages. The hierarchy of social class thus defines the elite. Henry
(1994) defended their right to have a larger share of the wealth
because they were smarter, harder working, more learned, more
productive, and harder to replace. To the degree that social class
is defined by racial groups and minorities are not among the
elites then elitism and racism are often found together. Henry
(1994) believed that minority groups should compete with and
equal the best in the majority culture.

The inherent assumption in such a statement is that the reason any minority has not assumed the same level of success as
the overclass is because they are not willing to work hard and
compete. Such statements fail to acknowledge any responsibility
for the plight of the underclass as a direct result of implementing systems that have been designed to favor the success of the
overclass.

Henry further supported elitism on the basis of its ultimate
good for society. This notion of individual worth being linked to
productivity is the underpinning of several "isms" including
ageism. Although this notion has also supported the "trickle down
theory" of economics, it has failed to produce desired results. He
stated, "In the delicate calibration of elitist toughness and egalitarian compassion, however, elitism ought to win out.... It directs
society's resources where they have the most chance of stimulating growth and change and making life better for everyone."
(Henry, 1994, p. 147).

Elitism can be found in other forms of discrimination. Willard
(1975) argued that attractiveness stereotypes lead to a phenomenon he called "aesthetic discrimination." He stated that beautiful people are often advantaged in society, and ugly people encounter both personal and professional discrimination.

Aesthetic discrimination can be defined as prejudging on the
basis of appearance. "If we deny the importance of physical
beauty in the culture, we avoid confronting a very real form of
discrimination" (Lakeoff & Scherr, 1984).

There are a variety of stereotypes about physical attractiveness that have direct implications for first impressions and for broader personal and social evaluations. Physical attractiveness affects jury decisions (Gray & Ashmore, 1976; Sigall & Ostrove, 1975), helping behaviors (Benson, Karabenick, & Lerner, 1976), and employment opportunities and job evaluations (Dipboye, Arvey, & Terpstra, 1977; Ilkka, 1995). Physical attractiveness is so potent that it even affects the attitudes that parents hold about their own infants (Stephen & Langlois, 1980).

Studies of children's skin color, especially Black children, also leads to evidence of a broader psychological heritage that encourages interethnic internalizations. Carl Jung (1954) referred to this as the collective unconsciousness. Humans are not only products of their personal histories but also of the heritage of the human species (Vontress, 1991).

Intraethnic internalizations are the constant reminders resulting from a series of inner conflicts of oppressed people passed on from generation to generation as a bag of psychological pain. With internalization the individual achieves a feeling of inner security. Once internalized, the conflicts are incorporated in one's personality as an inseparable integral. From this worldview, an individual's affective, cognitive, and conative behaviors are predisposed. This internalization allows the values and attitudes of society to reside uncensored within the individual. The negative side of this phenomenon is that individuals may lose their ability to recognize their own prejudices. The positive contribution is that each generation develops internalized regulators of conduct, and the order of society is preserved without external surveillance (Kochanska, 1994).

Ethnocentrism

Yinger (1994) suggested that when a subset of people act as if they are superior toward others, they are engaged in ethnocentrism. Kleg (1993) noted the self-love component of ethnocentrism that allowed one to feel superior about those in his or her ingroup while dismissing those in other groups as inferior. He felt that ethnocentrism created division in society because of the inherent separation into we/they, good/bad, and superior/inferior. Ethnocentrism seems to make it much easier to dismiss the "other" as unimportant and less worthy and to foster a competition for resources.

Locke (1992) extended the notion of ethnocentrism as the assertion of the superiority of a group's creativity or accomplishments. Ponterotto and Pedersen (1993) voiced a preference for Yinger's definition of ethnicity:

> [An ethnic group is] a segment of a larger society whose members are thought, by themselves and/or others, to have a common origin and to share important segments of a common culture and who, in addition, participate in shared activities in which the common origin and culture are significant ingredients. (Yinger, 1976, p. 200)

Some individuals believe that ethnocentrism constitutes the core of prejudicial attitudes and beliefs. Aboud (1987) defined the term *ethnocentrism* as "an exaggerated preference for one's own group and concomitant dislike of other groups" (p. 49). Aboud noted that ethnocentrism is tied to negative attitude development and can be explained by an individual's need to maintain self-esteem through the projection of one's own negative attributes onto others.

D'Souza said that ethnocentrism comes from the Greek word *ethnos*, which means people or nation. He said, "Ethnic groups are usually related by blood, kinship, or a common history, but these ties do not have to be racial—frequently they are not" (D'Souza, 1995, p. 33). He also identified nationality, religion, shared traditions, and geographical proximity as more potent common denominators for tribalism and ethnocentrism than race. He added, "Some scholars maintain that ethnocentrism is a survival instinct rooted in evolutionary biology" (D'Souza, 1995, p. 33).

When discussing group separation, Allport (1958) offered that this process occurs because of two central ingredients, erroneous generalizations and hostility. He felt these characteristics to be natural and common capacities of the human mind. Thus, both minority and majority groups may be guilty of perpetuating separation because the comfort with those of their own kind is enticing and fosters the sense of camaraderie and belonging.

Hostility toward the unknown may prevent the effort required to correct faulty generalizations.

Although group separatism may provide a sense of belonging, it also takes a toll on individuals and groups. In an interview sample of 2,078 people, Weiss, Ehrlich, and Larcom (1992) studied the psychological effects of "ethnoviolence" in the workplace. In addition to the obvious physical harms and financial costs, they found two major types of psychological effects. Negative psychophysiological symptoms include nervousness, depression, helplessness, sleep problems and nightmares, increased fear and anger, headaches, stomachaches, shortness of breath, body exhaustion and weakness, consumption of more prescription or nonprescription drugs and alcohol, increased anger and feelings of revenge, and unwanted changes in weight. Defensive behavioral changes and increased social withdrawal result in watching children more closely, becoming more cautious when walking in certain places, increasing safety and security of one's home, carrying a gun, taking self-defense classes, changing schools, quitting school, or dropping classes.

Members of both the mainstream majority culture and minority cultures glorify ethnocentrism and detest the idea of adopting other cultural values. Majority groups as well as minority groups often reject those who succeed through becoming linguistically anglicized or culturally "Americanized." Minority groups often develop labels to ridicule their own individuals for this behavior such as:

- Oreo cookie : an assimilating African American
- Red apple : an assimilating Native American
- Lemon or banana : an assimilating Asian
- Tio Tomas : Mexican Uncle Tom

The nature of race and its association with ingroups and outgroups has been debated. Gaines and Reed (1994) cited Du Bois as the source of the belief that race was more a result of human experience with particular cultures and histories than a biological entity. Du Bois essentially believed that race was more psychological than biological. Others view bias as an expected reality and have devalued the contribution of historical racism to the collective experience.

The process of developing racial identity in a diverse and racist population is extremely difficult. For many, marginal groups are expected to pull themselves up by their own bootstraps, regardless of societal bias against them. Other minorities are confused by the dual message of equality and inequality that is prevalent in society today. These people have not been able to resolve the internalized tensions between pride and shame.

This dualism was reflected in the views of Booker T. Washington and W. E. B. Du Bois. Washington often stated that White racism was a response to failings of Blacks and their culture and that if Blacks improved their economic status, racism would disappear. Du Bois rejected this notion, because individual Blacks who had overcome poverty and lack of education were also afflicted by White racist attitudes and behaviors.

Maldonado (1975) summed up the view of many in his statement, "Ethnic self-identity is central to the development of the personal identity of minority group members" (p. 621). Ultimately, it is one's personal identity that creates goals and brings dreams to reality. As long as ethnic identity remains a source of confusion, shame, and hostility, then the growth of the individual is thwarted.

Ethnic identity seems to be a problem only for minority groups. Phinney and Rotheram (1987) recognized that group norms and expectations are not recognized by Whites because the White group norms are the ones of the dominant culture. They stated, "Many majority group children are not even aware that they belong to an ethnic group" (p. 17).

Nationalism/Regionalism

Allport (1958) noted that the tie between nationalism and persecution of minority groups was seen in Germany and that this phenomenon could be found elsewhere in the world. While studies found evidence that insecurity and frustration do play a part in the nexus of anti-Semitism, investigators also found proof that the most important single factor was national involvement. He also noted that the anti-Semite was not merely a bundle of negative attitudes but was also attempting to find an island of institutional safety and security. Allport stated, "The research establishes the fact that the higher the degree of nationalism, the higher the anti-Semitism" (p. 381).

Nationalism need not exist only among individuals from different nations. West (1993a) spoke of "the class nationalist viewpoint," for which he gave the following description:

> It understands African American oppression in terms of class exploitation and national domination. The basic claim is that African Americans constitute or once constituted an oppressed nation in the Southern Black belt and, much like Puerto Ricans, form an oppressed national minority within American society. (p. 263)

Kleg (1993) addressed the role of geography in prejudice. He said that all geographic races are not necessarily tied to the three major groups of races, Caucasoid, Mongoloid, and Negroid. Many populations in the world possess unique physical traits. Because groups are often separated by physical or social barriers, little gene flow may occur between groups. Therefore, geographic populations have somewhat different dominant physical traits. The result of this phenomenon is that even among identical major groups, there will be significant differences in physical appearance and thus the tendency to identify ingroups and outgroups.

Allport (1958) addressed prejudice in terms of geographical regions of the United States and found that in regard to the extent of regional prejudice, there were conflicting studies. In general, he felt that it was fair to state that attitudes toward African Americans were less favorable in the South than in other regions and that anti-Semitism was greater in the Northeast than in other parts of the country.

Racism

Several credible definitions of racism exist. Kleg (1993) suggested that racism embraces the notion that some groups are innately, biologically, socially, and morally superior to other groups. He further suggested that this superiority can be attributed to racial composition. Racist thoughts that may ultimately contribute to some action include the notion that mixing superior and inferior groups leads to degeneration of the superior. A corollary of this type of racist thought is that superior groups have the right to subordinate inferior groups.

Racist thought usually, but not always, includes the belief that race establishes a group's potential level of development. In addition, it should be noted that not all people who hold racist thoughts are overt hatemongers. In fact, the most insidious form of racist behavior comes from those who harbor racist beliefs and subtly encourage others to commit acts of violence (Kleg, 1993).

Jones (1981) posited that racism was the use of power against a group defined as inferior by either individuals or institutions, with this definition supported by the entire culture. The notion that racism can only be practiced by those who have power to enforce their will is a more narrow definition and implies unidirectionality. Jones also delineated three forms of racism, which he named individual, institutional, and cultural, depending on the level of pervasiveness.

Ridley (1989) extended the role of power in racism. His definition included any behavior or pattern of behavior that intentionally limited the opportunities of one group while continuing privilege to members of another group. This definition is also limited by the notion of unidirectionality. However, it does describe the systematically negative application of power toward those groups defined as socially inferior.

Ponterotto and Pedersen (1993) also acknowledged the role of power in racism. They described it as the driving force. They further discussed the psychological research focus on Whites, which they believe to be due to the fact that Whites are the prime perpetrators of racism. They also recognized that racism has a behavioral component that when directed toward specific groups will result in dire effects and consequences. The cultural acceptance of racism then may lead to violence in addition to the lack of opportunities for members of the targeted group.

The role of power in racism seems logical. Without the ability to affect outcomes, prejudice would be impotent. In his discussion of this topic, Locke (1992) noted that racism was a blend of prejudice and power. His definition of prejudice reflected a pre-emptory decision without full examination. That ignorance perpetuates prejudice seems clear. School integration was believed to be a cure for ignorance; however, prejudice persists in schools today precisely because we have remained largely ignorant about one another. Stereotyping persists and judging without full examination is still the rule.

West (1993a) has suggested three White supremacist logics that support racism: Judeo-Christian, Scientific racist, and Psychosexual. He declares that each of these logics view Blacks as alien. Once viewed in this fashion, African Americans must overcome these myths in the minds of Whites before they can even be considered worth further exploration. Defeating the errors in these logics that are so embedded in our culture will take a colossal effort.

D'Souza (1995) described racism as "an ideology of intellectual or moral superiority based upon the biological characteristics of race" (p. 27). He further stated that racism involves a willingness to discriminate based upon an evaluation that determines superior and inferior races. He maintained that to be a racist, a person must do four things: (a) believe in biologically distinguishable groups or races; (b) rank these facts in terms of superiority and inferiority; (c) hold these rankings to be intrinsic and innate; and (d) seek to use them as the basis for discrimination, segregation, or denial of rights extended to other human beings (D'Souza, 1995, p. 28).

Fredrickson (1981) believed that racism results from a cognitive process that holds that population groups can be distinguished by ancestry and are likely to differ in culture, status, and power. Racists assign these differences to immutable genetic factors and not to environmental or historical circumstances.

Cross (1991) proposed a model of racial identity that explains an individual's conversion from Negro to Black. Each of the proposed stages is characterized by different racial identity attitudes, each of which is allegedly characterized by distinctive, conative, and affective elements. He identified these stages as (a) pre-encounter, (b) encounter, (c) immersion-emersion, (d) internalization, and (e) internalization-commitment.

The United States of America has become a multiracial, multicultural, and multilingual society. With increasing diversity, we see evidence of increasing racism. "It is a pervasive aspect of U.S. socialization. It is virtually impossible to live in U.S. contemporary society and not be exposed to some aspect of the personal, cultural, and/or institutional manifestations of racism in our society" (Tatum, 1992, p. 3).

Part of the problem in the United States is the discrepancy between our public documents and our lived reality. Our ideals create expectations that are not met for many minority groups, resulting in disappointment and disillusionment. The rhetoric of our public documents contains phrases such as "equality, liberty, and justice for all." There is a strongly held ethic of equality that underlies much of the fabric of American life—concepts such as "created equal," should have equal access to "life, liberty, and the pursuit of happiness," "one nation, under God, indivisible, with liberty and justice for all," "my country, 'tis of thee, sweet land of liberty." However, these expectations are seldom realized for certain subgroups who are the targets of racism.

It has long been a tradition in the United States that all ethnic groups melt into a new American collective culture, leaving their traditional culture and values behind. As David, the young Jewish immigrant in Israel Zangwill's (1912) play the *Melting Pot*, exclaims: " America is God's crucible, the great melting pot where all the races of Europe are melting and reforming!"

This concept of the United States as a melting pot was first challenged in the early 1920s by Marcus Garvey, an immigrant from Jamaica. He challenged Blacks to embrace their African roots. "In contrast to those who preached accommodation with White society, he encouraged them to resist White cultural and economic dominance" (Martin, 1976, p. 3). This movement resulted in part because, for Blacks, the melting pot was never a real option.

As racism increases, no portion of society is exempted from its concomitant violence. The National Institute Against Prejudice and Violence studied violence on college campuses and found that as many as one in five students of color were victims of some form of harassment on the campus of the college they attended. Nationally, 800,000 to 1 million students report annually that they have been victims of ethnoviolence. One in four students identify the incident as seriously affecting their lives (Brodie, 1991).

Other indicators of a rise in racism include the increase in special interest group movements. Recent examples include the Million Man March, the push to change the name of sports teams such as the Atlanta Braves and the Cleveland Indians, and the increasing visibility of the militia movement.

Perhaps as a response to increasing racism against them, there has been a renewed emphasis on the afrocentric movement. Since the 1980s, interest and focus on Black culture and Black consciousness has heightened. This emphasis has taken many forms. Some of these include the wearing of African clothing, a demand for Afrocentric curricula in higher education, more African American faculty and administrators, the institualization of African American holidays and celebrations, and a renewed interest in Malcolm X and his political philosophy (Tryman, 1992).

In response to this movement, some alienation has taken place. Many of the demands clash with perceptions of White students that Blacks are already receiving preferential treatment in admissions, scholarships and fellowships, and academic support programs. This brings up the cry of reverse discrimination, the antiaffirmative action movement, removal of quota systems, and reactivated KKK and skinhead groups. Unfortunately, threats to the power of the White male will intensify the likelihood of a response. Eisenstein (1994) said, "White male privilege is constructed in and through a racism that differentiates people of color as 'less than' at the same time as it constructs radicalized gender privilege" (p. 70).

Many of these reactions are part of the natural cycles of the U.S. political system. The political continuum from left to right begets special interest groups who battle for power to achieve their political agendas. Periodically, one group will achieve dominance and governmental policies come to reflect this position. As a response, the opposing forces create a backlash that "may manifest itself in small but significant ways at first, eventually snowballing into a full-fledged movement that develops momentum as the pendulum swings back the other way and influences public policies" (Dye, 1992, p. 42).

For African Americans, the traditional emphasis for achieving equality by the Black establishment was legalistic and civil-rights oriented (Kotkin, 1993). However, Kotkin has pointed out that "African-American leaders as different in temperament and approach as Booker T. Washington, Marcus Garvey, Malcolm X, Louis Farrakhan, and Tony Brown have emphasized the importance of developing a more self-affirming, and economically and intellectually self-sufficient social culture as the primary means of overcoming racial oppression" (1993, p.10).

Thomas Sowell (1989) described the behaviors of Blacks who do not have the academic qualifications to compete with their White counterparts. He felt that their frustrations and lowered self-esteem led them to behavior resulting in "continually attacking, undermining, and trying to discredit the standards that they don't meet, scavenging for and issuing a never-ending stream of demands and manifestoes" (Sowell, 1989, p. 116).

Hornblower (1995) reported that the University of California Board of Regents made history when it "ended affirmative action throughout the nine campuses thus prohibiting the consideration of race, gender or ethnic origin in admissions as well as in hiring and dealing with contracts" (p. 34).

It is obvious that much needs to be accomplished in race relations. However, over the past 40 years through civil rights laws, dramatic changes in racial attitudes have occurred. Since the criminalization of racial discrimination, the public generally condemns blatant racism. Most citizens of the United States have strong convictions about racial harmony, justice, and fairness and would respond with anger and shock at the scales and tests used to assess racial attitudes during the 1950s (Byrnes & Kiger, 1987).

For example, read these items taken from the *Ethnocentrism Scale* (Part B), which were used to determine participants' degree of agreement or disagreement:

1. Negroes have their rights, but it is best to keep them in their own districts and schools and to prevent too much contact with Whites.
2. It would be a mistake ever to have Negroes for foremen and leaders over Whites.
3. Negro musicians may sometimes be as good as White musicians, but it is a mistake to have mixed Negro-White bands.

4. Manual labor and unskilled jobs seem to fit the Negro mentality and ability better than more skilled or responsible work.
5. The people who raise all the talk about putting Negroes on the same level as Whites are mostly radical agitators trying to stir up conflict.
6. Most Negroes would become overbearing and disagreeable if not kept in their place. (Allport, 1958, p. 69)

Jones (1972) produced several examples of racial attitudes of Whites toward Blacks from interviews conducted by the Social Institute at Fisk University during 1940 and 1946. The following two quotes from those interviews show how much attitudes have changed since that time regarding appropriate language and opinion of Blacks:

Man, age 38, newspaperman in Newport News, Virginia:
The Negro is a Black and kinky-haired person from whose body comes a not entirely pleasant odor. He is always regarded as an inferior person and race mentally and morally, destined by birth and circumstances to serve the White people.... I don't understand the Northerners. How would they like a nigger to marry their daughter?

Woman, age 20, stenographer in Newark, New Jersey:
They aren't different, except for their color... most of the colored people I know are servants or laborers. I never knew any who did skilled work.... If I were a monarch and had power to do what I wanted to do with the Negroes, I don't know just what I would do. It would not be a good idea to send them back to Africa. It's necessary for them to mingle with the Whites, to learn each other's ways. (pp. 30–31)

Since the 1954 *Brown v. Board of Education* decision, people have increasingly supported the notion of egalitarianism in the schools through legislation and litigation favoring sex equity, school integration, bilingual and multicultural education, special education, and due process for students. Thus, we no longer worry about universal schooling under the law but we are concerned about universal quality schooling. Access may be a necessary condition but it is not sufficient to ensure that all races have quality education (Puddington, 1995).

Steele (1990), author of *The Content of Our Character*, noted the dual effects of a focus on race. Writing in *The New York Times*, he said, "America suffers as much today from a well-intentioned identification of its citizens by race as it does from old-fashioned racism" (Steele, 1995, p. A8).

Racism does not apply only to Black-White relationships. The experience of Native Americans with the dominant culture provides insight into its insensitivity regarding our shared heritage. Vine Deloria (1983) wrote:

> One day at a conference we were singing "My Country 'Tis of Thee' and we came across the part that goes, 'Land where our fathers died, Land of the Pilgrims' pride,'.... Some of us broke out laughing when we realized that our fathers undoubtedly died trying to keep those Pilgrims from stealing our land. In fact, many of our fathers died because the Pilgrims killed them as witches. We did not feel much kinship with those Pilgrims regardless of who they did in." (p. 48)

Gaines and Reed (1994) offered similar painful social scenarios of culturally oppressed people. For example, minority members may be repulsed repeatedly when they make friendly overtures towards Whites, and they may have feelings of being unwelcome in many places owned by members of the majority culture.

Deloria (1983) reflected the common belief among minorities that equality before the law is not a real expectation:

> Whites have had different attitudes toward the Indians and the Blacks since the Republic was founded. Whites have always refused to give non-Whites the respect which they have been found to legally possess. Instead there has always been a contemptuous attitude that the law says one thing, 'we all know better.' (p. 51)

Psychological Impact of Racism. Allport and Ross (1967) argued that feelings of compunction (i.e., guilt and self-criticism) arise when one's actual reactions are in conflict with how the person believes he or she should (and would) respond. It is also a possibility that dissonance is aroused when perceptions of some aspect of the self are contrary to internalized standards.

In his classic work on race relations, Myrdal (1944) described that dissonance as a struggle with the difference between "creed and deed." Contemporary examinations of these issues continue to show that the methods mainstream individuals use to cope with inconsistent cognitions is an integral part of expressions of racism.

Erickson (1968) pointed out the possibility that members of an oppressed and exploited minority may internalize the negative views of the dominant society, thereby developing a negative identity and self-hatred. A related theme has been expressed by social psychologists. Tajfel (1978), for instance, suggested that membership in a disparaged minority group can create psychological conflict; minority group members are faced with a choice of accepting the negative views of the society toward their group or rejecting them in a search for their own identity. The victims of prejudice suffer from a psychological syndrome of pervasive anger, depression, denial, loneliness, and isolation (Ehrlich, 1990).

Cultural indicators of status include accent, skin color, gender-biological characteristics, and physiological characteristics. "Skin color is the characteristic that can shape a child's experience more than any other with the possible exception of gender" (Phinney & Rotheram, 1987). These characteristics can be used to identify targets for prejudice. Skin color is seen, accent is heard, and therefore, warning signs are generated that allow the "less than" individual to be treated in ways that further define his or her inferiority.

Another contributor to the problem of racism is the role of power in relationships among individuals and groups. Ponterotto (1991) addressed the development of these issues within the African American community. From the time of slavery, African Americans (powerless) needed to both oppose and gain favor with the slave owners (powerful), which resulted in psychological duality. This phenomenon occurs today when respect for strong women is countered by the notion of male dominance/female subordination and may contribute to the weakening of the African American home. The stress of this duality is brought to the fore today when prejudice and discrimination have resulted in male economic powerlessness (due to lack of employability) and comparative female power.

Franklin (1993) recognized the development of a dual personality as a reaction to slavery. The slave had to displace aggression, deflect anger, deny his or her own feelings, and deal with both negative and positive emotions simultaneously. Ambivalence became a familiar coping mechanism not only in dealing with the master but in family relationships as well. Psychologically, slavery created lasting scars. Levine (1977) described the intense angers, hatreds, and frustrations that resulted from the violence and brutality inflicted on the slave population.

Racial Stress. The flight-or-fight response theory of racial stress (Ponterotto, 1991) predicts that White Americans who do not migrate away from interethnic contact (the flight response) have a natural tendency to feel threatened and resort to the fight response. This is an example of the principle that racial-ethnic based unfamiliarity resulting from segregated socialization will yield ignorance and fear.

White flight was a fear response that began in the late 1950s when predominantly White schools and communities were integrated with African American children. Some parents moved their families to all-White communities to avoid this integration, and some White parents moved their children to private schools. The frequency or effectiveness of White flight was drastically altered in the 1980s. All-White neighborhoods and schools were becoming more elusive and Whites and minorities were forced to coexist for economic reasons. Thus, in these integrated neighborhoods, with flight no longer an option, fight was the direct result. Conflict arose as individuals struggled to define differences among the races and thereby justify White privilege.

To a large degree, civil rights legislation has lessened the overt practices of discrimination and prejudice; however, it is leading to new styles of prejudice and conflicts. After the Civil Rights Act declared blatant racism, sexism, and ageism to be illegal, the present-day prejudice has become more insidious, subtle, and less identifiable. Sigall and Page (1971) suggested that improvement in racial attitudes can be dismissed as "superficial." Verbalizations might have changed, but racial attitudes and feelings still remain the same.

However, Tryman (1992) recognized that this country was established with *de jure* or legal racism as a part of its founding documents. Although legal racism has been addressed by civil rights legislation, the institutions founded before these changes remain in place and continue to develop and reinforce norms, attitudes, and values consistent with racism. Thus, institutional racism can be individual or group oriented and can also be conscious or unconscious. "This is true of the family, church, public and private schools, civil and social associations, and economic and political institutions" (Tryman, 1992, p. 224).

Most scholars and theoreticians of race relations agree that the threat of losing power, and thus privileges and resources, is generally the single most important reason for racial conflicts (Wellman, 1977). Access to power is a recurring theme when studying multicultural issues. Moghaddam and Taylor (1987) described theories of intergroup relations that attempt to explain prejudice and racism between more powerful and less powerful groups, rather than based on ethnicity.

However, power is a multidimensional construct. May (1967) identified five types of power. The first is exploitative and implies physical violence. Ethnoviolence is an example of this kind of power and may include assaults on individuals as well as property damage. Manipulative power, the second type in May's construct, pertains to power over resource distribution such as job and housing discrimination and institutionalized racism. Competitive power is power against each other in which one must win and one must lose. Both sexism and homophobia would be examples. Nutrient power is for the other and identifies a within-group support system. Parenting and teaching are good examples because they involve care for others. Integrative power requires collaboration with others and usually follows the thesis, antithesis, and synthesis process. One's own power abets a neighbor's power. Collaborative power with others exists between groups. This is a strongly held ideal in the United States today and is the underlying purpose for writing this book.

Modern Racism. After 30 years of the civil rights movement, the sad news is that racism remains a perennial problem. Anti-Black feelings and racial conflicts still persist (West, 1993b). Furthermore, several social scientists (Ashmore & McConahay, 1975; McConahay, 1986; McConahay & Hough, 1976) have noted a new form of racism called symbolic racism. Symbolic racism is a reaction to post-civil-rights policies, such as affirmative action and equal housing, when Whites feel that Blacks are receiving undeserved benefits and still are making unfair demands.

This symbolic racism or what McConahay (1986) now calls "modern racism" explains the vicious cycle phenomenon of prejudice. If you try to stop one set of problems, another set of problems related to prejudice starts. McConahay (1986) developed items to assess modern racism in the United States. Two examples from the Modern Racism Scale follow:

- Over the past few years, the government and news media have shown more respect to Blacks than they deserve.
- Over the past few years, Blacks have gotten more economically than they deserve. (McConahay, 1986, p. 108)

These items question the notion of attention and advancement for Blacks as a result of what they "should" deserve. The inability to respond to an individual's achievement outside of his or her race or ethnicity is in itself racism.

Brown (1990) characterized this modern racism as more subtle and elusive than in earlier times. He said:

> [This is] a racism that no longer manifests itself simply in the appearance of "White only" signs and utterance of epithets such as "nigger." It is a racism that is persistent and constitutes part of the social order, woven into the fabric of society, and everyday life. It is a racism frequently less intentional... but its victims insist that it is no less real, harmful, or in need of remedy. (p. 295)

Cohen (1995) observed that racism in America is both intractable and changing. He noted that the current popularity of Colin Powell with both Whites and Blacks is a phenomenon that should not be dismissed. Johnson (1994) also acknowledged the changes in race relations in America. He stated, "The civil rights acts of the 1960s and beyond did represent more than a Band-Aid on America's race problems. Racial conditions in America did change in ways that even the most cursory examination of places like Birmingham and Selma demonstrates" (p. 173). However, he also noted that when people are unable to feed their children, appeals to improve race relations are ignored.

It may be too early to say that we are a color-blind society. A culture- and gender-neutral society may be the ultimate goal, we have much work ahead. Affirmative action may not be fair in the long run, but it is a valuable tool now, at least to produce some new role models, to prove that the United States of America is a land where dreams can become a reality if given opportunities.

Sexism

The role of women throughout history has been one of inferiority and subjection. Some authors apply retrospective determinism and argue that whatever has happened to women is a result of their biological make-up. These authors refuse to acknowledge the role of society in denying women equal opportunity (Lauer, 1986).

Women have also been subjected to the beauty myth (Wolf, 1992), which is also highly destructive to their personal growth and development. In this myth, beauty is the source of all success. If a woman is both competent and beautiful, her success is attributed to her beauty rather than her competence. Women have made gains in equal access, but the reality of sexism is that beautiful women's bodies are still used to sell cars, alcohol, and almost everything else.

Women may also fear success because of the burden of social disapproval (Horner, 1972). A corollary of the beauty myth is that gifted women, unlike gifted men, may be required to hide their abilities to be accepted socially (Noble, 1987). Thus, success in a traditional male career may result in censorship by society and a loss of femininity in the eyes of others.

The reality is that by the year 2000, 80% of women aged 25–54 will be in the workplace (Hoyt, 1988). Unfortunately, most will still be concentrated in low-paying occupations such as clerical and retail sales, because the technical, higher paying jobs will still be held by men (Ehrhart & Sandler, 1987).

Betty Friedan, leading feminist and author of *The Feminine Mystique,* noted that women take the gains made over the past few decades for granted. However, she said, "Sexual politics— reifying women's oppression and victimization by men—has come to dominate women's studies and feminist thought" (Friedan, 1974, p. xx).

However, there is a growing resentment against women that could backlash against economic and political gains. This resentment likely stems from the notion that practicing gender preference to equalize past wrongs punishes the innocent. Regardless of the origin of the resentment, the women's movement will not fade away, and it should work now toward uniting us all. Women, after all, are only half of the population (Friedan, 1995).

Benokraitis and Feagin (1995), authors of *Modern Sexism,* described sexism much as racism has been defined. That is, the problems of sexism tend to affect more than the individual, and as such are embedded in all societal institutions. Once imbedded in our institutions, these concepts and behaviors about social roles and expectations become internalized and are such a fabric of our being that change becomes difficult. They further stated, "Some aspects of sex inequality have improved. There is, however, a great deal of evidence that sex inequality is still a major problem and may even be increasing in some areas. (Benokraitis & Feagin, 1995, p. 16)

Alexander (Hill & Jordan, 1995) described the condition of Black women in the United States. She described America's perception of Black women primarily as sexual beings who have no modesty, virtue, or intelligence, and little claim to respect or power throughout the last $3^1/_2$ centuries. She believes that Black women have always had to shoulder a dual load of demeaning perceptions and that they are the most consistently marginalized segment of our society. This has resulted in their unique disempowerment because of their presumed racial and sexual inferiority.

Another area of sexism particularly as it applies to women of African ancestry is in the area of sexual morality. From antebellum times, it was presumed that for these women, sexual morality was nonexistent, when in truth, a Black woman rarely had the option of saying no and making it stick when any man wanted to exploit her sexually. "The institution of slavery provided both a convenient venue for coerced sexual relations between White men and Black women and an authoritarian environment that sanctioned and even encouraged those encounters" (Alexander, 1995, p. 9). Unfortunately, the tendency to blame the victim and negative perceptions of Black women continued unchanged into the 20th century.

Although some African Americans tried to emulate the "idealized" patterns of middle-class White family life in which wives were expected to stay in the home protected from the world's corruption, economic necessity kept the majority of Black women employed outside their own homes. Realizing that these negative ideas were not likely to change, many Black women felt that the only way to protect their daughters was to repress even healthy expressions of independence and sexuality. Racism has always sullied reform movements for minority women.

Sexual harassment has been another ploy to prevent women from achieving equality in the workplace. Benokraitis and Feagin (1995) asserted that sexism is more than a problem experienced by some individuals. They believed that sexism is embedded in our institutions and organizations at all levels of society.

Although the workplace has not generally been receptive to the women's movement, the university may be the notable exception. Johnson (1994) said, "In just one generation, the women's movement has transformed the university. . . . The attitudes formed there carry over into the larger society, reinforcing a determination to fight sexism and gender discrimination not only on campuses but in communities and corporate offices" (p 249).

Some examples may help to explicate the impact of the university on women's rights. Today, almost every campus in the United States has a center for women's studies. In 1996, medical school classes are almost 50% female. Women are in the military flying fighters, helicopters, and cargo planes. Shannon Lucid recently set the U.S. record for space flight when she spent 188 days on the Russian space station Mir (Down to Earth, Oct. 7, 1996). There are more women in the Senate and House of Representatives than at any time in our history. Women today have more opportunities than ever before, yet the wage gap persists. Women still earn only about 77% of their male counterparts' wages.

Sexual Orientation and Prejudice

Gay men, lesbians, and bisexual persons have been the invisible minority (Fassinger, 1991). Negative societal attitudes have created a web of prejudice that requires secrecy to maintain safety and security. Herek and Berrill (1992) have documented the violence targeted toward gay men and lesbians. Studies have shown that as many as 92% of gay men and lesbians have been the targets of verbal abuse and over one third have endured physical violence. Even law enforcement officers may target these individuals for physical violence. The unfortunate fact is that these events are unlikely to be reported because of the reprisal that accompanies "coming out of the closet."

Pharr (1988) addressed the homophobia issue and wrote:

> When gay men break ranks with male roles through bonding and affection outside the arenas of war and sports, they are perceived as not being "real men," that is, as being identified with women, the weaker sex that must be dominated and that over the centuries has been the object of male hatred and abuse. Misogyny gets transferred to gay men with a vengeance and is increased by the fear that their sexual identity and behavior will bring down the entire system of male dominance and compulsory heterosexuality. (p. 19)

Chapter Summary

Prejudice exists today much as it has at any time in our history. We still harbor the belief that some groups are physically, intellectually, or socially inferior. We translate these beliefs into action as we target specific groups for maltreatment. These actions represent the various "isms." This treatment is most often in the form of denial of opportunity, but it can become violent such that targeted groups are at heightened risk of morbidity and even death.

The cause of prejudice is complex, and thus simplistic solutions have been ineffective. We know that prejudice may be individual, organizational, and cultural and to the degree that it has become institutionalized in the culture, it is that much more difficult to overcome. Prejudice may result from unresolved personality conflicts or flawed cognitive processes in the individual, and social sources may perpetuate prejudice within a group. Regardless of the source, the result is the same: inequity, pain, and loss.

Two models of prejudice were presented in this chapter that describe an existing prejudice, activating situation, and ultimately a prejudicial action. The first source of prejudice was due to feelings of self-superiority and inferiority of others. The second and newer model determines the source of prejudice to be fear of loss of power. In a changing world, security is derived from the belief that we hold sufficient power to affect our future. In a world of diminishing resources, we would expect that prejudice would increase if this model is true. The need is urgent for counselors to address and remediate prejudice.

CHAPTER 2

The Current Status of Prejudice in the United States of America

In the United States of America today, prejudice is alive and well. In the following pages, current theories of prejudice development will be explored using examples of the national political climate as well as current events and institutions that reflect our national attitude toward prejudice. In these events, we will see ourselves and our attitudes shaped by the media. No one would argue that we have not made progress through law in providing equal access, but there remains a deeply embedded thorn of prejudice that threatens the health of the nation. Despite the threat, sensitivity to our social attitudes can be helpful in educating a new generation to be free of this social disease.

Prejudice is probably as old as humankind and surely is one of human beings' most intractable problems. Nevertheless, the attention devoted to prejudice varies as society's competing needs change. Thus, at times prejudice has been assigned a low priority; however, current problems in our society have revived interest in its study. Today's society is vitally concerned about prejudice, and efforts to reduce it have a high priority for educational institutions as well as the criminal justice system.

King (1995b) spoke of the need to diminish prejudice when he contended that our support of societal fragmentation as a desirable outcome was a delusion. He felt that as we overidentify with those like us, those who share our values, we find an area of comfort. However, this leads ultimately to the exclusion of others. Sometimes, it is easier to assign the role of "other" not on the basis of values or character but on a visually identifiable characteristic such as skin color. Prejudice when manifested as racism is a particularly virulent form that can be found worldwide.

Ward (1995) spoke clearly and directly about the pathology of racism. He described it as the "eighth deadly sin" and felt that it deserved a higher ranking because it seems to be the motivation for the killing of so many over such slight variations in appearance. The violence associated with ethnic wars is so easy to impugn because we see it as distant; yet the racism that we tolerate in slighter doses is no different in origin. We are separated from these racial wars in our own land by a mere 130 years.

D'Souza (1995) described a fear shared by many that racism cannot be removed. He questioned whether racism might be a staple of the human psyche and so deeply ingrained in Western consciousness that it cannot be expunged. The danger associated with such a belief is that we would have no reason to encourage efforts toward eradication. Lacking definitive evidence to the contrary, efforts to abolish racism seem the best course of action.

Wilson (1993) also addressed the stance that genetic inheritance plays a role in racial differences. He described a study of Caucasian and Chinese newborns matched for gender and maternal characteristics. The study found that the Caucasian babies cried more, blinked more when exposed to a bright light, and were harder to control than the Chinese babies. He concluded that tempermental differences may follow ethnic lines. The implications of such a study are somewhat difficult to interpret, given the fact that within-group variability in large samples may be greater than between-group variance.

Johnson (1994) spoke about the current racial scene. He recognized the increase of racial polarization nationwide and attributed the problem as much to class and caste as race. However, he acknowledged the central role of race, especially between

Blacks and Whites. He further attributed much of the mutual anger and resentment to the failure of public education and the never-realized integrated society. These feelings were also complicated by separatist movements among both Blacks and Whites.

Thernstrom (1995) was more optimistic about the state of race relations. He maintained that although the Kerner Commission described America in 1968 as separate and unequal, the present day has much better news to report: Inequality has been greatly reduced. The median income of African American married couples with children is now only slightly lower than that for all American families. Since 1970, residential segregation has dropped sharply in 11 of the 13 metropolitan areas with the largest Black populations in the country. Twelve percent of all college students are Black—a figure proportionate to the Black population. He stated, "The media let the problems of the underclass define Black America, when by some measures many Blacks are doing well" (Thernstrom, 1995, p. A15).

The National Political Climate

The national political climate of the mid-1990s represents a confusing blend of political parties and their stances, the Dow Jones edging ever closer to 6,000, and a population in overdrive. President Clinton gave a metaphoric description of the mid-1990s: "What makes people insecure is when they feel like they're lost in the fun house. They're in a room where something can hit them from any direction at any time; they always feel that living is like walking across a running river on slippery rocks and you can lose your balance at any time" (Bernstein, 1995, p. XX).

In October 1991, Anita Hill testified before the Senate Judiciary Committee as a part of the confirmation hearings for the appointment of Supreme Court nominee Clarence Thomas. Her testimony described alleged incidents of sexual harassment that had occurred almost 10 years before. The testimony was dramatic and yet told with dignity. It was a defining event in the 20th century. Hill was both praised for her courage and vilified for her "lies." The entire country could be separated into two groups: those who believed Hill and those who believed Thomas.

The unfortunate reality was that Hill brought into the hearing room the burden of the historical treatment of Black women. Alexander (1995) described the marginalization of Black women into objects:

> Entrenched historical methodologies and skewed
> prioritizations that deny the significance and validity
> of nontraditional sources have helped to create a hierarchy
> of authenticity and believability in which Black women's
> experiences are misunderstood, doubted, downgraded,
> or ignored. (p. 19)

In 1995, Hill and Jordan edited a book titled *Race, Gender and Power in America*. The title of the second chapter states succinctly what happened to Anita Hill: "The Hill-Thomas Hearings—What Took Place and What Happened: White Male Domination, Black Male Domination, and the Denigration of Black Women." However, Anita Hill's testimony started a dialogue that changed the legal issue of sexual harassment forever.

Bernstein (1995) depicted the general political theme of this period when he described the 1996 election campaign as in danger of yielding to the class warfare rhetoric of Jesse Jackson or the economic nationalism of Buchanan or Perot. He noted that a large group of voters were dissatisfied and would vote for change as they did in 1992 and 1994. The volatility of the campaign was influenced by the rhetoric because the group supporting change has no strong party allegiance.

Johnson (1994) also wrote in the same pessimistic vein. He felt that our inability to solve racial tensions and economic disparities would ultimately cause greater social turmoil that would result in violence reminiscent of the Los Angeles riots of April 1992. The threat of violence between the races was another factor that may have contributed to the verdict in the O. J. Simpson trial.

The O. J. Simpson Trial

From the moment he was declared a suspect in June of 1994 until the trial was over, O. J. Simpson and the question of his guilt or innocence dominated the airwaves as well as public and private debate. On October 6, 1995, when the "not guilty" verdict was announced, an estimated 150 million people watched their TV screens. The long-term result of this trial on racism and belief in blind justice has yet to be determined.

Writing in *Newsweek* that week, Cose (1995) asserted that the methods used by the lawyers in the courtroom might be viewed as negative by the rest of the world because when those ploys used race as an issue, groups could be easily polarized. He hoped that the case would increase understanding and clarify misperceptions so that racial divisions could be healed. However, he stated, "Instead, we may be left to wonder whether, when race is an issue, the search for justice in a polarized society inevitably leads to cynicism about judicial process and pessimism about the possibility of bridging the racial divide" (Cose, 1995, p. 35).

Morrow (1993) described the O. J. Simpson event as the defining trial of the 1990s. He stated:

> The Simpson case offhand seems an unbeatedly lurid end-of-the-millennium American omnium-gatherium of race (the nation's oldest, most durable inflammation of the psyche) sex, celebrity, media hype, justice and injustice. A perfect demonstration of how the American tendency to moralize has gone into partnership with the American appetite for trash—the superego and the id so nicely morphed that they are indistinguishable. (p. 28)

In discussing the O. J. Simpson trial, *The Economist* ("Behind the Verdict," 1995) pointed out that the problem with race was on both sides of the issues: Whether or not the police department may have been racist in its investigation of the crime did not affect the guilt of Simpson, since these two events were not related. However, they also cautioned that progress in race relations was dependent on the recognition by both sides that police reform is essential and that evil can be performed by rich or poor as well as by Black or White.

The role of the race factor in interpreting the results of the O. J. Simpson trial was portrayed vividly by Whitaker (1995), who characterized the differences in how Blacks and Whites interpreted the issues. They felt that for Whites, the issue was domestic violence, but for African Americans it was all about the criminal justice system. Other authors drew some sobering conclusions regarding the uniquely American belief that we could remove the effects of 300 years of slavery in 30 years. They suggested, "if the races don't keep working at what divides them, it could easily be worse" (Starr, Smith, & Fineman, 1995, p. 35).

Gates (1995b) offered a most provocative summation of the Simpson trial:

> The Simpson trial spurs us to question everything except the way the discourse of crime and punishment has enveloped, and suffocated, the analysis of race and poverty in this country... the result is that race politics becomes a court of the imagination wherein Blacks seek to punish Whites for their misdeeds and Whites seek to punish Blacks for theirs, and an infinite regress of score-settling ensues. (p. 65)

Lewis (1995a) made several observations about the Simpson trial. He noticed that although Whites saw the evidence against Simpson as conclusive, Black Americans believed in the police conspiracy theory. He attributed this to the fact that Blacks (even upper-middle-class Blacks) have experienced victimization by law enforcement officers and found the conspiracy theory plausible. He suggested that for everyone's sake we should try to build trust beyond our differences if we want to live in the same country.

Lacayo (1995b) believed that the focus of the trial would ultimately come down to race. He said, "Even before the verdict, it was plain just how passionately the Simpson case pressed upon the sore spots of the American racial psyche" (p. 30). Streisand (1995) observed that nothing O. J. Simpson says will overcome the pain that the trial caused for both races.

Million Man March

Another commentary on race relations in our times was the Million Man March on Washington, D.C., in October 1995. At this event, Reverend Louis Farrakhan called for Black men to march on the capital for a day of atonement and unity. *The Economist* ("Voices in," 1995), described Black-White race relations in America as the poignant backdrop against which one of the major dramas of prejudice was performed. At the time the march was being televised, President Clinton was giving a speech in Texas encouraging unity. Earlier, Colin Powell had been televised, "speaking his mind on a difficult subject, sensibly and with apparent candor" ("Voices in," 1995, p. 26).

This backdrop would imply that much is right in America with race relations. However, Black men did march and they marched alone. This separatist trend was identified by *The Economist* ("The Other American," 1995) as born of sheer frustration. They stated, "Prejudice was driven by hate or disdain; now it is driven by fear "(p. 19). "Race is a deeply unhelpful concern—indeed, a profoundly counterproductive one" (p. 20).

A Harvard professor, West (1995) described his reasons for participating in the Million Man March despite the fact that he is a Democrat and a Christian who does not support xenophobia and anti-Semitism. He said that he was following Dr. Martin Luther King, Jr., who at the time of his death was meeting with Black nationalists to promote Black unity. Additionally, he said, "I have in mind the general invisibility of, and indifference to, Black sadness, sorrow, and social misery, and the disrespect and disregard in which Blacks are held in America and abroad. We agree on Black suffering" (p. A23).

Loury, professor of economics at Boston University and author of *One by One From the Inside Out: Essays and Reviews on Race and Responsibility in America* (Loury, 1995a), described his own feelings regarding the march as a time for pride. Writing in *The New Republic,* he said:

> As I beheld hundreds of thousands of Black men gathering in a crowd that ultimately stretched from the steps of the Capitol back toward the Washington Monument, I would be even more deeply moved. . . . It was a glorious, uplifting day, and I was swept up in it along with everyone else. It almost did not matter what was being said from the podium. For the first time in years, as the drums beat and the crowd swayed, I heard the call of the tribe. (Loury, 1995b, p. 20)

Hugh Price, president of the National Urban League, was quoted in *Time* when he described the march as "the largest family values rally in the history of America" (Lacayo, 1995a, p. 34).

Although the immediate association of the Million Man March may have been made with the civil rights marches of the poor in the 1960s, those marching in 1996 may have been very dissimilar. Marriott (1995) described the marchers as having higher incomes and education than average for Blacks. He found that 38% of 1,050 Black men surveyed said they had completed 4 or more years of college, in contrast to Black men in general age 25 or older, of whom only 13% completed 4 or more years of college in 1994.

Unity within the Black community was demonstrated by Louis Farrakhan, promulgator of the Million Man March. Walsh (1995, p. A22) reported that even though Farrakhan is a controversial figure, criticism by other Black leaders has been slight. In contrast, White America was highly critical of Farrakhan because he is considered a racist and anti-Semite and is unlike other civil rights leaders such as Reverend Martin Luther King, Jr., or Jesse Jackson.

Fineman and Smith (1995) were not so sanguine about unity in the Black community. They wrote:

> Leadership in the Black community, nurtured in the church-based civil-rights movement, is divided, confused, spent. Beset by economic fears and the chaos of the inner city, many Blacks are ready for talk of go-it-alone self-help. Farrakhan fits the near-hysterical tone of public life today, in which versions of the "paranoid style"—from Ross Perot to Pat Robinson to Pat Buchanan—are in fashion. (p. 33–34)

Patterson (1995) also discussed Black unity. He felt that the linking of economic and political self-determination with separatist ideas is a mistake that will ultimately benefit only separatist leaders and reactionary Whites.

West assessed Farrakhan's 2 ½ hour speech as "crazy" (Gates, 1995a). However, in the same article Wyatt Walker (minister of Canaan Baptist Church in Harlem) was quoted as saying, "When he had the men raise their hands and say, 'I pledge' it was incredible" (Gates, 1995, p. 35).

Colin Powell's Candidacy for President

In addition to the much publicized O. J. Simpson trial and the Million Man March, the potential presidential candidacy of Colin Powell permeated the national scene for a period of time. Powell represented the first serious possibility for a Black man to be president. Thomas, Barry, and Cohn (1995) stated, "As the 1996 presidential campaign season begins, voters are wondering the same thing: Is Powell launching a campaign to recapture the Truman Balcony, this time as President?" (p. 28).

Alter (1995) suggested that Powell's run for the presidency would be a double-edged sword. He said, "Powell's color cuts both ways. It hurts him by reducing his margin for error. . . . Yet Powell's color may also be a huge, almost hidden advantage. Many racists don't like to admit they're racist; voting for Powell is a way to show themselves they aren't" (p. 43).

Challenge to Affirmative Action

Puddington (1995) described the state of affirmative action in early 1995. He attributed the decline of support for affirmative action to a combination of the ascendancy of conservative Republicans, the disorganization of liberal Democrats, and the general public's overwhelming dislike of most federal racial policies. He said, "Over the years the proposition that affirmative action was necessary to combat discrimination, or even the effects of past discrimination, became increasingly difficult to sustain" (Puddington, 1995, p. 24).

Hornblower (1995) recognized California's contribution to the death of affirmative action. He felt that the decision of the Board of Regents of the California State University System (a divided vote) no longer to consider race, gender, or ethnic origin in admissions or in hiring and dealing with contracts was essentially the death knell for affirmative action in higher education. With this vote, they became the first university system in the country to eliminate race preference in college admissions.

Cohen (1995) took a strong stand on the role of affirmative action in education:

> A school such as [University of California at] Berkeley has an affirmative obligation to make society better than it found it. It cannot simply accept the status quo and then graduate it 4 years later. To take race into account when, really, it ought to be taken into account, is nothing less than good pedagogical practice. (p. A19)

Kennedy (1995) praised the civil rights movement of the 20th century as one of the most successful reform movements of modern times for achieving equality in educational opportunity. He documented the effect of *Brown v. Board of Education* and the civil rights laws of the 1960s in making bigotry unfashionable. However, he also believed that the deep-rootedness of prejudice in our culture meant that we must continue our efforts. The loss of such remedies as affirmative action may make that task even more difficult.

The Burning of Black Churches

One of the most difficult to understand series of events in 1996 was the burning of over 26 predominantly Black churches in the South (Morganthau, 1996). As if that is not bad enough, if January 1, 1995 is used as the reference date, then an additional 13 churches must be added to that total.

As of August 1996, the breakdown of these fires included 23 active investigations (no suspects were yet arrested), 8 cases had resulted in the arrest of suspects, and 8 cases were regarded as accidental. At this writing, the Bureau of Alcohol, Tobacco, and Firearms has been fully charged to uncover any sign of racist conspiracy. Not all suspects arrested so far have shown a pattern of group ideology or conspiracy, but the Bloomville, South Carolina, church fire in June 1995 has been attributed to two former Ku Klux Klansmen (Holland, 1996).

Evidence collected so far does support the fact that these church burnings have been caused by arson (Witkin, 1996). The source of the arsons are as yet unidentified. The ATF has investigated over 146 church fires since late 1991, and a federal official was quoted as saying, "In church fires, you see a whole spectrum of motives—insurance fraud, homeless people trying to keep warm, juvenile vandalism, or people lashing out" (Witkin, 1996, p. 32). However, for the recent spate of church burnings, there is national concern that racism is at the core.

The fear among many leaders of the African American community is that the church burnings are in fact attempts at intimidation. Nelson Rivers, director of the southeast region of the

National Association for the Advancement of Colored People (NAACP) was quoted as saying, "The burning of Black churches in the South has been used for years to try to intimidate us" ("No Sanctuary," 1996, p. 27).

Although many had believed that progress in race relations had been made in the South, there are many in the African American community who question that notion. Long the victims of injustice at the hands of law enforcers, they have little trust that these investigators will work intensively on discovering and resolving the source of the problem. Democratic Representative John Conyers of Michigan was quoted in *U.S. News & World Report*, "Remember from the view of 30 million Americans what you've got to overcome—a horrible, horrible legacy [of injustice]" (Witkin, 1996, p. 32).

Beyond the legacy of past wrongs, the current climate also contributes to mistrust. Reverend Terrance Macky, Sr., (pastor of the Mt. Zion African Methodist Church in Greeleyville, South Carolina, which was burned in June 1995) said, "Maybe they're embarrassed, but this is a time for people to take a stand. Even worse than silence has been a renewed tolerance of racism" (Fields-Meyer, 1996, p. 102).

Budiansky (1996) described the early frustration of Southern Christian Leadership Conference leaders about the weak response of the government and media to this problem. This inattention was viewed as tolerance. Jesse Jackson was quoted as saying, "The story would have broken much earlier if White churches or synagogues were ablaze" (Budiansky, 1996, p. 8). However, as the media have increased the attention given the church burnings, the number of burnings have increased dramatically. In the 2 weeks after President Clinton visited the Greeleyville church ruins, there were seven church burnings.

As the racism issue becomes more public, its depth is revealed. A White resident of one of the communities where a church was burned offered this explanation for the burning: "What I was expecting to hear was that it was more Blacks. I think that Blacks will do against theirselves just to look like it was racism" (Meredith, 1996, p. A10).

The violation experienced by the parishioners of these churches cannot be completely articulated. For generations, the church has been a place of safety for African Americans. Haizlip (1996) described this phenomenon as follows:

> For me as a child, those beautiful little structures were
> places beyond enchantment. As an adult, I understood that
> the churches were indeed the collective soul of Black folks.
> I never thought that this particular reality could end. . . .
> Where can we go now to be safe? (p. E13)

Lest it seem that no one has offered a constructive response to these events, a number of efforts do support rebuilding. The Mennonite Disaster Services are working with contractors to rebuild one burned-out church. At another site, volunteers with the Quaker Work Camp are helping rebuilding efforts. These workers are coming from as far away as Tanzania and Great Britain (Smothers, 1996). Additionally, funds for rebuilding have been set up in each community, and state governors and businesses are involved. A $500,000 reward has been established in Charlotte, North Carolina, for information leading to convictions ("No Sanctuary," 1996).

Some individuals have also credited these events with bringing African Americans and Whites together. Charles Mills, a White electrician from the Daystar Assembly of God Church in Alabama, was quoted as saying:

> The Devil may have started the fires, but the Lord is using
> it for good in bringing down walls. Your churches are the
> backbones of the community and a powerful symbol that, if
> they were stamped out, could weaken everything. But you
> folks didn't give up and we want to help. (Smothers, 1996,
> p. A10).

The Changing Social Climate of Prejudice

One of the most successful outcomes of the civil rights movement was the rise of the Black middle class. Merida (1995) noted that many people believe this phenomenon is proof that equality is now available to all. He said, "The current frustration of the Black middle class is that while they have been successful and may now be financially comfortable, disparities still remain that conspire to keep Blacks from accumulating wealth that can be passed on from generation to generation as Whites do in much larger percentages" (p. A1).

King (1995a) underscored the changing racial climate by reflecting upon his experiences at Banneker Junior High School in 1955:

> Though it wasn't a subject of constant attention or discussion,
> we believed deep down inside that because we were
> enmeshed in a segregated system not of our own making, we
> were on a mission. So we were driven by determination not
> to allow anyone, especially a White school official or teacher,
> to get away with believing we were in any way inferior. And
> our parents and teachers wouldn't let us forget that. (p. A17)

Estrada (1995) connected the destiny of the Black middle class to the Black "underclass." He stated, "It is the chronic deterioration of the Black underclass that is having such a dramatic impact on the way mainstream America views Blacks. And as upwardly mobile Afro-Americans are all too aware, this in turn can and does intensify prejudice against them as well" (p. A25).

West (1993b) referred to the general debilitating effect of nihilism, which he contends pervades Black communities. He held that, "Nihilism... is the lived experience of coping with a life of horrifying meaninglessness, hopelessness, and (most important) lovelessness" (p. 14). West also stated that this experience resembles a collective clinical depression in many areas of Black America.

Pressley (1995) offered a practical example of the impact of race-based tensions. She described an incident in western Texas in which a Black player was removed as quarterback of his high school football team. She said, "The quarterbacking has not only cast a shadow over everyone's favorite time of year in these parts, it also has thrust into sharp focus a subject most people prefer not to acknowledge or discuss—the state of race relations in this city of 85,000. The local leader of the NAACP commented that if you replace one person with another of another color, for no apparent reason, that's racism" (p. A3).

The complexity of the racial scene is increasing as other racial groups become major players in American society. Constable (1995) described the plight of Hispanics and Asian Americans as they struggle against negative stereotypes: "For Asian Americans the problem is exacerbated by their lack of a common language and religion. While Asians believe that they are the least likely minority to face prejudice, they do recognize a growing xenophobia that has caused the unions between foreign-born and native-born Hispanics and Asian Americans" (p. A1).

Johnson (1994) recognized the multirace factor in racial relations. As minorities face increasing racism from the majority culture, they tend to act it out on one another. Even minor events may result in a major escalation and tragedy. He described such an event:

> In one incident a teenage Black girl went into a liquor store owned by a Korean family and picked up a bottle of orange juice. The woman owner confronted the girl and accused her of shoplifting. An angry argument ensued. The Black girl slapped the store owner, slammed money down on the counter, and turned to walk out of the store. By then, the owner had a gun. She fired, striking the girl in the back and killing her. (p. 185)

The end of this story seems so needless, so preventable. Yet racism breeds violence and contempt for others.

Kennon (1995) discussed the difficulty of changing one's social designations. He said that as individuals leave their culture behind for economic or social advancement, they may feel treasonous. Those who do not make the transition may feel inferior. Though there are ways to transcend one's social group (changing race affiliation, changing class, or changing estate), there is a major price to pay emotionally.

If all the voices speaking about the ongoing national atmosphere agreed, the situation would be relatively simple. But many points of view exist. A prominent one is supported by conservatives. Henry (1994) asserted that the real policy debate in America has always revolved around the poles of elitism and egalitarianism. In his opinion, egalitarianism is being relied upon too often. He cited the most difficult issues of our time (feminism, multiculturalism, proposed bans on hate speech, affirmative action, racial quotas, the erosion of political parties, and the reenshrinement of the more aggressive forms of "progressive" taxation) as examples of this debate. He said, "To me, the real racism lies in the condescending assumption that we must equate all cultures to assuage African Americans or any other minorities, instead of challenging them to compete with, and equal, the best in the culture where they live now" (Henry, 1994, p. 14).

During 1995, one of the loudest conservative voices belonged to Dinesh D'Souza. He contended that liberal programs have not reduced prejudice and racism because they were based on the false assumption that racial generalizations are irrational. D'Souza held that groups can be defined by their traits and thus generalizations can be appropriate. He said, "Since groups do possess distinguishing traits, the liberal assumptions that greater contact between groups can be expected to eliminate prejudices and stereotypes turns out to be illusory" (p. xx).

Herrnstein and Murray were also prominent conservative spokespersons in that time period. They admitted that if affirmative action were abolished, fewer Black students would be admitted to the University of California at Berkeley or Yale. However, they felt that this would not change the opportunity for these students to go to college elsewhere:

> If affirmative action in its present form were ended, the
> schools at the very top would have smaller numbers of Blacks
> and some other minorities on their campuses, but many other
> schools in the next echelon would add the students even as
> they lost some of their former students to other schools
> further down the line. (Herrnstein & Murray, 1995, p. 477)

This stance against public policies to achieve racial equity stems from beliefs that genetic and environmental disadvantages cannot be remedied through intervention. Herrnstein and Murray (1995) cited as evidence the fact that certain endowments, including intelligence, are not distributed equally within the population. Therefore, they support the notion that inequality should be tolerated in the United States, since they interpret inequality as the natural order of life.

Carter (1993) compared the current role of religion in public debates about race with the stance taken in the 1950s by Joseph Rummel, the Roman Catholic Archbishop of New Orleans. At that time, he issued a pastoral letter condemning racial segregation, and he forbade Catholic legislators to support a pending bill that would have required segregation in all of Louisiana's public schools:

The rhetoric of the 1950s was just like the rhetoric of the 1990s, except that in 1956, the liberals cheered and the conservatives got mad. . . there is much depressing evidence that the religious voice is required to stay out of the public square only when it is pressed in a conservative cause. (p. 64)

The Multicultural Educational Climate and Racism

In 1967, the U.S. Commission on Civil Rights published a report titled "Racial Isolation in the Public Schools." The report declared that the isolation of children into single-race groups in their educational process was a negative experience. They specifically identified the harm to White children who grow up isolated from other races. They believed that this situation might lead to a false sense of self-esteem due in part to a false notion of racial superiority. This isolated school experience would not properly prepare White children to live in a world that is rich in human diversity.

The problem of achieving multiculturalism in schools may be traced to the make-up of faculties. Sleeter (1989) recognized the importance of the make-up of the school faculty reflecting the same diversity goals that are projected for the students in the school. All students need to see faculty members of their own ethnicity, but it is equally important that diverse faculties model the kind of multiculturalism they are trying to teach.

Another difficulty in achieving multiculturalism was addressed by several authors (Harris, 1995; O'Connor, 1989; Sizemore, 1990). They hypothesized that the overemphasis on a Eurocentric curriculum so influences minority children's thought patterns that they cannot value the life-style contributions of other cultures. This may result from the limited preparation of teachers to properly present the contributions of other cultures to the strength and diveristy of our nation.

One of the most favorable contributions of a diversified curriculum is the likelihood that exposure to cultural contributions from other ethnic groups will forever change children's thinking such that racism and sexism will be reduced in our society (Brislin, Landis, & Brandt, 1983; Sizemore, 1990).

The problem of defining a truly diversified curriculum is related to the concept of centricity. Asante (1991b) described this as placing the student in the center of his or her own culture to create a reference point for relating socially and psychologically to other cultures. For White children, this poses no problem because most content is approached from a White perspective. However, this phenomenon is further complicated by the fact that American education is in fact Eurocentric. For minority children, the contribution of their cultures to history is often diminished.

One of the most negative contributions of a Eurocentric curriculum is that it does not positively value cultural contributions made by women, African Americans, and other ethnic groups such as Native Americans, Latin Americans, and Asian Americans (Harris, 1992).

Although there have been efforts in recent times to include Afrocentricity (Asante, 1992) as a part of the educational process for African American children, a problem remains. How can each child be taught from his own unique centricity? Asante (1991a) proposed that students be taught to study the world from many different perspectives so that an appreciation could develop for each other's cultural struggles.

Minorities are often very sensitive to discrimination. When it is recognized as part of their daily lives as students, the whole experience of learning takes on a negative connotation. To be forced to read and drill and compute in an environment that is destructive can be debilitative and contribute to some minority students' disillusionment with the educational process in general. Unfortunately, these students can ill afford to eschew education when it is their primary tool for advancement and hope for a better world.

Chapter Summary

Chapter 2 has focused on the current expressions of prejudice in the culture of the United States as we approach the 21st century. We live in a time of access—to information, travel, education—and at no other time in our history have so many demonstrated possession of the American dream. Unfortunately, the gap between the "haves" and the "have nots" is increasing rapidly.

Prejudice in all its varied forms is played out against this backdrop. Major events such as the Hill-Thomas hearings, the O. J. Simpson murder trial, the Million Man March, the challenge to affirmative action, and the burning of Black churches have been a reflection of our society's deeply held prejudices and to some extent, it has frightened us. We are not as far along in our efforts toward a color-blind society as we thought we would be when the civil rights legislation of the 1960s was implemented. We had hoped for more, and yet we have hope that education and training will provide the means to reduce or perhaps even prevent prejudice in the next century.

COUNSELING STYLES AND PREJUDICE

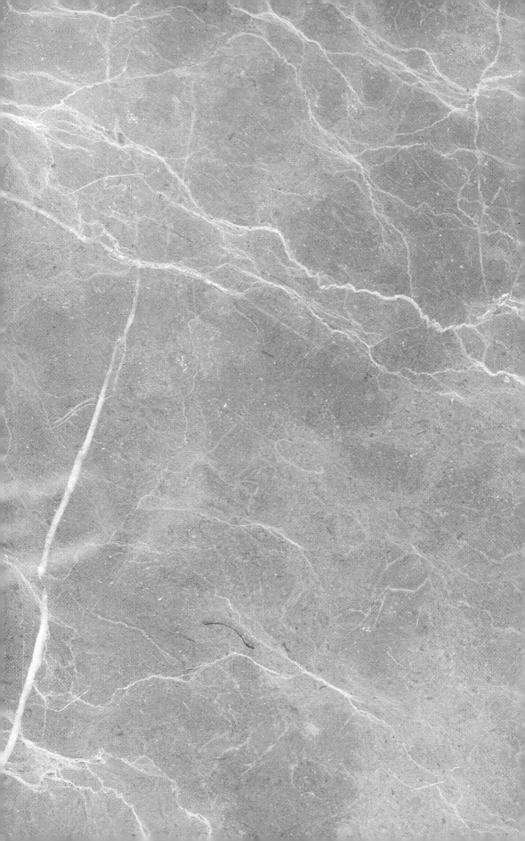

Introduction

The purpose of Section II is to review various counseling methods and their application for problems related to prejudice. This section begins with an overview of prejudice from the Maslowian perspective in Chapter 3. It is helpful to contrast prejudice in modern society with prejudice as it is found in more primitive societies. This theoretical development will be helpful for all counseling methodologies.

In the following chapters, nine counseling styles are presented in terms of their historical contribution, goals of therapy, assessment, perspective and treatment of prejudice, and a case presentation and therapy dialogue. Each area is discussed and examples are given. At the conclusion of this section, six case examples are presented as exercises for further skill building.

Figures 3.1 and 3.2 on the following pages provide a summary of the chapter information for nine

FIGURE 3.1

Views of Prejudice From Nine Counseling Orientations

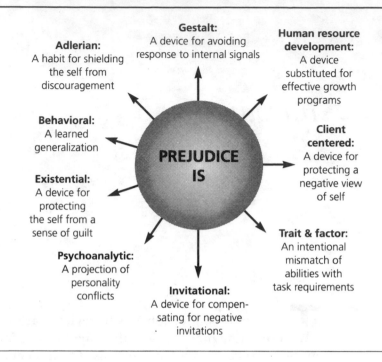

of the counseling orientations. Figure 3.1 addresses the nature of prejudice from each counseling technique. Figure 3.2 describes a treatment goal for each of those counseling orientations.

The chapters are organized to represent the three major theoretical orientations to counseling: (a) psychodynamic, (b) experiential and relationship-oriented, and (c) cognitive and behavioral. Chapters 5 and 6 address Adlerian and psychoanalytic approaches. Experiential and relationship methods are found in Chapters 7 through 11 and include existential counseling, gestalt counseling, human resource development (HRD) counseling, invitational counseling, and person-centered counseling, respec-

FIGURE 3.2

Views of Treatment of Prejudice From Nine Counseling Orientations

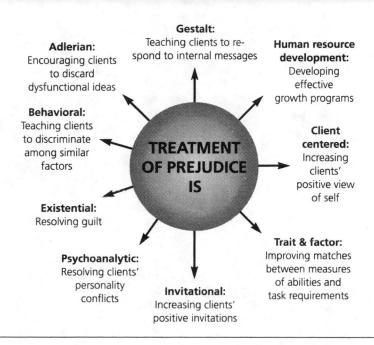

tively. Finally, cognitive/behavioral methods are represented by behavioral therapy and trait and factor counseling in Chapters 12 and 13.

The case presented in each chapter is the same so that methods can be compared. The case involves a 16-year-old girl, Jane S., who has gained weight in recent months and feels rejected by and hostile toward her former group of friends.

A Maslowian View of Prejudice in Modern Society

Prejudice is as old as the human race. The contention that prejudice is a constant in the human condition leads to another question: Do societies express their prejudices in different ways? Specifically, is it necessary to update our knowledge of prejudice to understand it in modern society?

It is reasonable to answer the forgoing question affirmatively. Prejudice changes with variations in social structures. For example, because of slavery, most African Americans in early America were in the same social circumstance. Today, African Americans are distributed across every social strata in American society. In early America, once a specific trait was attributed to African Americans only limited opportunities occurred to observe contrasts that would refute it blatantly. Currently, however, all stereotypic labels are challenged repeatedly and forcefully. The image of an African American peddling drugs on an urban street corner stands in sharp relief against stories of Colin Powell, Martin Luther King, Jr., Cornel West, Maya Angelou, Oprah Winfrey, and Barbara Jordan. Contemporary stereotypes are built and shattered constantly so that biases shift continuously. The intellectual tasks required for that process are enormously complex. In short, it is increasingly difficult to maintain stable prejudices, yet today's society is rife with prejudices. Why?

Maslow's Hypothesis of Prejudice Formation

Prejudices exist because human beings have needs. Abraham Maslow (1968) proposed five basic human needs: physiological, security, love and belongingness, competence, and self-actualization. He contended that healthy human development proceeds sequentially through each of these stages unless people's movement is blocked by circumstances that cause them to either fixate at a given level or regress to a lower one.

The deprivation of a need satisfaction can lead to the formation of a prejudice. For example, if people are unable to get food, they may conclude erroneously (through insufficient or inaccurate information and/or cognitive processes) that an individual is preventing them from obtaining it. If, after having concluded that one person is responsible for the deprivation, the individual then generalizes the same notion to all similar people, a negative prejudice against that group has been formed.

Prejudice may also have a positive valence. If the people in the food example believed erroneously that an individual helped them meet their need, then they can conclude that all such persons would be helpful. Thus, they would have developed a positive prejudice.

The illustration of food deprivation can be extended to all of the five human needs. When people conclude erroneously, either consciously or unconsciously, that some group will automatically either help them obtain or deprive them of basic or secondary needs, the "helpees" may become prejudiced toward or prejudiced against that group of people.

A notion put forward in the preceding section is that human beings are innately driven to satisfy their basic needs. In this sense, human beings are in a natural search for the portion of available resources they believe will satisfy those needs. Wherever resources are, or are perceived to be, inadequate, people compete for them. This competition can lead to a range of behaviors that pit one person against another and group against group. Therefore, the quantity of prejudiced behavior within a social group varies directly with the perception of the adequacy of that group's resources.

Within Maslow's framework, the remedy for prejudice is related to people's perceptions of their access to the resources needed to meet their physiological, security, belonging, competence, and actualization needs. This means that in counseling, prejudice reduction activities are directed toward first determining the nature of healthy human needs and second, developing constructive ways to acquire them. Such efforts have both expanding and narrowing dimensions. Clients presenting excessive demands for resources will moderate their appetites; those seeking too little will increase their estimates. It's a matter of adding a little here and subtracting a little there. Both types will need to develop specific programs for acquiring adequate resources.

The underlying assumption of the Maslowian approach to prejudice reduction is that people who have healthy need systems and who are able to satisfy them will live peacefully with others. Thus, there are two central tasks of prejudice reduction: (a) identification of healthy needs and (b) development of means to satisfy those healthy needs. The following case example will illustrate this point:

A 16-year-old girl has gained weight during the last few months since her mother died. She has experienced some rejection (belongingness need deprivation) from her friends who are thin. She generalized that all thin girls will reject her because of her extra weight (prejudice). The diagnosis of her problem reveals that the weight gain is related to the grief associated with her mother's death.

In counseling, the girl, Jane S., identified a healthy diet for herself with the ultimate goal of weight reduction. She devised an action program that included four basic steps to address her weight as well as her prejudice: (a) consult a dietitian, (b) check her weight regularly, (c) attend Weight Watchers, and (d) talk socially with a thin teenage girl for 10 minutes three times a week until she feels comfortable with thin teenage girls.

Prejudice in Modern Society

The number of prejudices in today's society is increasing because they are being related more often to secondary needs (substitutes) rather than to primary ones. Maslow's famous needs hierarchy is related to healthy growth tendencies, but he also discussed deficiency needs that develop when a growth need is impeded. For example, in our modern society, the general level of interpersonal responses is extremely low. Carkhuff (1993) and his associates demonstrated conclusively that most people either offer no response or a deteriorative one to the human beings they encounter. Indeed, Carkhuff's studies provide voluminous support for the contention that most people without specific training cannot respond effectively to each other because, quite simply, they don't know how. Every other serious investigator who has explored interpersonal relations in America has drawn similar conclusions. In short, most Americans live in an interpersonal world that does not and cannot meet their affiliative needs.

The number of compensatory activities for this deprivation is virtually limitless. One of the classic examples is the straight-A student who parades a perfect report card so that people will praise him or her. The real need, however, is for someone to affirm him or her as a worthy person. Why else would anyone excel at material that is not personally meaningful?

The proliferation of behaviors that substitutes for interpersonal satisfaction is very extensive. Among the prominent surrogates are professional accomplishments, monetary status, social status, political power, military power, athletic prowess, and marital image. Indeed, a vast number of activities that are directed consciously or unconsciously toward satisfying needs for social affiliation qualify as substitutes for that acceptance.

The general concept that emerges is this: Developed societies (i.e., U.S., Japan, Germany) produce a greater supply of resources that satisfy physiological (food) and security (police, armies) needs, but they have not mass-produced ways to meet belonging, competence, and actualization needs. In fact, the work of Carkhuff (1995) and others indicates that the developed nations are fixated at the belonging-need level. In other words, in developed societies, human relationships are the frontier; the paradox is that people tend to use the strategies that yielded satisfaction of the physiological and security needs.

This fixation at the belonging level means that the preponderance of prejudices emanate from the struggle to satisfy needs for interpersonal satisfaction. By contrast, in developing nations, most prejudices originate from conflict over physiological and security resources. Therefore, efforts to eradicate social prejudice must be tailored to the level of need manifest in the society.

According to Maslowian theory, to reduce negative prejudice, we must assist individuals in identifying healthy needs. Our social institutions, such as family, schools, churches, must collaborate to help individuals find ways to satisfy their healthy needs. Society's responsibility to the individual is reciprocated by the individual to society. As each helps to create the other, healthy need satisfaction is ensured.

Sources of Social Prejudice

A society's principle prejudice corresponds to the level of the society's dominant level of need deprivation. Table 3.1 identifies the sources of social prejudice. For example, if a society's dominant need is for security, then an arms race is likely.

A society's inability to satisfy its members' belonging needs often gives rise to a wide variety of substitute objects. This proliferation of sought-for objects also expands the types of competition among the people. Indeed, competition becomes almost omnipresent. Nearly everyone pursues many objects and in so doing develops a diverse array of situational opponents. For instance, a person who wants to buy a boat to satisfy a belonging need (get positive attention) may compete momentarily with a salesman to get it. During that period the buyer may develop a prejudice against all boat salesmen. After the boat transaction is completed the buyer may pursue a new car, at which time a boat salesman might become a confederate and all car salesmen might assume the prejudicial position. The general rule is that in a society in which belonging is the dominant need, there is apt to be a rapid turnover of prejudices, so that old types of bias are lost in the rush for new ways to satisfy affiliative needs.

TABLE 3.1

Sources of Social Prejudice

Society's Dominant Need	Society's Principal Prejudice
Security	Prejudice is against those who are perceived as controlling access to security resources (arms, property)
Belonging	Prejudice is against those who are perceived as controlling access to belonging resources (club membership)
Competence	Prejudice is against those who are perceived as controlling access to competence resources (education, certification)
Actualization	Prejudice is against those who are perceived as controlling access to actualization resources (experimental devices, frontiers)

The foregoing statement has huge implications for developed nations. First, traditional prejudices yield to transitional or temporary ones. This increases the possibility that enduring prejudicial structures such as slavery will be overturned. For instance, the implementation of security nets such as Social Security, Medicaid, and Medicare has been coincidental with the legal revision of a wide variety of established forms of prejudice (i.e., Jim Crowism, school segregation, sex discrimination, or age discrimination). It can be argued cogently that after the security needs were met the society moved to the belonging-need level where it is currently grappling with those problems.

By contrast, underdeveloped nations can be identified as those that have not yet arranged for physiological- and/or safety-need satisfaction. Thus, they contend with problems related to food distribution and protection from life threats. At this level, established social lines ensure survival of certain groups at the expense of others, and these cultural structures give rise to enduring prejudices against groups. These fixed demarcations generate stable biases that serve as impenetrable divisions between individuals and groups. Quite literally, survival is at stake.

This is not to contend that adequate food and security will eradicate all prejudice but rather to recognize that a new set of prejudices will emerge as belonging becomes the prime need of a society. The corollary is that belonging is a higher order need and represents progress toward a universal climate of actualization in which the premier activity is fulfilling constructive human potential.

Chapter Summary

This chapter has provided an overview of prejudice from the perspective of Maslowian theory. We presented the idea that societal prejudice is a product of unmet social needs. This view has implications for both individuals and society as a whole.

Individuals ultimately express the prejudice held by the larger group; the support (or lack thereof) of the larger group will enforce (or dissuade) individual prejudicial actions. As individuals learn to meet their needs in a healthy fashion, society as a whole is changed and a healthier environment will come into being. This growth-promoting reciprocity is our hope for prejudice reduction in the future.

Adlerian Counseling

Adlerian counseling is identified with the formulations of Alfred Adler (Ansbacher & Ansbacher, 1956) during the late 19th and early 20th centuries. Adler emphasized family relationships as the source of most psychological traits. He claimed that psychopathology was rooted in maladaptations to real-life problems. Adlerians assume a teaching role with their clients with the express purpose of convincing them of three things: (a) that previous experiences do not determine how people live, (b) that human beings are able to influence events, and (c) that therapy leads to more effective resolutions of human problems (Corey, 1991a; Dinkmeyer, 1987, Dinkmeyer & Sperry, 1986; Powers & Griffith, 1985, 1986).

Adlerians believe that people must face their life situations and delineate reasons for their successes and their failures. Therapy begins by establishing a compatible patient-therapist relationship, progresses to an understanding of patient's belief patterns, proceeds to the patient's confrontation of errors, and culminates in the development and implementation of better strategies, which are translated into more effective action. These stages can be characterized as (a) review of the life situation, (b) review of beliefs, (c) development of insight, and (d) formulation of new beliefs and behaviors.

The Adlerian search is for origins of pathological adjustments to family and community situations. This therapy is geared toward eliminating or modifying those maladaptations. In addition to being supportive, therapists can challenge clients' beliefs and suggest novel ways of assessing new and established behavior patterns.

Adlerians are criticized for their emphasis upon exploring past experiences. They are accused of being nonspecific in their diagnosis of patients' immediate responses and of offering too few alternatives to troublesome behaviors.

Goals of Therapy

The basic goal of Adlerian therapy is to assist clients in developing alternative ways of thinking, feeling, and behaving by encouraging them to translate insights into action. Additionally, therapists seek to help their clients gain insight into mistaken goals and self-defeating behaviors through a process of confrontation and interpretation. Key to this goal is the establishment and maintenance of a good working relationship between clients and therapists as equals. This facilitates a therapeutic climate in which clients can come to understand their basic beliefs and feelings about themselves and discover how they acquired these beliefs.

Assumptions

The following list contains a summary of some of the basic assumptions upon which Adlerian therapy is based:

1. Counseling involves teaching clients better ways to meet the challenges of life tasks.
2. Past experiences influence people but do not mold them.

3. Clients have the capacity to influence and create events.
4. The critical issue for clients is what they make of their endowments.
5. Clients create a unique lifestyle that helps them explain their patterns of behavior.

Assessment

The Adlerian model uses a life-style questionnaire to discover family influences, birth order, intrafamily relationships, early memories, social forces influencing the client's personality formation, summary of basic mistakes, and summary of assets.

Therapeutic Procedures

In the first phase of therapy, the most important procedure is developing a therapeutic relationship. This relationship is developed through empathic understanding. Additionally, the therapist helps the client develop a contract that specifies what he or she wants from therapy, enumerates client responsibilities, and guides the course of therapy.

During Phase 2 of therapy, the client is encouraged to explore his or her dynamics to see how his or her current life style is affecting his or her current level of functioning. This involves a process of continually reviewing the relationship between life style and functioning.

Phase 3 of therapy emphasizes insight as a precursor to therapeutic change. Through interpretations, the therapist suggests that the client examine the relationship between behavior and beliefs. Eventually, the client discovers the purposes of his or her behavior.

During the final phase of therapy, the client takes risks and changes behavior. Through these changes, the client experiences inner resources and the power to choose and direct his or her own life. The therapist will alternately challenge and encourage the client's attitudes, beliefs, goals, and behaviors to ensure that the client has integrated purpose and action.

Prejudice From an Adlerian Perspective

Adlerian counselors perceive prejudice as a manifestation of pathological belief patterns formed in early family and/or community relationships. As people attempt to cope with the demands of social contacts they encounter tasks they cannot accomplish successfully, so they develop maladaptive beliefs that lead to ineffective behaviors. When those maladaptive beliefs are used in relationships with people outside the family they engender prejudices. That is, the pathological beliefs are projected onto others to justify personal failures.

Adlerian Treatment of Prejudice

Adlerian counselors approach therapy for prejudice by searching for the person's beliefs that were formed as outgrowths of their early experiences. After the stultifying situations are identified, therapists attempt to evaluate them with their clients who use them for insight into their belief systems. Therapists encourage their clients to establish new beliefs and to translate them into more effective actions.

Case Study

A 16-year-old girl, Jane S., has recently gained some bothersome weight and a significant thin cohort has rejected her socially. The girl has drawn a connection between the two events and has concluded that all thin teenage girls reject overweight people. She doesn't like the social isolation from thin teenage girls and is seeking counseling for her problems.

Treatment

The therapist established an empathic relationship with Jane and determined significant relationships with her family. The therapist challenged Jane's belief that being overweight is a punishable transgression and that she deserved the rejection of her cohort.

The therapist encouraged Jane's decision to initiate both a healthy diet and a program to reestablish relationships with thin teenage girls by conversing with them regularly until she feels that her choice of friends is not based on the belief that all thin teenage girls reject those who are overweight.

Therapy Dialogue

JANE: I'm really shook up about the weight I'm gaining.

COUNSELOR: You sound like it's a hopeless situation.

JANE: It's always been that way in my family.

COUNSELOR: You learned early that people in your family are supposed to be fat?

JANE: Yeah. We're all fat. I knew I'd get too heavy some time. Now it's here.

COUNSELOR: So it was inevitable. You had no choice in the matter.

JANE: Well, I try to eat the right things.

COUNSELOR: So, there's no better strategy. You're convinced that your weight isn't related to your diet.

JANE: Not exactly. I work pretty hard sometimes, but at other times I eat what I want. I think I'm just bound to be fat—I can't control myself.

COUNSELOR: You sound depressed and sad, almost like it's your time to join the fat brigade.

JANE: It is depressing. All of the thin girls ignore me. They don't even see me anymore. I'm an outcast.

COUNSELOR: So, you're going to let your weight situation isolate you from a whole bunch of girls.

JANE: I don't care about them. They're all snobs and manipulators. If they can't get something out of you they ignore you. I really hate them.

COUNSELOR: Did you come to that conclusion after you gained weight?

JANE: Well, yes. It got a lot stronger because I could feel what they were doing to me.

COUNSELOR: It was O.K. as long as it was happening to someone else.

JANE: No, but it just wasn't as clear. I guess I've always known this would happen ever since I was a kid. It was like a cloud over me. Now, it's finally happened.

COUNSELOR: You've always felt like a time bomb that would go off and sure enough it did.

JANE: Well it's one thing to be fat and another to be rejected because of it. I hate them as much as they hate me!

COUNSELOR: Do you want to feel like this? Hating yourself and everybody else?

JANE: Of course not!

COUNSELOR: Then, let's get started on ways to turn this around. You've been very successful in other areas of your life. Let's build on that.

Chapter Summary

Adlerian counseling begins (as do most effective therapeutic techniques) with the development of a compatible client-therapist relationship and seeks ultimately to assist the client in developing more effective beliefs, feelings, and behaviors. Adler emphasized the role of family relationships as the source of most psychopathology. Adlerian therapy is a process, then, of discovering and rejecting psychopathology and learning new responses.

Adlerian therapists may use a variety of techniques to explore the life situation and current beliefs of the client. They may be supportive or confrontational. However, Adlerian therapists almost always adopt the role of teacher when helping clients learn the new skills required for healthier living.

5

Psychoanalytic Therapy

From a psychoanalytic point of view, humanity is basically evil and is governed by rudimentary instincts. Thus, people are destined to become victims of the interaction and conflict between these instincts and social forces. The only hope is to find a livable balance between our evil impulses and the demands of our environment. However, this solution results in only a tolerable life with little hope of profound happiness.

Balance is achieved by gaining a complete understanding of the factors that make us weak; thus we can arm ourselves against succumbing to them. We can accomplish this understanding and learn to apply it through psychoanalysis. Those individuals who achieve a reasonable balance between internal and external forces can help others achieve balance through insight and understanding.

Freud defined the unconscious as the portion of the mind that lies below normal awareness. Within the unconscious could be found the id, ego, and superego and the interactions of these components determine the internal balance and ultimately the sanity of any individual.

Freud identified and catalogued elements of the psyche that contribute to our understanding of the mind. He defined instincts as powerful and incessant inner stimuli. These stimuli were of course evil and if left unchecked would contribute to the ruin of the individual (Ivey, Ivey, & Simek-Downing, 1987; Prochaska, 1984).

The id is the source of all wishes and desires. It is unconscious and exists at birth. The id wants what it wants when it wants it and cannot tolerate delay. The infant is complete id.

Fortunately, the superego moderates and/or neutralizes behavior to conform to socially acceptable standards. The superego is analogous to one's conscience. It contains a set of principles gathered from interacting with others in society and serves as an internal gyroscope. The superego compares your behavior to your ego ideal, that is, what you think you should be like. The superego is perfectionistic, seeking to inhibit the id's antisocial desires and causing an individual to experience guilt when transgressing (or even when considering a misdeed) or pride when the person reaches a particular standard. Differences between one's basic instincts and society's rules are stored in the superego. These conflicts must be resolved to restore the individual's balance.

The ego comes into being within the first year of life. Some needs such as hunger can be satisfied only by interacting with the real world. The ego, which is partly conscious, operates through the secondary process, or reality principle. It is responsible for dealing with reality and satisfying the needs and desires of the id in a socially appropriate manner. Whereas the id knows only subjective reality, the ego must also understand the world outside the mind and the self. As the child grows and matures, the ego grows stronger becoming able to delay gratification and balance the desires of the id within the restraints of the superego. The ego has a difficult job. Sometimes it is overwhelmed and the tension that results is experienced as anxiety. If the anxiety becomes too great, the ego may defend itself by using a large number of protective maneuvers called defense mechanisms.

Defense mechanisms mediate and compromise instinctual drives. A defense mechanism is an automatic and unconscious process that serves to relieve or reduce feelings of anxiety or emotional conflict. These mechanisms protect the integrity of

the psyche until balance can be achieved through ego intervention. Repression is a defense mechanism that bars thoughts
and memories from the consciousness so that the individual
will not suffer from the pain they evoke. Projection is a defense
mechanism in which personally unacceptable wishes and
impulses are attributed to others. Transference is a process in
which conflicts experienced with one person are projected into
another relationship.

Major Theses

Freud believed that the mental life and the nature of humanity
could not only be understood but that insights gained could be
applied to alleviate human suffering to some degree. He postulated that the greatest part of humanity's behavior is irrational
and is governed by unconscious forces and processes. However,
he also believed that it is possible to depict the development and
maintenance of destructive forces in human beings and society.

Historical Contributions

Psychoanalytic theory has provided a base for the interpretations of fields of study beyond the helping professions (i.e.,
anthropology, economics, and religion). It also has delivered a
systematic focus for interpreting the symbolism in behavior and
interpersonal relationships.

Perhaps one of the most important contributions of psychoanalytic theory to the discipline is the comprehensive view of the
interpersonal relationships in the family and their implications
for psychological development. It was also the first system to deal
with and begin to comprehend the importance of affect. It has
also provided a meaningful framework from which to understand the means by which individuals attempt to maintain a
sense of uniqueness and ward off annihilation.

Psychoanalytic theory was the first to give focus and meaning
to the polarities of feelings and behavior and to emphasize the

common attributes of the sexes. It also provided an explanation of the implications and durable effects of trauma and thus provided impetus for intervention and remediation (Erikson, 1963). Likewise, psychoanalytic theory has provided an explanation of the durable influence of early childhood experiences for those who are minimally functional in society.

Perhaps one of the greatest contributions was the early emphasis on the development of standards for training and practice. This provided a systematic approach for research and results dissemination across a broader range of practitioners and has thus helped the development of the field in general.

The Therapy Process

Therapy supplies patients with painful frustration and resolutions of the frustration, such as that involved in working through a transference. Since a weakened ego constitutes the condition for the development of neurosis, therapists are committed to ally themselves with the ego against the id and the superego.

The role of therapists is largely a didactic one in which they uncover and integrate unconscious material. Therapists are also involved in making judgments as to whether or not a defense is appropriate or inappropriate. The question rests on the influence of the defense. If it weakens the ego, denies reality, or threatens to change the structure of the entire psychic system, it is maladaptive. In a real sense, therapists judge a defense as helpful or not in accordance with the difficulty or ease in making psychoanalytic interpretations. The patients most difficult to analyze are most sick.

Therapists using the psychoanalytic technique are somewhat distant but are considered to be all-knowing and understanding authorities by clients. Their theory and manner communicate to patients that they are truly superior. Therapists not only understands the patients' unconscious processes but also render irrational material rational. There is an implicit assumption that therapy cannot work if patients insist on questioning therapists' knowledge and authority. In such cases patients may be judged too resistant to be amenable to treatment. The level of intensity of any denial is a reflection of the validity of the interpretation (Linder, 1954).

The scientific basis of psychoanalysis separates it from therapies that rely upon human experience for their data. Objectivity is psychoanalysts' major tool and personal involvement with clients is an impediment to effective analysis. Analysts must be free to organize patients' verbal behavior into its component parts without distorting them because of personal needs.

Psychoanalysis contrasts with religious notions of human behavior and during its inception generated considerable controversy. The Freudian concept of the role of sexual drives clashed heavily with cultural mores, and many people objected strenuously to the notion that children were dominated by sexual instincts.

Psychoanalysis dominated the early attempts at psychotherapy; other schools of thought developed largely as reactions to its main tenets. Many of Freud's pupils and colleagues formulated neo-Freudian therapies that were permutations of the original concepts. Carl Rogers' (1951) work in person-centered counseling was stimulated in response to the Freudian notion that people were innately prone toward licentious behavior and that the prime task of civilization was to foster behaviors that would satisfy basic drives through socially acceptable means.

Considerable criticism of analytic counseling has stemmed from its objectivity, which necessitates an affectively distant client-counselor relationship. This style of association negates the possibility of the development of a human relationship by placing the therapist in an observer's role. Thus, clients' experiences are not viewed empathically, which makes an object rather than a person of them.

Prejudice From a Psychoanalytic Perspective

A person's prejudices emanate from unresolved personality conflicts developed in early childhood. The person uses a pathological defense mechanism (projection) to protect the ego against threats (anxiety) posed by possible activation of repressed personality conflicts.

Psychoanalytic Treatment of Prejudice

Patients must discover their personality conflicts and reintegrate themselves with the help of therapists who foster healthier means of resolving tensions between basic drives (id) and the demands of society (superego).

Case Study

Jane S., a 16-year-old girl, gained some bothersome weight and believed she was rejected by thin teenage girls because of it. Thus, she became prejudiced against all thin teenage girls.

Therapy Dialogue

JANE: I'm really scared about the weight I'm gaining. I'm getting as big as a horse.

COUNSELOR: Uh-huh (waits).

JANE: I don't know what to do. It's beginning to cause trouble with my friends. They're acting like I have something wrong with me. Maybe I do. I'm starting to wonder.

COUNSELOR: What do you think is wrong?

JANE: I don't know but it may have something to do with my mother. I read that food represents your mother's love and maybe that's what I'm trying to do. You know, substituting food for her love.

COUNSELOR: Does eating food make you feel loved?

JANE: I guess it does. When my stomach gets full I get sleepy and cuddly just like babies do after they eat. Sometimes I roll up in a ball and snuggle myself.

COUNSELOR: You're aware that there is some connection between your eating and thinking about being a baby.

JANE: Yeah. I worry about it sometimes. I wonder if I'm afraid to grow up. It may be easier to be a little kid. It's safer. Your parents protect you and you don't have to worry. I even dream about staying young forever just like Peter Pan. That would be nice. I could fly all over the place (laughs).

COUNSELOR: Right now Peter Pan is more appealing than adulthood.

JANE: Sure it is! Then I wouldn't have to face the cruelty of small-minded girls. Just because they're thin doesn't mean they are better then me. I hate them all.

COUNSELOR: It's easier to project blame on your thin friends than to search yourself for explanations for your weight gain.

JANE: O.K., it may be my fault for eating too much, but the way they treat me just makes me feel so bad. I want something to make me feel better.

COUNSELOR: Food brings back feelings of safety and security for you. It's easier to eat than to work on your relationships.

JANE: O.K. I get your point. You think my eating is tied to my emotions rather than to hunger.

COUNSELOR: We all want to get away from bad feelings that make us feel threatened, but meeting a physical need won't help with an emotional need. Somewhere along the way in your development, you've linked the two.

JANE: Well, what can I do now? I can't go back.

COUNSELOR: Understanding the problem is the first step toward solving it.

Chapter Summary

Psychoanalytic theory as described by Freud gave structure and function to the unconscious and provided a vocabulary for exploring the hidden processes that control behavior. The therapeutic end point of psychotherapy is insight and behavior change. Although some will note differences between counseling and therapy, their shared components focus on problem resolution as evidenced by emotional and behavioral change.

The therapist role in psychotherapy differs from other approaches in its almost exclusionary use of the didactic. The therapist remains aloof and distant from the client to remain outside the client's problem and thus serve as a better observer. Objectivity is crucial and involvement with the client is an impediment. Prejudice from this perspective is a projection of an individual's personality conflicts onto others in an attempt to protect the ego. Psychotherapy has been the target of criticism because of its concepts pertaining to sexual drives. However, it was also the first discipline in the field to require rigorous standards for training and practice.

CHAPTER 6

Existential Counseling

Existential counseling is based on the notion that life has no intrinsic meaning and that people must exercise their responsibility to choose a meaning for their existence. A corollary is that failure to make a choice results in guilt and anxiety. Existentialism is closely related to phenomenology—the study of subjective experience—but it also retains an association with science through its reliance on analyses of clients' processes for coping with their existence. Existentialism can be traced to figures such as Husserl (1929), Nietzsche (1967), Kierkegaard (1954), and Frankl (1959, 1967), but it was popularized in therapy by people such as May (1953) during the 1950s and 1960s. During that period there was a cultural emphasis upon the discovery of personal meaning, and existential counseling met that need very well.

Logotherapy, as developed by Frankl (1959), identified the search for meaning in one's life as the primary motivational force. The notion of a search for meaning implies that the meaning of one's life exists and must be discovered rather than created. Frankl (1959) associated logotherapy with existentialism in three ways. First, logotherapy was associated with existence itself. Second, it involved a search for the meaning of existence. Third, it was the struggle for meaning in personal existence or the will to meaning.

Frankl disassociated logotherapy from psychotherapy in two primary ways. Psychotherapy is concerned with one's past; logotherapy is concerned with the future. Psychotherapy believes the human concern is the gratification and satisfaction of drives and instincts, and logotherapy views humankind as fulfilling meaning and actualizing values. Even though existential counseling techniques may be didactic and confrontive, the essential ingredient is an authentic relationship between therapist and client.

Existential counseling strives to present its clients with an authentic human climate in which people can deal honestly with their own life choices. Therapists' authenticity is critical because it establishes an environment in which clients can manifest the genuineness required for honest consideration of their ways of living.

It is believed that when clients are immersed in a genuine human relationship they will experience four basic realities about themselves: (a) what brought them to counseling, (b) where they are in their life, (c) what they want to change about themselves, and (d) how they want to change. Therapists guide clients' development by facilitating their movement through each of those four stages. Therapeutic success is measured by the degree to which clients have formulated and taken responsibility for their life-style choices.

Criticism of existential counseling tends to focus around the contention that it is excessively verbal and intellectual. Theoreticians and practitioners are accused of relying upon cognitive understandings of life rather than primary experiences of it. The assertion is that existential counseling predisposes clients to become skilled observers and to substitute speculation for participation (Corey & Corey, 1990).

Goal and Focus of Counseling

The goal of counseling is to mold one's life substance into a caring and worthy existence. The purpose is to help people become aware of what they are doing and to prod them out of their stance as victims. The existential approach is the only counseling formulation that focuses upon the crucial questions concerning the nature of human beings.

According to existential theory, human beings, whose sense of self is developed through their relatedness to others, do not know themselves except in relation to others. Because of the importance of relationships, human beings' principal source of anxiety is a fear of losing others and being alone. Existentialists help their clients realize that their real guilt is that they cannot act and that they must face the fact that they are really alone. The task of therapy is to enable human beings to act and to accept the freedom and responsibility of acting.

Historical Contributions

Existentialism was the first counseling approach to attend to the depersonalization and isolation of modern human beings. It also filled a very real treatment void left by Freudian, behaviorist, and trait-and-factor approaches to counseling. It asks basic questions not asked elsewhere concerning the nature of humankind and develops in response a core of basic human values that are not developed in other therapeutic orientations. It also posits for the first time a unique combination of both the subjective and objective world in humankind's phenomenological existence.

Therapeutic Process

The therapeutic process begins with the formation of a significant one-to-one relationship in which both therapist and client "act" as if they were the only persons existing at that point in time. Through their fulfilled need for intimacy, clients experience their own existence as real. A false sense of guilt is relieved, and patients achieve a continuity with themselves. They must assume responsibility for their behavior with active decision making. The process is highly verbal, emphasizing words about feelings and exploration of values.

The Therapist's Role

Therapists communicate their understanding and full regard for their patients' human dignity. They work as tutors with clients, helping them to analyze the existential meaning of human experience rather than the direct expression of experience. Occasionally, therapists may share their experience with clients.

The counseling relationship is an unfolding and dynamic process that moves through three phases. The first phase is centered on understanding one's present modes of existence. This may be accomplished by assessing physical status, social status, personal integration, and values. Therapy helps individuals determine who they want to become and to elaborate the talents they have available to accomplish this goal.

The second phase addresses modifying and expanding these modes into a renewed direction for one's life to determine one's life values. The third phase deals with assessing and developing skills as a means to carry out this new life agenda and implementing values choices.

Contributions to Counseling

The existential approach offers both clients and therapists an opportunity for an honest human encounter and a developed cosmology for existence. This approach makes explicit values that are left implicit in other approaches.

Major Themes

Anxiety is a symptomless, deep feeling of unease that accompanies the awareness that one's existence is limited and frail and that one is ultimately responsible for the purpose and direction of one's own existence. Existential anxiety is the bodily response to the recognition that we are accountable for fashioning a worthy existence in a limited time without the surety of some authority telling us what worthiness is. In existential counseling, the experience of existential anxiety is understood as a positive sign. It means clients have begun to acknowledge the obligation to take charge of their own existence and have moved beyond the mere passive acceptance of social definitions of "who I am."

Authenticity is the kind of existence people have when they accept responsibility for choosing the constructs and assumptions that direct their actions. Guilt is the emotion felt when a person has not fulfilled the existential obligation to fashion a worthy existence. It is understood as a call from within to take control of one's own existence.

Prejudice From an Existential Perspective

Existential counselors consider prejudice a pathological condition that limits people's ability to engage their lives fully. It is viewed as a process in which people substitute an unjustified judgment of others for an authentic encounter with them. The assessment is that clients have chosen to avoid painful experiences by acting as if the responsibility for their situation belongs to others. In short, prejudiced clients have evaded their personal responsibility for confronting others and making personal judgments about them.

Existential Treatment of Prejudice

Existential counselors engage prejudiced clients in a dialogue during which they establish an authentic and caring relationship. The interaction provides an opportunity for therapists to demonstrate respect for clients and to gain an empathic understanding of their ways of establishing meaning. That is, therapists discern how clients derive their prejudice and communicate that understanding to the clients so that they can conceptualize how it distorts their personal responsibility for their choice of meaning.

Case Study

A 16-year-old girl named Jane S. has had a bothersome weight increase in the last few weeks. She is convinced that her thin teenage friends are rejecting her because of the weight gain. She has decided that all thin teenage girls will reject her and has developed a prejudice against all such people.

Treatment

The counselor established a trusting relationship with Jane and directed her to clarify her present status. The counselor provided a genuine and caring relationship in which she could gain an empathic understanding of her client's life choices. The client revealed that she was allowing her relationships with her friends to create stress, which she was handling by excessive eating. Thus, she connected the weight gain with her abdication of responsibility to make her own life choices.

The counselor has tutored Jane's assertion of her personal responsibility and actions. She concludes that she is healthy, though overweight causes self-doubt. She wants to do things that are consistent with her personal values. She initiates a weight loss program as well as an effort to get reacquainted with thin teenage girls. In the process she understands that her prejudice toward thin teenage girls stems from her failure to exercise her own freedom and responsibility to maintain a healthy weight level. She concludes that there is a relationship between her weight gain and her relationship with thin teenage girls but that she can control it.

Therapy Dialogue

> JANE: I'm really scared about the weight I'm gaining. I'm getting fat as a horse.
>
> COUNSELOR: It's like you're losing control of your life.
>
> JANE: Yeah. Everything seems to be running away with me just like my weight is.

COUNSELOR: You have a general sense that whatever is wrong is messing up everything.

JANE: I guess the biggest problem is that my weight is ruining my friendships, especially with thin girls. I can't stand to be around them.

COUNSELOR: Somehow this weight change is related to how you get along with thin girls.

JANE: Since I gained all this weight I have noticed that thin girls don't like to be around me. They used to be my friends and now they act like I'm contagious or something. They're all phonies. I've watched them and I can't trust a thing they say, any of them.

COUNSELOR: You think they're bad people but still you are letting them dictate the food you choose. It's as if they are in charge of your diet.

JANE: They are. I can't get out from under the pressure they create. I need friends. Everybody needs friends. The only ones I have are the people nobody else will talk to. They're not friends. They're just desperate people.

COUNSELOR: You're uncomfortable with your thin friends making your choices, and you want to retrieve your right to do that.

Chapter Summary

Existentialism emerged at a time in history when there was great emphasis on personal meaning. The struggle to find meaning in one's existence despite the dehumanizing forces that abound in modern society became a theme in the United States as industrialization peaked. The answer to the question, "Why have you not committed suicide?" is the beginning of the determination of the meaning of one's life.

Clients must determine what they want to change about themselves and how they want to change. Therapists work as tutors, mentors, and teachers to help clients assume responsibility for their choices.

Prejudice from the existential counseling perspective implies that individuals are avoiding responsibility for their situations by refusing to meet the targets of their prejudice and make authentic judgments of them rather than making unjustified ones without data. Treatment of prejudice involves helping clients discern the source of their prejudice so that it can be addressed. Ultimately, it is the responsibility of each individual to live an authentic life that has meaning as a contribution to society.

Gestalt Counseling

Gestalt therapy is associated with the work of Fritz Perls, who gained considerable recognition during the 1960s. In his book *What Really Matters*, Tony Schwarz (1995) made the following statement about Perls and gestalt therapy:

> Gestalt therapy was conceived around a simple premise: that people suffer because they have lost touch with their bodies and their feelings—and thus, in the deepest sense, with themselves. Therapy, Perls believed, should consist of an effort to help the patient recover this self-awareness.... What we are trying to do in therapy is to re-own the disowned parts of the personality.... Most defenses, Perls argued, reflected ways of using the mind to keep feelings at a distance.... Perls evolved an approach to working with people that had to do with truly bringing them into the present moment. He did it in a way that allowed them to experience their past suffering in the present, to work through it toward an opening and a letting go. (p. 95)

Rainette Fantz (Corey, 1991a) attributed specific characteristics to gestalt therapy. One of its emphases is to discover what a client sees, hears, smells, tastes, and feels in the present moment.

Polarities are critical: anger and depression, resentment and guilt, spontaneity and control, taking and giving, forthrightness and appeasement.

Fantz held that the central task of a therapist is to help clients to fully experience being in the "here and now" by first realizing how they are preventing themselves from feeling and experiencing in the present. A basic premise of gestalt therapy is that by experiencing conflicts directly instead of merely talking about them, clients will expand their own level of awareness and integrate the fragmented and unknown parts of their personality.

The goal of gestalt therapy is to move from environmental support to self-support and to assist clients in gaining awareness of their present experience. Therapy will provide the necessary interventions and challenge to help them gain awareness of what they are doing, thinking, and feeling now. As they come to recognize and experience blocks to maturity, they can then begin experimenting with different ways of being.

Gestalt therapy has been criticized for its harsh confrontations with patients. Schwarz (1995) believed that Perls abandoned the intellect altogether. He felt this resulted in a deprecation of self-consiousness and loss of the ability to reflect on decisions and actions, the characteristics that distinguish us from animals. He also felt that Perls' blatant honesty without compassion was cruel. It violated the first law of medicine, "First, do no harm."

Prejudice From a Gestalt Perspective

Gestalt counselors perceive prejudice as a mechanism for avoiding painful feelings about the self. It is painful to confront one's situational struggles in a world where limitations are disapproved. Thus, people develop prejudice as an intellectual device that softens or eliminates the conscious realization that others are inflicting pain to meet their selfish needs. That is, prejudice develops when it is easier to pretend that some class of people is causing the pain than it is to directly confront the source of the hurt. To be full persons, human beings must face the source of their pain and deal with it straightforwardly.

Gestalt Treatment of Prejudice

Gestalt counselors strive to bring experience into the moment, so they confront prejudiced clients with the feelings they experience while being prejudiced. The treatment might include an imagined conversation with the object of the person's prejudice so that there would be a clear-cut experience of the prejudicial judgments. One situation might be, "Look her in the eye and tell her how you feel when you hire a man because you think women are inferior to men."

Case Study

A 16-year-old girl, Jane S., had gained some weight and believed she was rejected by all thin teenage girls because of it. Thus, she became prejudiced against all thin teenage girls.

Therapy Dialogue

JANE: I'm really scared about the weight I'm gaining. I'm getting big as a horse.

COUNSELOR: What do you mean when you say "scared?"

JANE: I get tense and nervous.

COUNSELOR: Where do you get tense?

JANE: I get a knot in my stomach. Right here.

COUNSELOR: Is it there now?

JANE: It's getting there. It makes me want to vomit.

COUNSELOR: Why don't you vomit?

JANE: It's embarrassing and it hurts.

COUNSELOR: What are you embarrassed about?

JANE: You'd think I was some kind of nut.

COUNSELOR: Why does it matter to you what I think?

JANE: You're a psychologist. You might think I'm crazy or seriously sick.

COUNSELOR: How do you feel when you say "crazy?"

JANE: I get scared.

COUNSELOR: You don't sound scared. You sound angry.

JANE: Sure. It makes me angry when you think I'm crazy. I came to talk about my weight.

COUNSELOR: Why didn't you say you were angry? You said you were scared.

JANE: I was afraid you would get angry at me if I said I was angry.

COUNSELOR: Now you seem relieved when you say angry.

JANE: Yeah. It's like getting it out there.

COUNSELOR: Like when you throw up?

JANE: I suppose.

COUNSELOR: You're the authority on how you feel. Don't you know?

JANE: I know I don't like what's happening to me. I want to have friends and lose weight and get my life back the way it was before I lost my mom.

COUNSELOR: You're angry with her for leaving you, and since you can't get back at her, you turn it inside and you eat to make it all go away.

JANE: (Cries) I want it to go away some other way.

COUNSELOR: Then you'll have to bring out the pain, face it, and move on.

JANE: I don't think I know how.

COUNSELOR: Well, that's where we will begin.

Chapter Summary

Gestalt therapy was developed as a technique for helping clients to experience themselves fully in the here and now. The experiential component of these techniques was believed to be critical in helping clients integrate their cognitive descriptions of problems or negative experiences with their emotional response to problems. This integration of senses and cognition provides a therapeutic reality that clients can use to confront true problems and find personal authenticity.

Gestalt therapy has been criticized for its confrontive techniques that may "unmask" an individual's true feelings and emotions in ways the individual is not ready to assimilate. This phenomenon has resulted in charges of cruelty because brutal honesty is often used without compassion.

Prejudice from the perspective of gestalt therapy is a "cop out"—a refusal to take responsibility for one's own pain and perhaps failure. By attributing negative characteristics to minority groups, one can intellectualize and perhaps justify exploitation of them.

CHAPTER 8

Human Resource Development Counseling

The human resource development (HRD) counseling model was founded in the late 1960s by Robert Carkhuff (Carkhuff & Berenson, 1976; Carkhuff, 1993). The HRD model of therapy defines two major purposes in life: to grow and to learn. A corollary of this belief is that life is to be valued above all else. The HRD model is an integrative, generative approach to helping relationships. It integrates person-centered, analytic, and behaviorist concepts into the helping process and differs from eclecticism in that it systematically includes contributions from each of those orientations. The helping process begins with person-centered responsiveness, progresses to analytic insight, and culminates in step-by-step action programs.

The historical significance of HRD formulations was that they occurred at the height of contention among three main approaches to counseling: Rogerian, Freudian, and Skinnerian. The HRD model maintained that each individual orientation made a significant contribution to the helping process. This integrative stance might have diminished the competition among the contending positions, but most followers of other models resisted being subsumed under a larger canopy as much as they resented each other.

However, the HRD model made unique contributions to the field of counseling as well as incorporating dimensions of other models. It was the first to integrate human values with scientific rigor in counseling. The scientific focus supported a skills-based training and required that counselors demonstrate their skills and that they be accountable for their counseling activities.

Another focus of the HRD counseling model was to systematically extend counseling activities into organizations and community programs so that community change was promoted. This interest in community development as well as individual development helped encourage the notion that responsivity and initiation were both important dimensions of counseling.

The focus on research aided the accumulation of the largest database available to document counseling's efficacy. Furthermore, the database was used as a feedback loop to revise formulations as necessary to increase effectiveness.

Major constructs identified by the HRD counseling model included designation of the counselor as a "helper," an individual who is more knowing and can help others improve in an area of functioning. A "helpee" was defined as a less knowing individual who wanted to improve in some area of functioning. Counseling or helping was defined as a systematic activity intentionally designed and directed toward the improvement of a person's physical, emotional, or intellectual skills. Since helping is skills based, a skill is defined as a behavior or task that can be replicated at will to a high degree of efficiency and effectiveness.

The "art of helping" uses a learning model identified by Carkhuff (1993) as exploration, understanding, and action. Exploration involves identifying where the helpees are. Understanding is the identification of where they want to be or the determination of a goal. Action is the development of a step-by-step plan to take the helpee from where they are to where they want to be or a plan for goal achievement. Feedback is an information loop about the efficacy of the programs or action plans so that they can be revised as necessary to ensure goal attainment.

The helper's role in therapy is to establish an atmosphere that is alternately responsive and initiative as indicated by the helpee's needs as well as to use appropriate helping skills that can be assessed by observers. The role of the helpee is to be open to the possibility that the helping process will improve his or her quality of life and to commit resources fully to the helping process.

Since HRD is skills based, the helpers' skills are delineated clearly; and the main task is to teach skills to helpees. Helpers' skills include attending, responding, personalizing, and designing programs. Clients progress through exploration, understanding, and action. The counseling process begins with helpers attending, observing, and listening. While clients explore, helpers respond. When clients gain understanding, helpers personalize both the meaning of their experience and their goals. When clients must act, helpers design action programs. Thus, at every point in the helping process, the tasks of helpees and helpers can be clearly articulated and are observable and measurable.

Assessment, then, is an essential part of the HRD model. Helpees' levels of physical, emotional, and intellectual functioning are assessed throughout the helping process as a measure of the effectiveness of the program. Changes in specific target skills are also assessed throughout the helping process to ensure that helpees are on target toward their goals.

Likewise, at each stage of the counseling process, helpers' actions can be rated according to their levels of functioning. This aids both process and outcome information that can be used for feedback.

The effectiveness of HRD is judged objectively by changes in measures of helpees' physical, emotional, and intellectual skills. This comprehensive approach examines helpees' total effectiveness rather than improvement in an isolated symptom or condition.

Objections to HRD are directed toward its systematic approach, which some observers contend makes it seem mechanical or methodical rather than spontaneous. The concern is that helpers are cast into a rigid role with precise behavioral expectations. Application of these prescribed skills in the counseling interview have been characterized as a limit upon helpers' use of creative responses.

Prejudice From a Human Resource Development Perspective

Prejudice from the HRD counseling model perspective is a mental process in which individuals learn to blame others for their failures rather than investing the resources necessary to learn the skills required for success. Thus, it would follow that treatment would involve helping clients to understand that their prejudice has them mired in defeat that can be remedied by their acquisition and use of appropriate skills. Then helpees are assisted to design and implement their growth programs that will remedy the learning deficits that fostered their prejudice.

HRD counselors view prejudice as a symptom that indicates an area in which a helpee has a skill deficit. It is assumed that there will be no prejudicial behavior whenever a person has skills sufficient to meet the challenges offered by the situation. Prejudice is defined as an externalization of a personal skills deficit. That is, the inadequacy is projected onto others.

Human Resource Development Treatment for Prejudice

Human Resource Development counselors approach therapy for prejudice by responding empathically to facilitate exploration of clients' situations. After helpees have comprehended their current circumstances, helpers personalize the problem by underscoring the helpees' ownership of a skill deficit. That is, helpees are aided in understanding that they are the ones with the specific skills deficit. After helpees acknowledge their skills deficit, helpers assist them in designing action programs that will help them learn the necessary skill.

Case Study

A 16-year-old girl named Jane has recently gained some weight, and her thin cohorts have rejected her socially. The girl has drawn a connection between the two events and has concluded that all thin teenage girls are prejudiced against people who are overweight. She doesn't like the social isolation that has ensued and is seeking counseling for her prejudice.

Treatment

Treatment for this helpee would begin with the helper responding empathically to her by communicating an accepting understanding of her problem. When Jane accepts responsibility and expresses a desire to change her behavior, the helper and she will design programs to attain two goals: (a) to lose the unwanted weight, and (b) to learn how to identify teenage girls who are not biased against overweight cohorts.

A weight loss program would be developed with a physician or nutritionist. The other goal would be addressed by Jane talking with teenage girls for 10 minutes three times a week and identifying those girls who are biased and those who are not. At the end of the program, Jane will have lost her unwanted weight and learned to discriminate between accepting and rejecting teenage girls.

In the following therapy dialogue, the helper is responsive to the helpee, Jane, until she decides that she does not have the skills to control her weight and that she needs to learn new skills that will accomplish that goal. When this understanding is attained, the counselor assists Jane in designing a weight control program that will teach her how to maintain her desired weight.

Therapy Dialogue

> JANE: I'm really scared about the weight I'm gaining. I'm getting fat as a horse.
>
> HELPER: You're upset because you're heavier than you'd like to be.
>
> JANE: Not just heavier then I'd like to be but heavier than my friends want me to be.
>
> HELPER: You feel rejected because of your weight gain.

JANE: Yeah. Some of my friends have started acting like I'm contagious or something. Even my best friend has joined them.

HELPER: You have some anger about losing these friends.

JANE: Sure, I have noticed that all thin girls stay away from me. I've come to believe all the thin girls are selfish and deceitful.

HELPER: You're suspicious of all thin teenage girls because they all seem to let you down.

JANE: Yeah, It's really discouraging. I try to lose weight but nothing works.

HELPER: You feel defeated about your weight situation but you'd like to lose weight so you could feel like a winner.

JANE: Would I ever! But I'm hopeless.

HELPER: Your weight-loss skills are pretty low and you know you need to learn some better ones.

JANE: If only that were possible! Nothing has worked so far, but if there is something I could do that would work, I'd start this minute.

HELPER: O.K., you know what your goal is, let's review what you've tried and decide what should be done to get you to your goal.

Chapter Summary

Human resource development counseling was founded by Robert Carkhuff as an integrative, generative approach to helping relationships. The helping process begins with person-centered responsiveness, progresses to analytic insight, and culminates in a behavioral action program. Carkhuff was the first to explicate a skills development model for counseling that allowed comparison of counselor effectiveness. Also critical to the model is the notion of the "helper," defined as a skilled, high-order functioning individual who may not necessarily have traditional therapist credentials but by the virtue of his or her level of functioning and skills could help others to reach at least that level.

Prejudice from an HRD perspective is a coping strategy for lack of skills to function effectively in a complex world. Treatment would involve a diagnosis and prescription of skills to be learned so that prejudice would become dysfunctional. Key to this model is the continual developmental approach such that everyone involved (helpers and helpees) is pursuing his or her own unique skills development program.

CHAPTER 9

Invitational
Counseling

Invitational counseling was founded by William Purkey during the 1990s. It developed from a positive view of humankind that holds that people are able, valuable, and responsible. It is based on many of the concepts espoused by "third-force" psychologists, such as Arthur Combs (1994), Abraham Maslow (1968) and Carl Rogers (1951, 1954, 1961). In general, it concurs with self-theory and focuses considerable attention on constructs such as self-esteem and self-concept. The uniqueness of invitational theory is its focus on the positive and negative signal system that triggers emotional responses in human beings. The intent is to systematically investigate those systems and to optimize those that maximize positive self-perceptions and minimize those that diminish them (Purkey, 1995).

The assumptions upon which invitational counseling are built revolve around some basic components required for therapeutic relationships. Respect is the belief that people are able, valuable, and responsible and should be treated accordingly. Trust is reflected by a counseling model that is a collaborative, cooperative activity in which process is as important as product. Optimism is supported by the belief that people possess untapped potential in all areas of human endeavor. Finally, intentionality is the belief that human potential can best be realized by places, policies, programs, and processes that are specifically designed to invite development and by people (counselors) who are intentionally inviting with themselves and others, both personally and professionally.

Therefore, invitational counselors are optimistic and intentionally strive to immerse their clients in a surplus of signals that invite them to do things that will improve their self-image. The belief is that if counselors can intentionally replace disinviting signals with inviting ones they activate or reactivate their clients' innate desire to seek positive growth.

Invitational therapy relies on the notions that each client has the potential for growth and that by nature, clients are growth oriented. This orientation is enhanced by one's belief in self, which is fostered by relationships imbued with realistic and genuine levels of optimism, trust, and respect. However, in the context of relating, people are in the process of continually sending positive and negative messages to others, and the view we hold about ourselves is the direct result of the impact these messages have on us.

In addition to others' messages of worth, the value we place on ourselves is proportionate to the degree that we feel we have control over our destiny. Our sense of control is reflected by our willingness to plan and to be goal directed. The more value individuals attribute to themselves, the more they are willing to risk their minds and hearts with others, and thus the more likely they are to develop into fully functioning, healthy human beings.

Therefore, the healing dynamic of invitational counseling lies in the ability of one constructive person to intentionally generate growth in another by using people, places, policies, programs, and processes as invitational vehicles. The critical factor is the presentation of a preponderance of invitational signals that encourage clients to do positive things. One essential ingredient is individuals' ability to discriminate and respond to positive signals.

The effectiveness of invitational counseling is measured by the frequency with which clients treat themselves as respectful, trustworthy, optimistic, and intentionally inviting. Also, the frequency with which clients treat others as respectful, trustworthy, optimistic, and intentionally inviting is an indicator that counseling has been effective.

Critics of invitational theory hold that it is a rehash of self theory, which was popular during the 1960s. There is concern that it relies more on the charisma of its leaders than on objective investigations. Its recent move toward more precise definition of its basic constructs will strengthen its position and provide a firmer base for further research.

The Counseling Process

The first step in invitational counseling is to generate a climate that is realistic, optimistic, trusting, and respectful. In this environment, the counselor will transmit positive messages to the client and provide clients with opportunities to control activities. Counselors will also help their clients plan and establish goals. Because invitational counseling also views clients as social agents, it is important to provide clients with opportunities to affiliate with others and plan cooperatively with them for a better future.

Prejudice From an Invitational Perspective

Invitational counselors believe that prejudice develops when a person receives a preponderance of similar negative signals from a given source. The similarity of signals leads to a conclusion that every person with similar characteristics will possess the same traits. Thus, if a person or group consistently transmits the same negative signal, then they are apt to engender prejudice in others. Therefore, prejudice is the withholding of respect, trust, optimism, and intentional invitations from people because they are members of a group that has erroneously been given a negative label.

Invitational Treatment of Prejudice

Invitational counselors approach therapy for prejudice by believing that if they intentionally establish a trusting environment, their clients will accept invitations to behave constructively. Counselors will offer constructive invitations as will the policies, places, and programs involved in the counseling relationship. In essence, invitational counselors will communicate to clients that they are valued and trusted. Specific behaviors let clients control activities through cooperative planning.

Case Study

A 16-year-old girl, Jane S., has gained some unwanted weight and feels that a thin teenage cohort has begun to reject her because of it. Therefore, Jane has developed a prejudice against all thin teenage girls because she feels they will reject her as well. She seeks counseling for her dissatisfaction with her life.

Treatment

The invitational counselor establishes a relationship characterized by respect, trust, optimism, and intentional invitations. The counselor provides positive feedback to Jane and gives her opportunities to initiate activities she has planned as well as to work cooperatively with her. Jane is encouraged to express affiliative needs toward the counselor. She plans a diet control program and discusses the semiweekly conversations she holds with thin teenage cohorts.

Therapy Dialogue

JANE: I'm really scared about the weight I'm gaining.

COUNSELOR: Well, I'm glad a nice person like you came to talk about it.

JANE: I don't think I'm a very nice person. I'm getting too fat.

COUNSELOR: You're sending yourself signals that you're really bad for gaining some weight you don't want.

JANE: I'm not the only one who's sending me those signals. I'm getting them from lots of other people. All of my thin friends are staying away from me.

COUNSELOR: So, a really fine person like you with all your talents is being told by some of her friends that they don't want to hang around with you. That makes you feel alone and sad.

JANE: Sure (cries). I'm losing all my thin friends and I'm stuck with fat ones like me. We choose each other because we don't have any other choices.

COUNSELOR: There are some people who send you good signals, but you don't believe they're real. They're more like cries of desperation.

JANE: Yeah. We all hate the thin girls. You can't trust any of them. They use everybody.

COUNSELOR: You have some friends who send you some good signals, but you don't trust them. Have you ever tested them to see if those signals are real?

JANE: Yeah. Some of those fat girls are good friends. They really like me. I'd like to get to know them better but I'm afraid to get too close. We might all just get fatter (laughs).

COUNSELOR: Maybe the challenge is to use the good signals you get to help everybody improve. You know, spend more time with the people who send you positive signs and less with those who tell you bad things. You could change your atmosphere. Maybe you could send more good signals to the people who make you feel good.

JANE: Yeah. I should do that. Everybody likes to hear good things about themselves.

COUNSELOR: I'll bet you'll be surprised at how much your praise means to your friends.

JANE: Well, I'd like some praise, too. Lately, I only hear bad things.

COUNSELOR: Maybe others are sending you some good signals, but you can't hear them now because you feel so bad about gaining weight.

JANE: You may be right. I guess I expect that everybody hates fat as much as I do.

COUNSELOR: You are more than how much you weigh. You are a very talented young woman.

Chapter Summary

Invitational counseling is a recent addition to the therapy modalities and is based on the precepts of many third-force psychologists. Its focus is on building self-esteem with the intent of optimizing the positive signal system so that positive self-perceptions are maximized. Invitational counseling recognizes four therapeutic components: (a) respect, (b) trust, (c) optimism, and (d) intentionality.

Prejudice, according to invitational theory, results from a preponderance of negative signals from a given source resulting in generalization and association of these negative signals with others who are similar. Treatment of prejudice involves establishing a therapeutic relationship between client and therapist. Through this relationship, the client will accept invitations to behave in a constructive fashion, and in time clients learn to discriminate positive from negative invitations throughout their environment.

10

Person-Centered Counseling

The person-centered approach to counseling is most frequently associated with Carl Rogers (1961), who asserted that empathic understanding, congruence, and unconditional positive regard were the three necessary and sufficient conditions for constructive personality change.

Historically, Rogers' formulations were offered at a time when counseling and psychotherapy were dominated by psychoanalysis (Rogers, 1951, 1954). We may contend that the original ideas underlying nondirective counseling were diametrically opposed to those of psychoanalysis. Rogers believed that people are prone toward behaviors that maintain the self; psychoanalysis contends that aspects of the human personality are innately antagonistic to each other.

Person-centered therapy asserts that inherent in individuals are the abilities (a) to understand the factors in their lives that cause them unhappiness and pain, and (b) to reorganize their self-structure in such a way as to overcome these negative factors. People's inherent powers will operate if empathic, congruent therapists can establish with them a relationship involving a depth of warm acceptance and understanding.

The process of therapy is one in which the structure of the client's self is relaxed in the safety and security of the relationship with the therapist, and previously denied experiences are perceived and by means of a verbal, symbolic analysis, are integrated into an altered self (Rogers, 1951).

The curative effect of nondirective counseling is based on the belief that clients have within themselves innate abilities that allow them to understand the problems that are causing difficulty and overcome those problems by reorienting the self. Thus, the cure lies within the clients. Therapists withhold themselves from the relationship in order not to interfere with the healing processes that are intrinsic in individuals who are freed from retarding influences.

Historical contributions of person-centered therapy include the notion of counseling's central core of empathy, congruence, and positive regard. It has also provided a fuller attention to the whole person of clients, particularly to the fundamental belief in their constructive capacities.

Another unique contribution of the person-centered approach is the focus on providing clients with an opportunity to find their own mode of expression. That is, whatever direction clients pursue, therapists provide them with immediate and concrete feedback of what they have just communicated. The person-centered approach provides clients with an opportunity to explore previously denied experiences in that it draws their attention to many things to which they have not attended or they have not communicated. This approach provides clients with opportunities for the discovery and correction of faulty generalizations.

The person-centered approach is not without limitations. First, it does not provide an opportunity for clients to have an impact upon their therapists or for therapists to give fully of themselves. The most substantial limitation is the lack of commitment to action; the nondirective stance of therapists does not allow intervention or suggestion toward more effective behavior. However, the offering of empathy, congruence, and positive regard is believed by proponents of this model to bring about therapeutic change without direct therapist intervention.

Objections to nondirective therapy contend that it is based on a false assumption that all people have the resources to understand and rectify the factors that are generating problems in their lives. In fact, considerable data casts doubt on the efficacy of nondirective counseling with deprived client populations. Conversely, the effectiveness of Rogerian-style counseling with high-resource clients such as college students has been demonstrated extensively.

Prejudice From a Person-Centered Perspective

Prejudice originates with individuals' experiences of themselves as having to preserve their sense of self by distorting their perceptions of others. Person-centered counselors assume that prejudice is a condition that interferes with a person's functioning. Therefore, prejudice is a process people use to compensate for negative self-perceptions that have developed from their inability to interpret their experiences accurately. The concept is that prejudiced people have been unable to interact openly with their environment and have developed distortions that have led them to conclude that data about others needs to be skewed systematically to maintain self.

Case Study

A 16-year-old girl named Jane S. has gained some extra weight and believes she has been rejected by all thin teenage girls because of it. Thus, she has become prejudiced against all thin teenage girls.

Treatment

The counselor provided empathy with a caring and honest atmosphere in which the client explored her prejudice against thin teenage girls. The client first discovered that she was defending herself by automatically rejecting all thin teenage girls. She then understood that she could cope with the various reactions of that cohort without losing or distorting her self.

Therapy Dialogue

JANE: I hate this. I hate the weight I'm gaining. I'm as big as a horse.

COUNSELOR: It's pretty disturbing to lose control of your weight.

JANE: Yeah. I'm getting so I eat all the time and I eat the wrong things. I know better but I can't stop (cries).

COUNSELOR: It's really sad to see yourself doing things that hurt you.

JANE: Uh-huh. It's like I'm trying to make myself ugly. I'm driving my friends away. Maybe I'll be all alone if I get too fat.

COUNSELOR: You're scared that maybe there's more to it than just gaining weight.

JANE: Maybe so. I'm getting so I can't stand to be around my thin friends anymore. They make me feel uncomfortable, like they're better than me.

COUNSELOR: You get really angry at those thin friends, but there is some pain too.

JANE: Sure, they're all snobs. I hate them all. They think they're a privileged class. Miss Americas in training. I don't trust any of them. They're all out for themselves. Selfish. It took me a while to discover that, but it's true.

COUNSELOR: So, it goes beyond your friends. You don't trust any thin girls.

JANE: I can't trust them. When I do they cross me up. They leave me alone when they have other people around. They say they like me when they want me

to do something, but then they desert me. So, I just
don't give them a chance to let me down.

COUNSELOR: You've cut off contacts with thin girls to
protect yourself from being hurt.

JANE: Yeah. But I have learned to fight back (laughs).
Sometimes I set them up for a disappointment like they
give me. I arrange to meet them and don't show up.
Then they feel how it is to be deserted. I shouldn't tell a
psychologist this but sometimes I stand where I can
watch them while they wait for me to show up. They
get really uncomfortable and I really enjoy it.

COUNSELOR: You're a little worried about what I think
about what you're doing.

JANE: I guess so. I don't want you to think I'm all bad.

COUNSELOR: You're afraid there may be so much bad
inside you that others have to reject you.

JANE: I don't want to be an awful person. I want to laugh
and have a good time. I don't want to be so fat.

COUNSELOR: You're convinced that being fat and being
bad are the same thing.

Chapter Summary

Carl Rogers introduced person-centered counseling in the 1950s
with his specification of the necessary and sufficient conditions
for therapeutic personality change, which included empathy,
congruence, and positive regard. Rogers believed that in the presence of these conditions, individuals could understand the causes
of their unhappiness and reorganize their behavior to overcome
them. The use of reflective technique is key in the therapeutic
process to provide clients with immediate feedback about their
explorations.

Person-centered therapy has been criticized because of its
focus on clients as the source of resources for solving their problems. For many clients this is a reality, but clients who are de-

prived physically, intellectually, or emotionally may not have these resources. Another criticism is the lack of intervention on the part of therapists to suggest more effective strategies and behaviors.

Prejudice from this perspective is a process of self-preservation by distorting their perceptions of others. Thus, prejudice is a form of compensation for negative self-perceptions. Treatment involves offering the necessary therapeutic conditions and facilitating clients' restoration of positive self-worth. Prejudice will disappear as the clients' self-perception improves.

11

Behavioral Therapy

Behaviorism began as a science in 1912 when the objective psychologists rebelled against introspective psychology as a discipline because it could never arrive at verifiable conclusions. A science should deal with those things that are observable and measurable, and only behavior met those criteria.

John B. Watson (1916) built upon the works of Russian physiologists Pavlov and Bekhterev to formulate the essential components of behaviorism. He held that mental processes were essential components of bodily movements or behaviors. Thus the proper subject matter for psychology is human behavior, which contrasted with the ideas of the introspective psychologists who claimed that consciousness should be the major construct of study.

In general, behavioral therapists ask if behavior can be described in terms of stimulus and response (Krasner & Ullmann, 1965). The purpose of therapy is to identify unhealthy responses to stimuli and substitute new, healthier responses through a process of conditioning or unconditioning as the case demands.

Watson (1916) described personality as the sum of activities that can be discovered by actual observation of behavior over a long enough time to give reliable information. Essentially, he believed that personality is the end product of our habit systems. Thus for Watson, a change in personality could be accomplished by changing the situation that calls out a particular habit system or by the conditioning of new habit systems.

Modern behavioral therapists may find Watson's formulations restricting, and thus may be more comfortable in therapy with a multimodal system (Lazarus, 1976; Schaffer & Lazarus, 1952). This eclecticism incorporates the major goal of behavioral therapy as change in behavior with much less emphasis on the notions of conditioning as the change agent. However, if the term *learning* were substituted for *conditioning* then agreement would be significant among both camps. Thus, behavioral therapy proceeds from (a) the identification of ineffective behaviors (specification of goals); (b) establishing a baseline from which to initiate change; (c) identification of treatment techniques to establish new, more effective behaviors; and (d) systematic measurement of the relative success of these treatments.

Wolpe (1976) has supported the use of a variety of techniques in behavioral therapy. He has applied the reciprocal inhibition principle to the treatment of human neuroses with great success. This principle was developed from the realization that the excitation of a particular group of muscles automatically involves inhibition of an antagonistic group. Thus, to treat a neurosis, one may oppose the behavior with an incompatible response. Laughter, for example, inhibits sadness and may itself be inhibited by sadness, anger, or anxiety. Wolpe (1958, 1976) also pioneered the use of systematic desensitization as well as behavioral rehearsal.

Although observation of clients is always essential for accurate diagnosis of their behaviors, behavioral therapy for adults also focuses on clients' roles in selecting behavioral change goals. The therapists' diagnoses and clients' selection of goals must merge to ensure that the goals are appropriate for predictable success.

Thus, therapists become "teachers" of new, more appropriate behaviors. This form of teaching may also involve homework and self-instruction carefully guided by therapists. Ultimately, adults must learn to diagnose their own behaviors and must self-instruct the required new behaviors (Watson & Tharp, 1989).

The Goal and Focus of Behavioral Therapy

The goal of counseling according to behavioral therapy is simply to bring about behavioral change. The primary technique involved in this process is the systematic manipulation and control of the therapy situation such that behavioral change can occur.

The primary focus of behavioral therapy is the application of principles of learning to induce behavioral change. Clearly, the most important aspect and the measure of success is whether or not a specific behavior has been modified. Insight and understanding of the behavior is not the target of this counseling modality. In fact, behavior is viewed as the only clearly observable and measurable aspect of the person and thus the only appropriate target for change. There are three principle assumptions of behavioral therapy:

1. Psychotherapy should be investigated in a learning-theory framework.
2. The factors that influence psychotherapy are reinforcement, extinction, and acquisition.
3. Empirical procedures are required for theory building.

Historically, behavioral therapy was the first model to realize and promulgate that focus away from the "inner" person allowed freedom from speculation about philosophical issues and client psychodynamics. Thus, the integration of theory, practice, and feedback brought a clear focus on the relationship between practice and outcome.

Behaviorial therapists were also the first to inform their clients in detail concerning the therapeutic process. This process included detailed information on what is observable and measurable. The direct approach to behavior change or symptom extinction provides a ready measure of therapy success.

Since the focus has been on the observable and measurable in the form of behavior change, behavioral therapy has provided a means for studying and testing social engineering by manipulation of the social and physical environments. This has been a major contribution to the social sciences and to their acceptance as "true" science.

Contributions to Counseling

The contribution of behavioral therapy to the field of counseling has been seen in three primary ways. The first area of contribution focuses on client information and involvement. In this counseling modality, clients are completely informed about the nature, process, progress, and expected outcome of therapy. Additionally, clients are involved in every decision about behaviors to change, timelines for change, and rewards.

The second area of contribution concerns the nature of the theoretical approach. In behavioral therapy, the learning theory approach provides a more easily acceptable and understood explanation of the acquisition and maintenance of a particular symptom. Because the theory is reflected in the process, by practicing the techniques outside therapy clients may markedly speed up the counseling process.

The third area of contribution involves the set of specific skills and techniques available to therapists. The focus on symptoms rather than inter- or intrapersonal dynamics is objective and gives the counselor knowledge of and confidence in clients' progress. The transference-countertransference neurosis is eliminated by this approach.

Limitations

Behavioral therapy is limited to those who can emit public cues and is focused on a narrow behavioral spectrum, thus limiting clients' abilities to progress in a multifactorial way. The approach does not address client creativity or self-actualization in the therapy process. The process may encourage clients to externalize responsibility for behaviors and become dependent on highly mechanistic techniques and applications.

The model assumes that therapists can become potent reinforcers and yet does not account for a poor therapist who may design an inappropriate model or schedule. Behavioral therapy does not provide a relationship or personal involvement between therapists and clients and may be used destructively by society toward its own ends.

Prejudice From a Behavioral View

Behaviorists view prejudice as dysfunctional behavior with a change potential. If prejudice were only manifested as an attitude, it would not be a target of change. Behaviorists believe that the process of behaving prejudicially would begin with a series of stimuli that elicit a particular response that is reinforced. Over time, the stimulus might be transferred or generalized to other stimuli that would yield the same response; thus the behavior becomes a habit, separated from the original stimulus.

Behavioral Treatment of Prejudice

As in other maladaptive behaviors, behaviorists would identify a specific behavior to change and develop a learning program to retrain the individual's behavior. Baseline rates and goals for change would be established and a specific strategy engaged to ensure that the new behavior is reinforced.

Case Study

Jane S., a 16-year-old girl, has had a bothersome weight increase in the last few weeks. She is convinced that her thin teenage friends are rejecting her because of the weight gain. She has decided that all thin teenage girls will reject her and has developed a prejudice against all such people.

Treatment

In this example, the client must select the behaviors she wishes to change. The process may begin with the counselor helping her define the problem. This may be completed by having Jane keep a food diary for a week and bringing the information to the next session. During the session, Jane and her counselor would look for specific behaviors to change (e.g., eating while watching television or eating high fat foods). The client might also be given homework reading assignments that relate to overeating or need for exercise.

The diary would be used to set baseline frequencies for behaviors that will be targeted for change. A program would then be developed to ensure that the targeted behaviors will be changed along with appropriate rewards for goal achievement.

It is critical to the process that the goals be self-selected based on sound practices related to goal achievement. Jane must learn new skills of food selection and exercise participation, and if these behavior changes are not personally selected, then it is likely that she will not be motivated to follow the program. Another aspect of goal selection is the incremental nature of goal achievement. Clients are more likely to be successful if success is built into the change process by ensuring that the goals are achievable. It is unlikely that Jane can change all negative food choices overnight. By deciding on realistic changes, achieving success, and experiencing a reward, she will be on the path to self-control and will have learned self-management principles.

Therapy Dialogue

> JANE: I hate the way I look and I hate all those skinny little snits who used to be my friends. I've taken down all the mirrors in my room.

COUNSELOR: What do you see when you look in the mirror?

JANE: A big, fat pig!

COUNSELOR: Have you always felt this way about how you look?

JANE: No. It's just been this past year. Nothing has gone right! And on top of everything else, I've gained all this weight.

COUNSELOR: Do you know what made you gain weight?

JANE: Not really.

COUNSELOR: Have you changed the way you eat or the way you exercise?

JANE: Well, I guess I have. I love to run and last year I had to quit because I hurt my ankle. I never went back to running.

COUNSELOR: Has anything else changed?

JANE: Well, when my mom died, I was really angry at everybody for a while. All my other friends were no help at all and now that I've gained weight they treat me like dirt. They weren't my friends at all. They aren't to be trusted. Every really thin girl I've ever known is a jerk. They think you're nothing if you're not tiny.

COUNSELOR: What would you like for them to think about you?

JANE: I want them to like me for who I am, not how I look.

COUNSELOR: You aren't relating to them at all now. How would you like to relate to them?

JANE: Well, I guess I would like to talk with them at least once in a while.

COUNSELOR: How do you envision that happening?

JANE: I don't know. Maybe I could sit with them at lunch at school again. Like I used to.

COUNSELOR: O.K. Your goal is to reestablish contact with your old friends. You want this to be successful, so you'll have to plan it carefully. How do you think you should begin?

JANE: What if I sit with them just on Fridays for a while? We can talk about the game or movies and such. But I'm also going to lose weight. That's for me though. I'm still the same person, fat or thin.

COUNSELOR: Ok. You have a plan for seeing and talking with your old friends. Now, let's determine your goals for your weight loss.

Chapter Summary

Behavioral therapy developed from the works of Pavlov and Watson, who recognized the inherent connection between mental processes and bodily movements or behaviors. More recent contributors such as Wolpe and Lazarus have recognized that behaviors are learned and can be unlearned when conditions are supportive.

The multimodal techniques used in behavioral therapy today include conditioning and reinforcement as well as life review, reciprocal inhibition, behavior rehearsal, and systematic desensitization to name a few. These techniques are used with a well-designed program consisting of goal setting, technique selection, and systematic evaluation. This insistence upon evaluation has provided a means for studying and testing outcomes and thus has made a major contribution to the social sciences and their acceptance as true science.

Prejudice is viewed by behavioral therapists as a dysfunctional behavior learned in and supported by the environment. Treatment is a process by which learning should correct misconceptions about the target of prejudice. In the process of change, therapists function as teachers and facilitators.

12

Trait-and-Factor Counseling

rait-and-factor counseling arose in the first part of this century as a part of the scientific movement that included an increased interest in measuring human traits and abilities. The original focus was on the decision-making process for vocation choice. The discovery of statistical distributions of human traits led to the conclusion that human choices could be enhanced by identifying an individual's location along those distributions and matching him or her with alternatives that require a corresponding level of that trait. One of the early pioneers in this area and proponent of the Minnesota approach was Williamson (Williamson & Darley, 1937). This approach to counseling was primarily vocational in nature and was concerned with educational and vocational adjustment. They developed tests of aptitudes and abilities based on the notion that in vocational guidance, everyone needs (a) clear assessments of their aptitudes, abilities, interests, and resources; (b) accurate knowledge of job requirements and opportunitites; and (c) assistance in merging the previous two into a personal, rational choice.

Counseling, then, was seen as a rational, problem-solving process that required data for accurate decision making. The primary focus of trait-and-factor counseling became the process of matching individuals to an appropriate occupation or educational program (Caplow, 1954; Super, 1957; Williamson, 1965).

The underlying assumption was that the whole human realm is composed of measurable factors. That is, people differ along measurable and relatively stable dimensions. Because jobs or occupations differ along these same dimensions, then a matching process would ultimately yield a satisfying career selection.

The rationality of the trait-and-factor approach was highly compatible with a technologically dominated society, and so it gained extensive popularity. It was used widely by industry and military forces and attained broad acceptance in academic circles, particularly in college admission activities.

The purpose of counseling from a trait-and-factor framework involves identifying important variables upon which individuals and jobs vary, developing reliable and valid measuring instruments, and applying these tools along with occupational information to the job-matching process. Counseling from a trait-and-factor frame of reference is relatively precise and gives clients objective information about both themselves and the alternatives under consideration. This mode stands in sharp contrast to other approaches that use ambiguity as a therapeutic factor.

Historically, the trait-and-factor approach contributed the notion that problems and dissatisfaction derive from a mismatch of an individual with his or her environmental or occupational demands. Thus, counseling is not a process of individual or environmental change, but the application of specific information to make more informed choices from options that already exist. Through the application of psychometrics, individuals can learn much about their talents, skills, and knowledge. Counselors are usually experts in available options and thus counsel clients about more appropriate choices or matches between abilities and opportunities.

The emphasis of trait-and-factor counseling on information and reality does much to reduce anxiety for clients. The decision-making process becomes concrete, based upon specific data that may have been unavailable to clients previously. The counseling process may provide an increased understanding of clients' values as well as specific talents and aptitudes. With the increasing availability of technology to assist the matching of abilities with jobs, client advising is made much simpler.

Trait-and-factor counseling has been criticized as presenting clients with a false picture of the world. Its precision is not an accurate reflection of real life, which includes much ambiguity. Indeed, it can be argued cogently that life's most crucial decisions involve ambiguous components that force individuals to resolve uncertainty by declaring their personal choice among equally desirable, or perhaps undesirable, choices.

Prejudice From a Trait-and-Factor Perspective

Trait-and-factor counselors perceive prejudice as a systematic error in decision-making formulae. Their faith is in the mathematical computations that lead to choices; inaccurate outcomes are traceable to incorrect data or processes. Thus, the quest is for formulae that will yield perfect decisions that require precision throughout the process. Prejudice injects errors into the decision-making process and is eliminated when identified.

Trait-and-Factor Treatment of Prejudice

Trait-and-factor counselors approach therapy with prejudiced clients by assessing that trait systematically. They present evidence that indicates the amount of inaccuracy the prejudice introduces into the clients' choice processes. They also calculate the degree of improvement clients could achieve by reducing the prejudice factor.

Case Study

A 16-year-old girl named Jane S. has gained some bothersome weight and believes she is being rejected by all thin teenage girls because of it. Thus, she has become prejudiced against all thin teenage girls.

Therapy Dialogue

> JANE: I'm really scared about the weight I'm gaining. I'm getting big as a horse.
>
> COUNSELOR: You'd like some help with losing weight?
>
> JANE: Not exactly. I'm more concerned about the friends I'm losing. I can't stand to be around thin girls. They make me uncomfortable. They are so deceitful.
>
> COUNSELOR: So, you'd like to know how to get along with thin girls.
>
> JANE: That's part of it, but I don't want to get along with all of them. I need to learn how to pick out the good ones.
>
> COUNSELOR: The basic problem is how to discriminate between genuine and ingenuine thin girls.
>
> JANE: Yeah. Do you have a test that will tell me how to do that?
>
> COUNSELOR: Maybe we ought to begin by testing your decision-making skills. That will tell you how your bias against thin girls is influencing your decisions. You could improve your decision making by altering your bias against thin girls.

Chapter Summary

The belief that rational decision-making regarding educational programs and careers could be enhanced by complete self-knowledge combined with facts about vocations and educational programs was the original basis for the development of trait-and-factor counseling techniques. The development of tests to measure every conceivable human trait became the task of those in the field. They believed that an accurate diagnosis and matching of interest and talent with a specific career could best be obtained with objective tests. The rationality of the process was intriguing, and instruments for measuring aptitudes and abilities gained extensive popularity in industry, the military, and educational institutions.

This approach may eliminate anxiety for clients because of its focus on reality and on an observable process that may be familiar to clients. Criticisms have focused on the lack of precision of the process, because jobs or career satisfaction is much more complex than tests can measure validly and reliably. The limitation of tests to completely measure the attribute of interest has also been recognized.

Prejudice from the trait-and-factor perspective is a systematic error in the decision-making formula. This systematic bias is due to imperfect prediction and as such must be countered by error reduction. Treatment is a process of studying the error introduced into the decision by prejudice and determining the improvement in accuracy to be gained by reducing the prejudice.

Exercises for Section II

These case presentations are true stories collected from individuals who have been the targets of prejudice. Each case has its own unique problem presentation, and the questions provided at the end will help you to focus the application of any of the models presented previously to this particular case. In each case, both the victim and perpetrator of prejudice are seen as potential clients.

Case 1

An African American woman with a doctorate in counseling held membership in a national professional counseling organization but was not a member of the state chapter of that group. The state chapter planned to hold its annual meeting in her city, and the guest speaker was a former professor and friend of hers. To attend the meeting the woman applied for membership in the state chapter. She was denied membership because the state chapter's constitution prohibited Blacks from joining the group. Her check was returned with a clear statement of the group's constitutional prohibition. Upon discovering the situation, the national president urged the woman to attend the conference, which she refused to do. The president switched his keynote address to the campus where the woman was employed, and he invited her students to attend. In this case there are two clients: the perpetrator of prejudice (the organization) and the target of prejudice (the woman).

1. Select a model of counseling for each of these clients.
2. What approach would you take with each person?
3. What would be your goal for the counseling process with each?

Case 2

At 11:00 p.m. a Black teenage girl and her father were waiting to board a train in a large metropolitan city. Because all restaurants inside the station were closed, the father and daughter went to a small restaurant outside, in which they were the only Black patrons. They waited for 20 minutes and still no one took their order even though the restaurant was nearly empty. Finally, a waitress told the father and daughter they could not be served. The father asked to speak to the manager but was told he had just left. The father and daughter left the restaurant without food. In this case there are two clients: the pepetrator of prejudice (the restaurant personnel) and the target of prejudice (the father and daughter).

1. Select a model of counseling for these clients.
2. What approach would you take if working with the restaurant personnel?
3. What approach would you take if working with the father and daughter?
4. What would be your goal for the counseling process for each client?

Case 3

A 9-year-old Caucasian girl attended an elementary school sponsored by a fundamentalist religious group that had a very conservative political stance. The girl supported Bill Clinton for the presidential nomination, and her classmates were solidly Republican. The students began calling her a "baby killer" and argued that all liberals were anti-American. The girl stood her ground for several weeks, after which she began to have difficulty sleeping and eating. Her teacher told her not to argue with the other students, and the girl was afraid to tell her parents about the problem because she feared they would believe it was her fault. The girl finally told her parents about the incidents. The family discussed the situation and began to explore the problem with the teacher, who told the parents that their child would have to learn to be more "thick skinned" about teasing. Several staff members privately indicated they did not like the school's harsh conservative posture but felt unable to alter it. The family transferred the girl to a public school where she was happy and productive. In this case there are two clients: the pepetrators of prejudice (the school teacher and students) and the target of prejudice (the 9-year-old girl).

1. Select a counseling model for this situation.
2. What would be your approach for each of the clients?
3. What would be your goal(s) of therapy for each?
4. How would your goal(s) of therapy change if you were using another technique?

Case 4

A teenage boy from a lower socioeconomic background was ranked highest in his sophomore class at a school located in an upper-income neighborhod. The boy was a member of the school's football team and vice president of the student council. But when Honor Society members were selected, he was omitted. The avowed reason was that he objected to a teacher's practice of using classtime to complete projects for her favorite club rather than covering the subject material. However, the boy attributed his rejection to the staff's rejection of all lower socioeconomic students. After this situation, the boy withdrew socially and became a near recluse. In this case there are two clients: the perpetrator of prejudice (Honor Society selection committee) and the target of prejudice (the boy).

1. Select a model of counseling for this case.
2. What approach would you take with the selection committee and the boy?
3. What would be your goals of therapy for each client?
4. How would your goals differ if you were using another approach?

Case 5

A middle-aged Caucasian man was superintendent of a small school system in a largely rural community. The system held the state's highest accreditation, and its costs were the lowest in that geographic region. The superintendent's school system was invited to become a member of a group of schools that were implementing a new curriculum that emphasized thinking skills. He took the proposal to the board of education, which decided to accept the invitation. A fundamantalist religious group heard about the proposal and interpreted the program as anti-Christian. They called the superintendent a "liberal" and argued that all liberals were dangerous to America and were harmful to developing children. The group began an active campaign against him. The superintendent developed disturbed sleep patterns and mild hypertension. He resigned after 2 years of the dissension. In this case there are two clients: the perpetrator of prejudice (the fundamentalist group) and the target of prejudice (the superintendent).

1. Select a counseling model for this case.
2. What approach would you take with each client?
3. What would be your goals of therapy for each client?

Case 6

During the Iranian hostage crisis (1979 and 1980), an Iranian graduate student was writing her dissertation. The chairman of her committee continuously found fault with her chapters, returned them late, wouldn't be persuaded of the legitimacy of her contention that Ralph Waldo Emerson's writing was heavily influenced by the 14th-century Persian poet, Hafiz. The student documented her case by citing "marginalia" in Emerson's own handwriting on a copy of the Persian poet's work. The student added other legitimate supporting documents. The chairman refused to accept the evidence, and the student had to change her dissertation topic. There are two clients in this case: the perpetrator of prejudice (the dissertation chairman) and the target of prejudice (the graduate student).

1. Select a counseling model for this case.
2. What approach would you take with the chairman and the student?
3. What would be your goal(s) of therapy for each client?
4. How would your goal(s) differ if you were using another counseling method?

THE MULTI-
DIMENSIONAL
MODEL OF
PREJUDICE
PREVENTION AND
REDUCTION

Introduction

This section of the book presents a new model to prevent and/or reduce prejudice. This model is an example of multimodal therapy that incorporates components of trait-and-factor, person-centered, psychoanalytic, and behavioral therapies. These therapies are embedded within personal, social, and political arenas, thus enhancing the likelihood that prejudice predisposition in these areas will be addressed.

The model is presented in theoretical and practical detail in Chapter 13 along with an instrument to assess the likelihood of the clients' propensity for prejudice perpetration or prejudice victimization. Chapter 14 uses the case presented in the previous section for a complete case study. This case includes all phases and components.

This multimodal model was developed primarily because most counseling approaches have rehabilitation rather than prevention as their primary purpose. Although rehabilitation is a worthy and necessary reactive effort, it is an insufficient one. Counseling also needs a proactive capability designed to reduce the occurrence of prejudicial behavior. The adage "an ounce of prevention is worth a pound of cure" is highly appropriate for the current national climate of prejudice.

Most models of counseling were developed as reactions to presenting problems and focus on the individual or small group dimensions of client-presented situations. The conventional view seems to be that if counselors can help clients move successfully through the processes required to activate their own resources, then healing will occur and the prime counseling task is completed. In this sense, counseling is dominated by the notion of independence through reactive responses to crises. A related assumption of such counseling is that human difficulties revolve primarily around personal or small-group deficits and that the answer is to shore up those inadequacies after they are exposed.

The foregoing image of counseling ignores or greatly diminishes the role of preemptive interventions, especially those directed toward large-group factors, such as societal and political issues, which focus on power allocations. Many counseling orientations are inadequate for coping with some of the more complex prejudice-related difficulties, and we need a counseling model that focuses more fully on a wider range of factors that effect reduction of prejudice. This is not to criticize other counseling models but rather to infuse into the field a wider range of comprehensive ideas and practices from allied professions. Precedents have been set for such efforts. Perhaps the most renowned work was done by B. F. Skinner (1948) who presented *Walden Two* as a conceptual model of how his theoretical formulations might look in the broader community. Another effort was *Summerhill*, in which Neil (1970) described the application of psychoanalysis to an educational setting. During the 1980s, Carl Rogers (1983) addressed the same task for person-centered formulations. In essence, these writers stretched the counseling envelope by extending the implications of the field.

New and specific factors support the attempt to formulate a more comprehensive model of prejudice reduction activities for counselors. First, if the United Stated is to prevail as the world's super power, it cannot overlook racial, ethnic, and gender-related concerns and conflicts within its own society. Prejudice as a form of human rights abuse can cause emotional and physical violence as well as consistent denial and deprivation of opportunities. Tolerance of prejudice is a direct violation of the American ideals of justice, equality, and the glorification of the individual (Bryant, 1994).

Second, according to the U.S. Bureau of the Census (1993), Whites will become America's numerical minority by the year 2010. The new demographics produced by continued immigration from other countries and higher fertility rates in some ethnic minority groups indicate that America will be a multicultural, multiracial, and multilingual society (Ponterotto & Pederson, 1993).

Third, the social melting pot theory of America as supported by Crevecoeur (1904) and popularized by Israel Zangwill (D'Souza, 1995) seems to have yielded to the cultural pluralism of the civil rights movement. There is now a realization that the strength of America lies in its diversity. Furthermore, "Diversity is here to stay and America is learning to build on it, to appreciate its potential, and to validate and affirm it" (Ramirez, 1991, p. 5).

Finally, the term *equity* is gaining momentum. We believe that equity is the process of empowering minority groups to participate equally with the majority. Special provisions for some ethnic groups have to be made to create equitable conditions.

Of course, total prevention is the ideal goal of all programs directed toward ameliorating the effects of prejudicial behavior, but prejudice is one of the continuing frailties of the human condition. That is, the best we can hope to do is to reduce prejudicial behavior because it probably cannot be totally eradicated. Ponterotto and Pedersen (1993) stated, "The view of many social scientists is that you cannot be socialized into a society stratified along racial lines and not be influenced by a racist ideology" (pp. 18–19).

13

The Multidimensional Model of Prejudice Prevention and Reduction

To meet the need for a more active role for counselors in the reduction of prejudice we offer a paradigm for prejudice prevention and reduction. The basic premise of this model is that prejudice is developed, maintained, and perpetuated by a combination of three major factors: (a) individual personality variables, (b) social mores, and (c) political systems. A second proposition is that prejudice reduction requires that all three variables be addressed simultaneously. A corollary is that professional helpers have to collaborate with those from social and political arenas to succeed in combating prejudice and racial discrimination proactively. The bottom line is that concepts of equity, fairness, and mutual respect among various ethnic, racial, and gender groups should become an active part of the nation's social, educational, and political agenda, and counselors should have a significant role in that effort.

The basic concept of the Multidimensional Model of Prejudice Prevention and Reduction (MMPPR) is that prejudiced behavior derives from the three primary sources noted, and it is possible to determine either a person's or a group's predisposition

FIGURE 13.1

Multidimensional Model of Prejudice Prevention and Reduction (MMPPR)

Individual factors (IF)	+	Social factors (SF)	+	Political factors (PF)	=	Total prejudice quotient (TPQ)

toward prejudicial behavior by tabulating the sum total of the primary prejudice predisposing factors present in a situation. Those factors are related positively and significantly. This relationship is depicted in Figure 13.1.

MMPPR counselors offer a range of services based on the needs of their clients. They are also prepared to provide services appropriate for social and political circumstances. For individual or group therapy, any of the counseling modalities described previously may be used as appropriate for the client. When the problem occurs at the societal or political level, however, skills related to teaching and advocacy may be required (See Table 13.1).

The proactivity of MMPPR counselors is related to the identification of preexisting conditions that predispose situations toward prejudicial outcomes. Once these factors have been diagnosed, it is possible to develop an intervention to prevent the prejudicial behavior from occurring. Counselors are not limited in the techniques available for developing the intervention, because all counseling methodologies will have application for

TABLE 13.1

Types of Services Offered by MMPPR Counselors

Client Deficit Area	Type of Treatment
Individual personality	Individual and small group counseling
Societal	Education and guidance
Political	Advocacy and lobbying

specific problems. A partial listing of such conditions can be found in Table 13.2.

Reactive services are appropriate when the prejudicial event is either completed or is ongoing. MMPPR counselors (as in other methodologies) will attempt to rehabilitate both victims and perpetrators. For example, in a case of spouse battering, counselors would work toward restoring the health of both the battered spouse and the abuser. If the event involved an unfair justice system, then MMPPR counselors would not only treat the perpetrator and victim but also initiate actions to rehabilitate the justice system. Table 13.3 describes existing conditions for which individuals and systems may need a counseling intervention.

Two primary types of clients exist for MMPPR counseling: (a) potential victims of prejudicial behavior, and (b) potential perpetrators of prejudicial behavior. Essentially, potential victims are those who may be objects of prejudice and perpetrators are those who probably will commit prejudicial acts.

A third concept underlying MMPPR is that the probability of the occurrence of prejudicial behavior is related positively and significantly to the sum of a potential victim's total prejudice pre-

TABLE 13.2

Preexisting Conditions for Which MMPPR Counselors Offer Proactive Services to Potential Victims and Perpetrators

Individual Conditions	Social Conditions	Political Conditions
Maladaptive ego defenses	Fostering negative social/cultural identity	Misuse of economic rewards
Presence of frustration/ aggression	Negative intergroup experience	Retarding power structure
Irrational beliefs	Dysfunctional child-rearing	Ineffective justice system
Poor self-concept	Dysfunctional family	Dysfunctional educational system
Instinctive fears	Dysfunctional religious system	

TABLE 13.3

Situations for Which MMPPR Counselors Offer Reactive Services

Individual Personality	Social Settings	Political System
Improper defense mechanisms	Negative cultural/ social identity	Misused economic rewards
Frustration/ aggression	Negative intergroup experience	Retarding power structure
Irrational beliefs	Negative child- rearing	Unfair justice system
Self-identity issues		
Instinctive fears	Dysfunctional family	Dysfunctional educational system
	Dysfunctional religious system	

disposing factors (individual, social, and political) and a potential perpetrator's total prejudice predisposing factors.

In traditional terms, potential victims may be thought of as masochists or enablers, and potential perpetrators are analogous to sadists or addicts. The key concept is that victims of prejudice and perpetrators of it are complementary roles in a prejudicial scenario. A corollary is that both need treatment.

Factors That Affect Prejudice

Individual Predisposing Factors

Individual prejudice predisposing factors are the traits that may increase the likelihood that a person will become either a victim or a perpetrator of prejudicial behavior and can be both specified and measured. They include the following:

- Unresolved personality conflicts
- Negative racial/ethnic identity
- Negative self-concept

- Low-order interpersonal skills
- Low-order cognitive skills

Unresolved personality conflicts are derived primarily from psychoanalytic literature that describes prejudice as a projection of incomplete or pathological ego development. Negative racial/ ethnic identity as proposed by Ponterotto and Pedersen (1993) is a person's negative interpretation of his or her racial background. According to Purkey (1978), negative self-concepts contribute to prejudice through the definition of oneself as incompetent and therefore worthy of punishment by others. Carkhuff (1983) demonstrated that low-order interpersonal skills interfered with all interpersonal relationships. Allport (1954) reported that low-order cognitive skills (simple categorical thinking) were related to prejudicial behavior.

Social Predisposing Factors

Social prejudice predisposing factors are those group characteristics that predispose its members toward becoming either victims or perpetrators of prejudicial behavior. Those group traits can be specified and measured reliably and validly. They include the following:

- Traditions of group superiority (e.g., Nazis)
- Traditions of group inferiority (e.g., "Okies" and "hillbillies")
- Negative child-rearing practices (e.g., child abuse and neglect)
- Traditions of ignorance of others (e.g., mid-19th century Japan)
- Traditions of paranoia (e.g., Ku Klux Klan)

Political Predisposing Factors

Political prejudice predisposing factors are those group characteristics related to allocations of power (decision making), and which can be identified and measured reliably and validly. They include the following:

- Disputes with other nations over military power (e.g., Cold War)
- Disputes over financial power (e.g., U.S.-Japan trade wars)
- Disputes over legal power (e.g., elections, police)
- Disputes over information control (e.g., Internet security disagreements)
- Disputes over disease control (e.g., rights of AIDS patients)

Quantifying the Predisposing Factors

It is reasonable to assume that each of the prejudice predisposing factors are equally applicable to both potential victims and perpetrators. The operational difference is that victims internalize the emotions of the predisposing factors; perpetrators externalize them.

Aspy, Aspy, and Sandhu developed the Multidimensional Prejudice Predisposition Scale (MPPS) as a diagnostic tool for counselors, teachers, and individuals to determine how predisposed a given individual is toward prejudice.

We can describe two dimensions to the measures of prejudice predisposing factors: its magnitude and its direction. Thus the score for each factor must address those two elements. To meet those criteria, the magnitude of the factors are expressed numerically on a 5-point scale and each is assigned either a positive or negative value to indicate its direction (positive being outward, and negative being inward). Therefore, a score of +3 designates a moderate level of the predisposing trait that is directed outward. Figure 13.2 outlines this scale.

This instrument is designed as a diagnostic tool and may be used by counselors, teachers, or individuals to determine how predisposed an individual is toward prejudice.

Scoring Example for the MPPS

For Item 1, a score of −3 indicates that the individual has a moderate number of personality conflicts that were directed inwardly. Conversely, a score of +3 indicates that the person has a moderate number of personality conflicts that are directed outwardly. A

FIGURE 13.2

Multidimensional Prejudice Predisposition Scale (MPPS)

Directions: Circle the appropriate number for each item.

Section I: The individual has:

	Internalized	Factor	Externalized

1. −5 −4 −3 −2 −1 Unresolved personality conflicts +1 +2 +3 +4 +5
2. −5 −4 −3 −2 −1 Negative racial/ethnic identity +1 +2 +3 +4 +5
3. −5 −4 −3 −2 −1 Negative self-concept +1 +2 +3 +4 +5
4. −5 −4 −3 −2 −1 Low-order empathy +1 +2 +3 +4 +5
5. −5 −4 −3 −2 −1 An inclination toward cate- +1 +2 +3 +4 +5
   gorical thinking

Section II: The person's native society has:

6. −5 −4 −3 −2 −1 Traditions of group superiority +1 +2 +3 +4 +5
7. −5 −4 −3 −2 −1 Traditions of group inferiority +1 +2 +3 +4 +5
8. −5 −4 −3 −2 −1 Traditions of exclusion +1 +2 +3 +4 +5
9. −5 −4 −3 −2 −1 Traditions of ignorance about +1 +2 +3 +4 +5
   others
10. −5 −4 −3 −2 −1 Traditions of paranoia +1 +2 +3 +4 +5

Section III: The person's native society has disputes with other nations over:

11. −5 −4 −3 −2 −1 Military power +1 +2 +3 +4 +5
12. −5 −4 −3 −2 −1 Financial power +1 +2 +3 +4 +5
13. −5 −4 −3 −2 −1 Legal power +1 +2 +3 +4 +5
14. −5 −4 −3 −2 −1 Information control +1 +2 +3 +4 +5
15. −5 −4 −3 −2 −1 Disease control +1 +2 +3 +4 +5

Scoring scale:
   1 = trait present but very weak
   2 = trait present but somewhat weak
   3 = trait present and moderate
   4 = trait present and somewhat strong
   5 = trait present and very strong
   + indicates that the emotion of the trait is directed outwardly
   − indicates that the emotion of the trait is directed inwardly

total MPPS score of –18 indicates that a person was moderately predisposed toward becoming a victim of prejudiced behavior.

Scoring Procedures

I. Self-Scoring:
    Clients rate themselves on the MPPS questionnaire.
II. Counselor Scoring:
    Counselors rate their clients on the MPPS questionnaire. This is called the inferred score which is derived from the counselor's knowledge of the client.
III. External Instrument Scoring.
    Information for each of the items can be obtained from instruments designed especially for that trait.
A. Personality conflicts: Rorschach Inkblot Test
B. Racial/ethnic identity: Ponterotto R/E test
C. Self-concept—Tennessee Self-Concept Scale
D. Empathic understanding—Carkhuff Scale
E. Cognitive functioning—Blooms Taxonomy

Interpretation of MPPS Scores

Individuals

A person's total MPPS score consists of the sum of scores for all 15 items. The subscore for Items 1–5 indicates the individual's amount of predisposition toward prejudicial behavior derived from the person's unresolved personality conflicts. The subscore for Items 6–10 indicates the individual's amount of predisposition toward prejudicial behavior derived from his or her native society's interpersonal traditions. The subscore for items 11–15 indicates the individual's amount of predisposition toward prejudicial behavior derived from the power disputes in that person's native society. The algebraic sign of the scores indicates the direction of the person's predisposition toward prejudiced behavior.

An example of a possible scoring scheme for the MPPS is presented in Table 13.4. Item scores are summed for each dimension (individual, social, and power), and then the scale scores are summed for a total MPPS score.

TABLE 13.4

Sample Score Sheet for MPPS

Item		Score
1.		−1
2.		−2
3.		−2
4.		−3
5.		−1
Individual subscore	=	−9
6.		+1
7.		+1
8.		+2
9.		+1
10.		+2
Social subscore	=	+7
11.		+4
12.		+4
13.		+3
14.		+5
15.		+4
Power subscore	=	+20
Total score	=	+18

This individual's score (+18) indicates that the person is mildly predisposed toward prejudicial behavior and that the emotion is directed outward indicating a tendency toward becoming a perpetrator.

Groups

A group's score for Items 1–5 consists of the means of the individual scores of its members or a sample of them. The interpretation of a group's score is identical to the procedure used for individuals.

In general, with the data supplied by the MPPS, counselors are prepared to (a) identify individuals who may be predisposed toward prejudicial behavior, (b) specify the magnitude of the predisposition, and (c) determine whether the affect associated with the predisposition is directed inward or outward.

Use of MPPS Results

After counselors have determined their clients' MPPS scores they are equipped to specify their target individuals and/or groups as well as to designate their target behaviors. They will have answers to two questions: (a) With whom should they work? and (b) What behavioral traits should they attempt to modify? The remaining issues are how to select their clients and how to treat them.

Selecting Clients

Three dimensions offer important information about client selection: (a) How predisposed to prejudicial behavior is the potential client? (b) How aware is the client of the predisposition? and (c) How willing is the client to discuss the predisposition? Figure 13.3 depicts the diagnosis process for two of these variables.

Figure 13.4 depicts the multidimensional relationship among these three client characteristics. To the degree that a client has prejudice predisposition, is aware of the predisposition, and is willing to discuss the predisposition, therapy to reduce the pre-

---

FIGURE 13.3

Awareness of Predisposition and Level of Predisposition Toward Prejudice

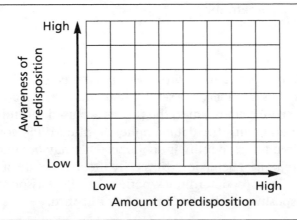

FIGURE 13.4

Awareness by Degree of Predisposition and Willingness to Discuss Predisposition

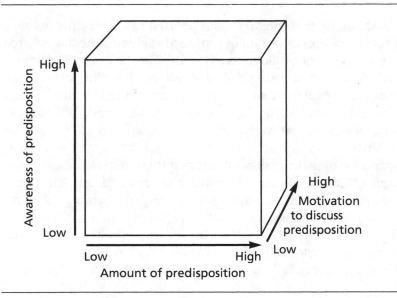

disposition and prevent prejudicial behavior is more likely to be needed. However, counseling may address any of the three characteristics to prepare for later therapy.

Using the three client dimensions in Figure 13.4, eight groups emerge:

1. High awareness, high predisposition, high willingness to discuss
2. High awareness, high predisposition, low willingness to discuss
3. High awareness, low predisposition, high willingness to discuss
4. High awareness, low predisposition, low willingness to discuss
5. Low awareness, high predisposition, high willingness to discuss
6. Low awareness, high predisposition, low willingness to discuss

7. Low awareness, low predisposition, high willingness to discuss
8. Low awareness, low predisposition, low willingness to discuss

Assuming that the MPPS can be used to identify the amount of prejudice predisposition of prospective clients, the data related to awareness and willingness to discuss may be gathered during a clarification of the results of the MPPS. At that time, clients may be asked to explore their past discussions of their predispositions toward prejudiced behavior. The number and depth of those previous discussions as well as the client's inclination to participate in future ones are both behavioral indicators of the clients' awareness of their predispositions and their motivation to discuss them. Of course, direct questioning is always available. The counselor can simply ask: (a) How aware are you of your predisposition toward prejudicial behavior? and (b) How motivated are you to discuss that predisposition? Both responses yield behavioral indexes and historically, direct questioning has been used extensively and successfully to select counseling clients.

Counseling With Clients Who Are Predisposed to Prejudicial Behavior

The MMPPR counseling model incorporates procedures from trait-and-factor, person-centered, psychoanalytic, and behavioral approaches into its procedures. The five-phase process for prejudice-reduction counseling using the MMPPR is as follows:

Phase 1: Trait-and-Factor

The counselor administers the MMPPR Prejudice Predisposition Scale to a client(s). The goal is to identify a potential client pool.

Phase 2: Person-Centered

The counselor provides a warm, genuine, and empathic atmosphere while discussing the MPPS results with the members of the prospective client pool. The goal is to identify the degree to which the prospective clients are aware of their predisposition to prejudicial behavior and are motivated to discuss it.

Phase 3: Person-Centered

The counselor offers an atmosphere of warmth, genuineness, and empathic understanding so that clients can explore their predisposition toward prejudicial behavior. The goal of these sessions is for clients to become aware of their unresolved personality conflicts, their native society's interpersonal patterns, and their native society's ways of allocating power.

Phase 4: Psychoanalytic

The counselor offers interpretations of the relationships between clients' present ways of coping with their prejudicial predispositions and the ways clients would like to behave. The goal is to delineate a set of specific prejudice-reducing behaviors the clients are prepared to learn.

Phase 5: Behavioral

The counselor helps clients devise step-by-step programs they can use to learn their new, self-selected behavioral goals. The counselor helps clients monitor their attainment of their prejudice-reducing behaviors. They are prepared to use feedback to assist in clients' learning of the prejudice-reducing behaviors. The goal is the implementation of the prejudice-reducing behaviors as chosen by the clients.

Case Study Overview

In this case, Jane S. presented with a problem related to her weight gain, feelings of rejection by her peers because of her weight gain, and growing prejudice against them because she believed that all thin teenage girls were shallow.

In the personal area, the client explores her situation while the counselor uses a person-centered approach. Through this process, she gains insight (psychoanalytic technique by counselor) that negative self-talk is one of her problems. The counselor uses behavioristic methods to help the client devise and execute a learning program to change her negative self-talk into positive self-talk.

Jane's social situation is explored in much the same fashion. She discovers that one of her social problems is that she has learned to withdraw from people who are different and that she does not want to do this. She devises and executes a learning program with the help of the counselor to change her withdrawing behavior to approaching behavior with people who are different from her.

The political area is also explored in turn. Jane discovers that she has learned to exclude individuals and information from her decision-making process and that as a result, her decisions are sometimes flawed and incomplete. With the help of her counselor, Jane devises and implements a learning program to change her exclusive decision-making process to an inclusive one. Through these steps, Jane has resolved her presenting problem as well as learned skills that will help her solve future problems without assistance.

Chapter Summary

Because prejudice is a multidimensional problem consisting of individual, societal, and political components, we have introduced the Multidimensional Model of Prejudice Prevention and Reduction. This model is designed to address predisposing factors in all three areas. It also acknowledges that these factors may be inwardly directed, resulting in the likelihood of an individual becoming a victim of prejudicial behavior; or it may be directed outwardly, resulting in a perpetrator of prejudicial behavior.

The Multidimensional Prejudice Predisposition Scale was developed to diagnose an individual's or group's predisposition toward prejudice in all three components. Scoring methods and interpretation procedures were also provided.

In the following chapter, a case is presented and each of the steps in the MMPPR counseling methodology is presented. This case is presented in great detail to highlight the steps of the technique.

14

A Case Study

In this chapter, the Multidimensional Model for Prejudice Prevention and Reduction is demonstrated through the case described in Section II. The model contains five phases that correspond to both the type of information needed in that phase and the specific counseling technique used to obtain the information. This case is presented in great detail to highlight the steps of the technique.

A 16-year-old girl named Jane S. has gained some bothersome weight and is concerned about this change. She has scheduled a visit with a counselor to discuss her situation. As part of the intake procedure she has completed the Multidimensional Prejudice Predisposition Scale (MPPS) and her scores for all three sources (personal, social, and political) of prejudice predisposition were somewhat elevated.

Jane has completed Phase I of MMPPR counseling by completing the MPPS.

She now enters Phase III by exploring her situation. The counselor provides a warm, honest, and empathic relationship. In this case Phase II will come later.

COUNSELOR: Hello, it's good to see you. Please come in and have a seat where you feel most comfortable.

JANE: I'm kind of nervous. It's the first time I've been to a counselor.

COUNSELOR: It's a bit a scary to try something new.

JANE: Yeah. I don't want to think I'm losing it. I'm just worried about all this weight I've gained. I want to stop it before it gets beyond me.

COUNSELOR: You're afraid the weight change might get out of control.

JANE: Uh huh. I don't seem to be eating much more but I'm eating the wrong things. I just can't get enough sweets. I've always liked them but now I crave them.

COUNSELOR: You're mystified by this new pattern that has emerged.

JANE: It's like a different part of me is gaining control and I don't like it.

COUNSELOR: There's a struggle inside you.

JANE: The sweets lover is winning. The health-food advocate is in trouble. I need to wake it up.

COUNSELOR: You want the health-food advocate to win.

JANE: Sure. I don't want to be fat and ugly. I want to be thin. I'm sort of pretty when I'm not so big.

COUNSELOR: You know that you can be more attractive.

JANE: Yeah. The guys liked me until I got fat. Now they're shying away.

COUNSELOR: You have more space now.

JANE: Boy, do I have space (laughs). They don't even look at me. I can only imagine what they say behind my back.

COUNSELOR: You think about what the guys say about you when you're not around.

JANE: They probably call me a cow or a pig. I don't blame them. I'm starting to look like a cow.

COUNSELOR: It's not just other people. You're putting yourself down.

JANE: It's the truth. I'm letting my pretty side get swallowed by the ugly side. I should be ashamed. I guess I am.

COUNSELOR: The struggle inside you is causing you to feel guilty.

JANE: Yeah, I'm smarter than that. I can control my weight. I know how. I'm just not doing it. It's awful!

COUNSELOR: *It's* awful or *you're* awful?

At this point, Jane explores the meaning of the MPPS results. This is Phase II.

JANE: I guess it's me. That test I took shows that I'm prejudiced. That's awful.

COUNSELOR: That test showed that you're prone to be prejudiced, not that you are prejudiced.

JANE: What does that mean?

COUNSELOR: It means that if you're placed in a situation where you have a chance to be prejudiced then you might act that way.

JANE: Give me an example.

COUNSELOR: If you had the job of selecting members of a team you might screen out some of them because of things that were not true. For example, you might exclude all thin people because you think that none of them could like you.

JANE: None of them do! They think I'm too fat and they make me feel ugly.

She then continues in Phase III by exploring her situation.

COUNSELOR: You are not satisfied with your belief that all thin people are bad.

JANE: No. It blocks them out of my life. It's like a wall.

COUNSELOR: You're not sure what you want to do with the wall.

JANE: Sometimes I want to make it higher and other times I want to tear it down.

COUNSELOR: You're not sure what's behind that wall.

JANE: If I tear it down, the people behind it might hurt me.

COUNSELOR: But you're not sure about that. Your feelings are mixed.

JANE: Yeah. I wish some of them would be my friends.

COUNSELOR: Your prejudice against thin people has cut you off from some people you would like to meet.

JANE: Yeah. I think we could like each other.

COUNSELOR: So, you'd like to cut through that wall and be able to make friends with some thin people.

JANE: Sure. But I don't know how.

Here counseling enters Phase IV, in which the counselor makes an interpretation about the client's situation.

COUNSELOR: Well, it seems that your weight gain may be related to the stresses in your life. You've found food as a source of safety and security. You've also decided that thin people can't like you because you can't like yourself. What you really want is to get back in control and earn you own respect. You're just not sure how to do that right now.

JANE: Yeah, I gues that's right. It doesn't sound too good, though.

Counseling moves to Phase V, the action phase. Jane and her counselor plan a learning program for Jane.

COUNSELOR: You are prejudiced against thin people, and you want to be able to meet them just as you would meet anyone else.

JANE: That would be great.

COUNSELOR: There are three areas where people learn to be prejudiced: ourselves; our society; and the political situation we live in. We have to learn new ways to deal with our hang-ups. New ways to get along with others.

New ways to share power. We have to start with our own hang-ups. You have said that you don't like yourself because you have gained weight, so maybe you should start by learning new ways to talk to yourself about yourself. How many times do you talk to yourself about yourself now?

JANE: Every time I look in a mirror.

COUNSELOR: What do you say?

JANE: "You're too fat."

COUNSELOR: Let's try this. Every time you look in a mirror say this to yourself before you say anything else: "You're a fine person."

JANE: That sounds easy enough.

COUNSELOR: Every time you do that give yourself a point, and when you get 10 points put on some of your favorite perfume. Then start over again. Can you do that?

JANE: Yeah. I think so, but I'm going to smell awfully good.

COUNSELOR: Good, maybe others will notice and compliment you for it. Let's give it a try and we'll talk about it next time.

Jane successfully completes a series of programs geared to help her learn to improve her own self-perceptions and has been able to relate more effectively with thin people. At this point she begins to explore the social sources of her predisposition to prejudicial behavior. Here, she enters Phase III again to explore a new area.

JANE: It feels good to be able to have at least one friend who is thin. It feels like my walls are breaking down.

COUNSELOR: Your world is getting bigger.

JANE: Yeah, but I'm still wondering about the other sources of things that make me prone to prejudice. You mentioned that the test showed that I had social hang-ups. What does that mean?

COUNSELOR: You learned some ways to be prejudiced from the people around you.

JANE: I probably did. They were pretty prejudiced. They hated everybody who was different.

COUNSELOR: You feel resentful about those attitudes.

JANE: Yeah. Those hateful attitudes filled me with hate that have kept me in a shell. The only people I feel comfortable with are people just like me.

COUNSELOR: Your wall is showing up again.

JANE: Yeah. I guess it was outside the other one. Now I have to break down another one (sighs).

COUNSELOR: The thought of more work is exhausting.

JANE: Sort of, but it's also exciting. It's like unlocking doors that have had me locked inside.

COUNSELOR: It's freeing to know that you can get outside those walls.

JANE: Yeah. What do I do this time?

COUNSELOR: Talk about what you learned about prejudice from your family. .

JANE: My parents were suspicious of people who did things different from us. They told us kids to stay away from weirdos like people who liked strange music. Man, if it wasn't music from the 1960s it was bad, and the people who listened to it were bad. The same things about clothes. If they weren't in style they were bad and anybody who wore them was bad.

COUNSELOR: Your parents closed themselves off from different people, and you resent that behavior.

JANE: I love my parents but they had their hang-ups. I'm worried that they gave them all to me and I don't want them.

COUNSELOR: You want to be healthy but you don't want to reject your parents.

JANE: Well, now it's just my dad since Mom died, and he's trying so hard, but he just won't understand why I want to be friends with the people he thought were bad. It puts me in a bind. I'm damned if I do and damned if I don't. Sometimes it's easier to just pull back and shut your eyes and ears.

COUNSELOR: It's painful to do things that will cause stress between you and your parents even when you think they're the right things to do.

JANE: Yeah. It's easier to get fat and dumb.

COUNSELOR: Sometimes choosing health is harder than dying slowly.

JANE: Ohhhh. Sometimes I just want to go to sleep and let the world go by.

COUNSELOR: But you keep hearing that part of you that wants to be healthy. It's still alive and functioning.

JANE: It won't go away. I know it's my best part. So what do I do to get rid of the prejudiced stuff I learned from my parents?

The counselor offers an interpretation (Phase IV) of the client's present situation and the client's goal.

COUNSELOR: You feel tied up in the prejudices you learned from your parents, and you want to be free from them. Specifically, you learned to pull away from people who are different and you want to be able to associate with them openly and honestly. Is that about it?

JANE: That's about it.

Jane enters Phase V to plan a learning program.

COUNSELOR: Let's start with your self-talk again. What do you tell yourself when you meet somebody different?

JANE: I say, "Pull back."

COUNSELOR: O.K. Now what do you think you ought to do to change that behavior?

JANE: Tell myself not to pull back, that they're O.K.

COUNSELOR: That's a good first step. Now what will you do to reward yourself?

JANE: After I say, "Don't pull back. They're O.K." 10 times I'll put a dollar in my left pocket and when I see something I want, I'm going to buy it out of the money in that pocket. That'll be my mad money.

After successfully completing several learning programs in the social area, Jane reenters Phase III to explore the political source of her predisposition toward prejudice.

JANE: I'm freeing myself from the prejudices I learned in the social area; what about the political stuff? I know I don't want to be a politician.

COUNSELOR: The political area is not about getting elected to office. It's about how to share power with others. It concerns things like money and decision making.

JANE: Now this is down to the nitty-gritty. When you get into my cash we're getting personal.

COUNSELOR: Talk about how your community shares its power.

JANE: Well, most of the decisions seem to be controlled by people with money. Everybody else just follows along and gripes (laughs).

COUNSELOR: You seem to have mixed feelings about that process.

JANE: I'm not sure about it. I don't want a bunch of idiots making decisions; I'd like to be in on more of them. I'd like to see more of us have an opportunity to share the power.

COUNSELOR: You trust some people and you don't trust others. But the group you trust is bigger than the group making the choices now.

JANE: I guess I'm more democratic than most people.

COUNSELOR: But you don't trust democracy all the way.

JANE: You mean where everybody gets an equal voice? I do, but it scares me sometimes.

COUNSELOR: You'll have to stretch to include everybody in the community's decisions.

JANE: Yeah. But I'd like to. I think that's American.

They move back to Phase IV in which the counselor makes an interpretation of the client's situation.

COUNSELOR: You learned that decision making is controlled by a privileged few, and you're not satisfied with that. You want to learn how to share decision making with everyone affected by the decision. You think that is the way an American ought to behave. Is that right?

Jane enters Phase V to plan a learning program to share decision making.

JANE: Yes. And I think I'm going into another one of those periods of changing my behavior.

COUNSELOR: Talk about your thoughts when you get into a decision-making situation.

JANE: I just want to get a decision made. I hate to dilly-dally around. I want somebody to tell the group what to do. I hate discussions with people who don't know what they're talking about. I want to get up and leave.

COUNSELOR: O.K. Let's try this. When you start to think that you want to leave say to yourself, "It's important to stay and let everybody speak."

JANE: I know. After I've done that 10 times I get a reward (both client and counselor laugh).

COUNSELOR: You've got the hang of it. I'd like to know what reward you're going to give yourself.

The client has gone through a successful series of changing from negative self-talk to positive self-talk about including everybody in the decision-making process. She returns to discuss her situation.

JANE: I think I've learned to include everybody in the decision-making process. But, I'm still overweight, which was why I came to counseling in the first place (laughs). But I think I know how to get rid of it. I'm going to tell myself how much I like my thoughts about losing weight and after I do that 10 times I'm going to buy myself a Diet Coke. I think it will help. I'll let you know if it works. By the way, I like myself a lot more, and I have a lot more friends.

Chapter Summary

The Multidimensional Model for Prejudice Prevention and Reduction is a method that incorporates several well-established counseling methodologies. This model recognizes that prejudice is a function not only of individual factors, but social and political ones as well. To address the problem of prejudice completely, all of these areas must be addressed. The client is both a target of change and a change agent, as individual contributions to prejudice are conquered and energy is then focused on the social and political changes essential to remove support for prejudice in the environment.

Prejudicial attitudes may contribute to predispositions toward prejudice perpetration as well as victimization. The Multidimensional Prejudice Predisposition Scale provides an assessment of clients' likelihood of perpetrating prejudice or becoming a victim of such acts. This knowledge can be critical as part of the diagnosis process of determining those individual, social, and political factors that must be changed to reduce the likelihood of prejudicial behavior. The case presented in this chapter demonstrated the use of the MMPPR to facilitate effective change within an individual predisposed toward prejudicial behavior. The model recognizes the complexity of change and addresses it systematically through the application of several counseling modalities at critical phases in the change process.

CASE EXAMPLES
OF THERAPY
FOR PREJUDICE

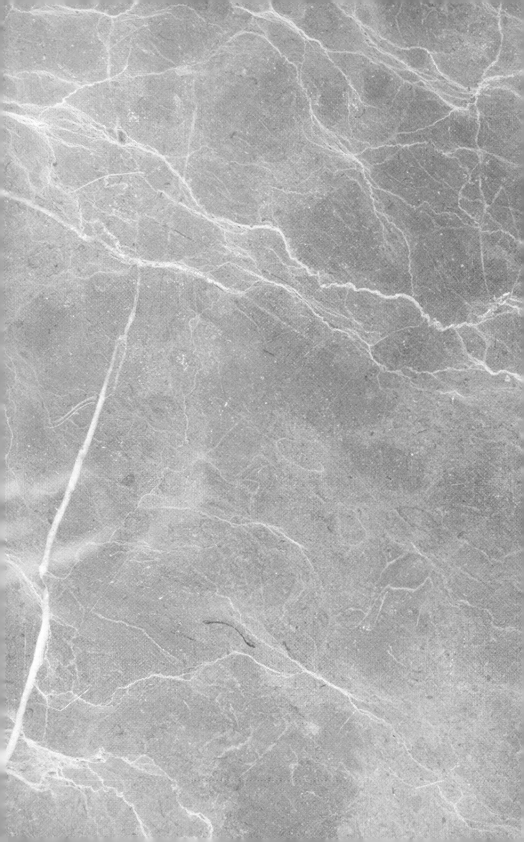

Introduction

The purpose of this section is to demonstrate selected counseling methods as they might apply to two cases in which prejudice is part of the presenting problem. We selected these methods to exemplify the three basic categories of counseling: psychodynamic approaches, experiential and relationship-oriented approaches, and cognitive and behavioral approaches. The three methods are Adlerian, rational-emotive therapy, and human resource development counseling.

Each chapter addresses one model, and the same two cases are used throughout, so the approaches can be compared and contrasted. The two cases represent a victim and a perpetrator of prejudice. The first case deals with homophobia; the second case represents racism. These cases were selected as representational of problems often seen by counselors today. The rights of gay men, lesbians, and bisexual persons have become part of a national debate, and legislation has been initiated on both sides of the issue. Recent Supreme Court rulings (Kaplan & Klaidman, 1996) have prevented states from abridging these rights, but the debate continues. Racial violence is also on the rise among adolescents, and juvenile justice programs have been developed to include rehabilitation rather than focusing on punishment.

In the following paragraphs, both cases are presented, and in the following chapters they are described in greater detail as appropriate for each counseling method. In each case, the goal of therapy is to address the needs of the client for growth and problem resolution. The client-counselor interaction dialogues are representative of various time intervals of therapy to reflect particular aspects and stages of the counseling approach being demonstrated.

The Case of Angelica

Angelica W. is a 27-year-old Caucasian woman who is a lesbian. For most of her life, she has been cautious about disclosing her sexual orientation to new acquaintances until she was confident of not being rejected. Recently, she applied for a position for which she was well qualified. She was interviewed by an extremely conservative woman, who asked her the usual questions but was very formal. At the end of the interview, the woman thanked her for coming in, but said she felt that Angelica would not be appropriate for this position. Angelica was surprised at such a complete dismissal because her education and experience made the job seem ideal for her. She asked the interviewer what specifically was lacking. The interviewer responded by saying, "I think we both know what the problem is. You don't fit our image. This is a family organization." Angelica knew the woman had assumed she was a lesbian because of her appearance, and it made her angry. She thought about filing a complaint with the Equal Employment Opportunity Commission (EEOC), but realized that any complaint would require public disclosure of her sexual orientation. Her parents and older brother did not know, nor did any of her extended family. She was sure her parents would be crushed by the news that their only daughter was a lesbian. The risks of public disclosure were too great, and Angelica did not file the complaint. However, 3 weeks later, she is still so angry and resentful that she cannot eat or sleep well. She has decided to enter counseling.

The Case of John

John H. is a 17-year-old, Caucasian high school junior who was referred to the juvenile diversion program for a racial incident that occurred at a high school football game. John and several of his friends attended the game with their school's most intense rival. At the concession stand, John saw one of the cheerleaders from the opposing team, who was African American. John stood close behind her and asked her (in vulgar, descriptive language) what she would charge to have sex with him. She told him that "no little White boy would ever be worth the bother." An African American man who witnessed the exchange laughed out loud and yelled, "Way to go" to the cheerleader. Johnny was embarrassed and angry. He yelled racial epithets at both the cheerleader and the man, but they continued to laugh. John was furious and pulled a knife from his pocket and pointed it at the cheerleader. He threatened to cut her "ugly Black face." The man told him to put the knife away, but John turned and made a swipe with the knife toward him. Instinctively, the man dodged the knife, and in doing so he bumped into the cheerleader, which caused her to slip. The knife grazed her arm, and blood immediately flowed from the wound. John was frightened. He dropped the knife and started to run away, when he was caught by a security guard who had been notified of the altercation. John was taken into custody. Because he had no previous legal problems, he was referred to the juvenile diversion program, which required counseling and community service.

Psychodynamic Model:
A Case Approach to Adlerian Counseling

The first step in Adlerian therapy is an assessment of the client's life style. This may be accomplished by having the client complete a life style questionnaire that addresses (a) life situation, (b) presenting problem, (c) life tasks, (d) family constellation and early development, and (e) early recollections (Powers & Griffith, 1986). This information provides a rich tapestry for interpreting the client's perceptions of life that are faulty and ultimately dysfunctional for his or her growth.

Adlerian therapy focuses on the individual as a social being who has created a life style as a means of meeting life tasks. Unfortunately, the life style created may not be based on a whole reality, but has been formed by the client's response to the events and circumstances experienced in childhood through the family constellation.

There are four goals of therapy in the Adlerian approach: (a) establishment of a good working relationship based on cooperation and mutual respect, (b) development of a therapeutic climate in which the client can come to understand his or her faulty beliefs, (c) evolution of client insight into self-defeating behaviors through confrontation and interpretation, and (d) translation of insight into better ways of meeting the challenges of his or her life tasks (Corey, 1991b; Corsini & Wedding, 1989; Prochaska, 1984).

The four goals of therapy are translated into phases. The first phase focuses on the development of an empathic relationship. The goals of therapy are individualized and made specific for the mutual benefit of counselor and client. Both must be congruent with the expected outcomes, and the responsibilities of each must be clear.

This agreement sets the stage for the second phase of counseling. This is a phase of summarizing and interpreting the information from the life style questionnaire to determine how the patient's current life style affects his or her functioning.

The review and analysis of functioning should lead to insight into the faulty understandings that have led to self-defeating behavior. This insight is a step toward action. Once the misunderstandings have been uncovered, the client is free to develop healthier approaches to life.

The fourth phase of counseling requires the client to take risks and make changes that will lead to a more satisfying life style. The therapeutic process begins with thinking, moves to feeling, and finally involves behaving.

Counseling techniques used by Adlerian therapists are drawn from many other modalities. These include questions, confrontation, interpretation, advice, encouragement, and homework. Psychodrama and role-play may also be used to help the client determine mistaken beliefs and faulty perceptions. Any technique that will enable the client to better understand his or her current dynamics, mistaken perceptions, and dysfunctional strategies could be used by the counselor.

The Case of Angelica

Summary of family constellation and early development

Angelica is the younger of two children born to Bill and Judy. Judy was 23 years old when their first child, Tom, was born, and 37 years old when Angelica was born. Angelica never really knew Tom as a sibling, because he went away to school when she was 4 years old. Bill and Judy started a bakery when Tom was a baby and it consumed most of their waking hours. By the time Angelica was born (resulting from an unplanned pregnancy) the business had expanded to three stores. Bill and Judy still focused their life around the main plant activities, but the additional stores increased the time they devoted to work.

When Angelica was a baby, they put a crib in their office and cared for her there. As she grew older, they added a play room for her and she continued to amuse herself with toys. When they could, Bill and Judy (and other employees) would spend time with her, but mostly she spent her time alone with her toys. She learned quickly not to bother her parents at work. If they were especially busy, even her physical needs were delayed. Sometimes she had wet diapers, and she learned to ignore her own hunger and to eat according to her parents' schedule.

On Sundays, the only day they did not go to work, the family would go to church, where Angelica met other children. Her early advances toward other children were not very successful. Other children made demands, unlike the toys in her playroom, and she found them unsatisfactory playmates. She began preschool at age 4 and was a very good student. Angelica liked adults more than children, but she had few expectations. She was surprised by the interest her third-grade teacher showed in her, and for the first time she was excited by school and miserable when vacations came around. Angelica developed a strong affection for her teacher that her parents could not understand.

Although they were not openly affectionate with each other or with Angelica, they cared for her deeply and placed few demands on her except that she not interrupt their schedule. If she did, they would get angry and chastise her for being inconsiderate. Angelica learned to keep peace by keeping her feelings to herself. As long as she reported only good news from school, everything seemed fine.

For all their personal inattention, her parents were eager to involve her in activities. Angelica took piano lessons, riding lessons, and ballet instruction; and though these were welcome activities, she did not excel. She also went to camp every summer, but spent as much time as possible reading and hiking alone.

Angelica and her parents took one vacation a year, usually to some foreign country that would enhance her education. She liked to travel, but her parents were not adventuresome and they often sent her on educational tours while they spent time alone relaxing. She felt excluded from their relationship.

In high school, Angelica participated in dramatics and found she loved the stage, where she could be someone else for a while. Acting was something at which she excelled. However, when she played the lead in the senior play opposite a very handsome, popular boy she found these scenes extremely uncomfortable. The teasing by cast members was difficult, but she pretended not to hear the frequent unpleasant remarks. She had no close friends among her peers, and her parents were always involved with the business when these feelings needed to be explored.

Angelica and her older brother had little in common, and Tom was always away. He married after college graduation and moved across the country to be near his wife's parents. By the time Angelica graduated from high school, Tom had three children whom she saw only once a year at Christmas.

Angelica was awarded a scholarship to a college several hundred miles from her home. She enjoyed the opportunities on the campus and found in her roommate a soul mate. Her roommate, Shelley, was cute, outgoing, funny, and a good student; she took Angelica to new restaurants and campus pubs that had never been a part of her life. She learned to drink and enjoyed the feeling of intoxication.

The first time Shelley approached her sexually, Angelica was curious, but afraid. She had ignored her sexuality like many other parts of herself. However, she liked the touching and eventually she and her roommate became lovers. Angelica felt contented in this relationship. She identified herself as a lesbian and thought this explained many of her unresolved feelings as she was growing up.

She also found that there were other lesbians on campus, and they provided a social support group for Angelica. She found identity in this group and was so involved that she did not even notice the intermittent disapproval targeted toward them. For a while, she was involved in the women's rights movement and liked being politically active.

After college graduation, she and Shelley moved to a large city for graduate school. They loved the environment and when class responsibilities permitted, they volunteered their time with an AIDS support group.

Angelica brought Shelley home for visits but never told her parents about their relationship. She knew her conservative parents would disapprove. She was not sure what form this disapproval would take, so it seemed easier to keep this part of herself from them because they did not attend to subtleties.

The Counseling Process

Over the first several sessions as Angelica and her counselor developed a working relationship, it became clear that Angelica's anger was overwhelming. She could not understand being denied a job for which she was highly qualified. For the most part, her life had been lived alone with few demands made on her to be a part of a family. She had resented her parents' aloofness and had interpreted it as selfishness. She had managed the early years of her life by being quiet and obedient. Now she felt that she had a real family in the group of lesbians she knew who cared about her and with whom she could share her life and her secrets. Her one-on-one experience with prejudice brought to the surface her anger at all those who had previously rejected her and who would reject her in the future because of her sexual orientation.

As she moved into the second phase of therapy, Angelica faced her anger and its consequences. She had lost weight, was not sleeping well, and was irritable with Shelley and other friends. Every relationship that was important to her was strained to the breaking point. She was afraid to talk with her parents because of her anger, so when she was sure that they were not home, she left brief messages on their answering machine telling them she was fine. She had not sought other employment, and she knew that soon she would have to ask her parents for financial help.

Angelica had adopted an independent life style to compensate for what she thought was rejection. She believed she did not need the approval of others, and yet the reality of rejection from someone who hated lesbians and who did not really know her had stunned her into almost total withdrawal from the world. She was afraid to be herself and afraid of losing the relationships that had become important to her. Angelica explored her sexual orientation to be sure that she was not just acting out her anger against her parents. Through questioning and interpreting, she arrived at an understanding of her anger and her life style adjustments.

These understandings marked the transition into Phase III of the counseling process. The following dialogue occurred at the beginning of this stage of therapy.

COUNSELOR: So you think you have a handle on your anger. What makes sense to you about your life?

ANGELICA: Well, I have decided that all my life I adjusted to whatever happened by believing that if I could keep everything under control—it would all work out O.K.

COUNSELOR: But that wasn't how you really feel, was it?

ANGELICA: No. I thought all my parents cared about was each other. I felt left out most of the time. They didn't have time for me, teachers didn't have time for me, Tom didn't have time for me. No one did. I thought it was because I was different, you know.

COUNSELOR: But that wasn't true either. You found freedom in having no demands.

ANGELICA: Yes, I was free, but I was lonely too. It is also easier to judge others and find them wanting rather than looking at yourself. For the first time in my life, I have to ask what I have done to make my life the way it is.

COUNSELOR: And what way is that?

ANGELICA: Well, I am miserable. I am furious. I am a pathetic victim. I really thought I could keep it all together. I thought I had learned how to do that at least. And now, I've seen it fall apart. But I also feel something else. I can't explain it exactly. It's that, well, I think I feel free in a new kind of way. Before, I was free because I created distance from other people. Now, I feel that I don't need that distance. It's O.K. if people know me, who I really am. They may like me or they may not. But if they do, I will really be able to relate in a whole new way. I won't have to be afraid that they will find out about me and reject me. Now, I won't have to live with the prejudices of other people. I can fight them openly.

COUNSELOR: So you are ready to come out of the closet?

ANGELICA: Well, I guess I've been out longer than I thought. The woman at the interview had little trouble knowing who I was.

COUNSELOR: Did she *really* know who you were?

ANGELICA: No, you're right, she didn't know me. She rejected me because she assumed I was a lesbian, and who knows what that means to her? She didn't really reject me. She didn't know me well enough.

COUNSELOR: What does that mean to you now?

ANGELICA: Well, she was wrong. She is prejudiced against lesbians. But I guess I should have had better sense. I guess I've always known there is prejudice in the world, and I didn't have to rub her face in it. I could have gotten that job by playing along a little. Maybe I did it on purpose. I wanted the confrontation, but I wasn't ready for it, really. I am a lesbian. That isn't going to change. But, I am a lot of other things as well. I don't even know what some of those things are (laughs). I need a job. I want to work. There are places that will be more open to me than that agency. I can fix myself up a little without sacrificing who I am. And once people get to know me, they might like me.

COUNSELOR: What about your parents? Are you ready to talk with them?

ANGELICA: I'm still angry at them in some ways. They didn't really want me in their lives. I was an intrusion. But they did want good things for me. I don't think they knew and still don't know what I need from them. I'm not sure I should tell them I am a lesbian. I think I want them to know how I feel first. If we can work through that, then there will be hope for more. I think that's what I want to do first.

COUNSELOR: You are prepared for their rejection of your experience. Things may seem very different to them. They did give you everything (laughs).

ANGELICA: That's not so funny. I think they will say that. I think they thought all those things were good for me. They did work hard to get them. They were both poor growing up and things do mean a lot to them. But I wanted time and they didn't have that to give!

COUNSELOR: And now you don't have time to give to them.

ANGELICA: No, that's not fair (pause). Well, I haven't wanted to spend time with them because I was afraid of what they would think about me. They are prejudiced against lesbians, too.

COUNSELOR: Maybe you should go home and ask them what they think about you. You can't live in fear your whole life, can you?

ANGELICA: No, but this is a big risk. If they reject me I'm not sure what I'd do next. It's one thing for the world to hate me because I'm a lesbian, and it's quite another to get the same thing from your parents. I've lived my life independent of them, but now I want them to be a part of my life, and they may not want to because I'm a lesbian.

COUNSELOR: Well, let's practice what you will say to them.

At this point, the counselor put two empty chairs in front of Angelica. Angelica told the empty chairs about her hurts and fears growing up. Then she sat in each of the empty chairs as one of her parents and responded. This exercise took quite some time and emotional energy. At the conclusion, she agreed to write a letter to her parents telling them about her hurts and fears.

Angelica lived her life as though her own interpretations of others' behaviors were absolute facts. This was characteristic of her even before she acknowledged to herself that she was a lesbian. She needs to find the courage to talk with her parents and face reality with them. She may not begin with the issue of her sexual orientation, but this too must be a part of their mutual reality at some point in time if she really hopes to have a relationship with them. A week passed and Angelica returned for a counseling session.

ANGELICA: Well, I did it!

COUNSELOR: I give, what did you do?

ANGELICA: I went to see my parents. I took them out to dinner and told them how I felt excluded from their lives and that I thought they didn't want me and that I had been an intrusion and... (stops). That was a lot all at once, but they didn't seem surprised at all or defensive. In fact, it was weird. They seemed guilty I guess. My mom said she was sorry and that they knew the business was taking up too much time, but it didn't seem to matter to me, so they stayed with it. I never had a clue they were paying that much attention. Even Dad said I always seemed so independent and never seemed to need them for anything. I did act like that and now I don't even remember why. Isn't that the craziest thing? We were all acting. I guess that's why acting was so easy for me; I'd been practicing my whole life.

COUNSELOR: It's great to see you so happy with yourself.

ANGELICA: I really am. I was afraid, and we talked, more than we ever really had before. I wanted to tell them I was a lesbian, but things were so good, I just wanted to enjoy it. But I can. I know I can. And I think they'll be O.K. with it. Disappointed probably, but not so much that they will reject me. I think they will like their daughter even if she is a lesbian. I don't think they'll be prejudiced against lesbians once they find out they are just like other people. They can come and visit me. They will love this city. I will enjoy showing it to them.

COUNSELOR: That would be a new level of relationship with them. O.K. Now, what about the prejudice of the rest of the world?

ANGELICA: Well, I am who I am, but I still don't want to file the complaint. I guess I should, but I don't want to do that. I hate red tape and waiting. It will just tie up my life when I'm finally ready to live it. I guess that's the coward's way out.

COUNSELOR: You feel guilty because you're not willing to expose the interviewer's prejudice.

ANGELICA: Yes, I guess I do. I suppose I owe it to those coming after me.

COUNSELOR: Is that the only alternative you can think of to influence this woman? What about a one-on-one? Could you talk to her directly?

ANGELICA: I never thought about doing that. You mean, just go up there and tell her off?

COUNSELOR: Not exactly what I had in mind. What if you talked to her about prejudice and judging people for their appearances instead of their capabilities? You could mention the law and let her know that you know what she did was wrong.

ANGELICA: Now that would be a challenge for me! She could throw me out I guess, but I could also let her know what a wonderful opportunity she missed by not hiring me. It gives me chills to think about it. What if I fainted dead away? No, I could do this. Maybe next time, she'd think twice about her own prejudice. I really have nothing to lose. She can't really hurt me any more. But I think I will wait until I have a job. That will make me feel better, you know, more secure. But I will do this. It will be great!

COUNSELOR: O.K. Let's practice again. That seemed to help last time. You did a wonderful job with your parents.

Summary

Angelica has learned new, more authentic ways of relating. She struggles to refrain from rejecting others before they have a chance to reject her. She finds that she must continually monitor her behavior to ensure that she has not returned to playing a role. She must continually be courageous enough to be honest with her circle of friends and check her assumptions before acting upon them.

Angelica told her parents that she is a lesbian. They were not surprised. They had guessed it long before, but they were too uncomfortable to bring up the subject themselves. At one level, they were relieved to have everything out on the table. It took a burden away, and though this reality was a disappointment for them, her parents were not disappointed in Angelica. They were proud of her accomplishments and supportive of her new career. They realized that they had not brought up the subject because of their own prejudices. That fact shocked them, but they are working to overcome their prejudgments, primarily because of Angelica's experience.

For Angelica, the final goals of therapy will be to help her remain committed to her own growth. She must set goals for herself and then translate them into tasks that she can accomplish. A critical part of this process will be her dedication. She must monitor herself for old, ineffective ways of behaving and seek solutions to her problems that will help her challenge and overcome misguided perceptions.

The Case of John

Summary of family constellation and early development

John is the oldest of three children born to Ted and Jane, who had been childhood sweethearts and married as soon as they graduated from high school. They were both Catholics from the same neighborhood and shared extended family ties. Both families believed in hard work and traditional male and female roles. Children were expected to do what they were told and to do it well. Children were also expected to go to school and do well, but there was no expectation that college and a profession was a possibility.

Jane became pregnant very soon after the wedding, but the pregnancy terminated with a miscarriage in the third month. She was terrified that she might not be able to have children, and when John was born 2 years after her marriage, she was ecstatic. She indulged him in every way possible. Ted disapproved of permissive child-rearing and thought that discipline and hard work were the ticket to a happy life. He often criticized Jane for "babying" John.

After John was born, Jane suffered three more miscarriages before a daughter was born 6 years later. After the miscarriages, Jane had been put on birth control pills to ensure that she could regain her health. This was difficult for Jane, who thought birth control was wrong, but it was a better choice than abstinence, which was her only other option. Ted disagreed with the treatment and would have forbidden it if the doctor had not called him and told him it would kill Jane to have another pregnancy at the time. This experience caused a strain in the marriage. Gradually tranquillity was restored, and Jane became pregnant. A second daughter was born 9 months later. Following another miscarriage, Jane had a hysterectomy. Ted had expected to have more children, especially sons, and hinted that Jane had let him down. She maintained a stoic attitude and accepted his criticism as her due.

Ted's father had worked all his life in an automotive assembly plant, and Ted began work in the same plant as soon as he finished high school. He worked there for almost 18 years before a change in company products caused him and many others to be laid off. Since his forced unemployment about a year ago, Ted's drinking, which had been weekends only, has become a daily occurrence. He is angry because he believed the company owed him more than it gave for the 18 years he worked there faithfully.

Although Ted was a hard worker, he was never promoted to a supervisory role despite his seniority. This was due primarily to his poor relationships with his co-workers. Ted was known to hold racist attitudes and he continually criticized the work of

African Americans. He believed they were given preferential treatment and spoke out against them at every opportunity.

Jane's life revolved around her husband's schedule. She rose to fix him a full breakfast prior to his leaving for work at 6:30 each morning. She took care of all chores inside the house while Ted and John maintained the house exterior and yard. She worked hard to ensure that the house was spotless, meals were plentiful and on time, clothes were washed and ironed, homework was done, shoes shined, diapers changed, and all the other indoor chores finished. Most days her chores were not completed until she put the girls to bed at 8:00 p.m. John was her helper when Ted was not around. Ted thought these activities were not masculine and he did not want his son to participate. When he found out that John had helped with a domestic chore he would yell at Jane and criticize her until she cried. If John tried to intervene, he was spanked and sent to his room. Despite this, Ted considered himself a model husband and father.

John was afraid of his father's anger, but he also thought his mom worked too hard and helped her when he could. She rewarded him with special treats and spending money that she saved from her household allowance. Ted was never aware of this and yet she knew she would be punished if he found out.

John was not close to his sisters. Their games were for girls, and his father insisted that John participate in "manly" things. He was taught to hunt and fish with his father, which he enjoyed even though these trips often ended with his father getting quite drunk. Because the trips were taken with uncles and cousins, there was additional freedom from his father's tyranny. However, John was expected to perform the same tasks as the grown-ups because he was the oldest child. Ted took pride in his son's abilities and bragged to his brothers about them.

John grew up in a neighborhood culture that generally did not believe that African Americans were equal in any way. This neighborhood was the last White enclave in an area of the city that was now mostly Black. Ted's family resented the changes and worked hard to ensure the exclusion of all African Americans from the neighborhood. African Americans attended the parish church, and eventually Black priests led mass, but

Ted's family would only attend services with a White priest. Under no circumstances would they accept communion from an African American.

John attended schools with about 50% Black students but he had very little contact with them. He and his friends stayed together, as did the African Americans, and they passed one another in the halls with a mutual consent to ignore.

John did very well in school until his sophomore year in high school. When his dad was laid off, he took a part-time job after school, and his mother began a waitress job at a cafe nearby. Both of these acts were criticized by Ted, but he did not attempt to find another job other than minimal trips to the unemployment office. When the unemployment insurance and his severance pay were gone, he spent increasingly more time at his father's house, where he and two of his brothers drank and played cards most of the day.

John also tried to help his mother with the household chores and sometimes had to do these after his father had returned home and passed out. He did not complete his homework, and though he still managed to do well on tests, his grades fell. John became increasingly angry with his father and at life in general. The incident at the football game was not surprising.

The Counseling Process

When John first went to his counselor, he was somewhat anxious, not knowing what to expect. His communication was tentative at first with very little personal involvement. He was angry about his circumstances and willing to blame the African Americans for their complicity in framing him. The counselor's role was to build rapport to start the process of therapy. John did recognize the authority of the courts, and he realized that his freedom could only be gained by his compliance with the terms of the program. Over several sessions, he and the counselor discovered that they shared an interest in swimming, and gradually John opened up and began to talk about himself and his predicament. His recognition of a goal signified his readiness to begin the work of interpreting his life style to determine self-defeating behaviors. The following excerpt occurred early in the second stage of therapy.

JOHN: O.K. I know I shouldn't have had the knife at the football game. It was against the rules to carry it, but I heard some rumors and I thought I should be able to protect myself.

COUNSELOR: What kind of rumors?

JOHN: You know, the usual stuff. Guys from their school were going to take us on. That kind of stuff.

COUNSELOR: You believed that this was a real threat?

JOHN: Well, maybe not exactly. If something did happen, I just wanted to be prepared.

COUNSELOR: You don't usually take a knife with you to school events?

JOHN: No. I never had before. It was a lot of things. I was mad about everything and the knife made me feel better.

COUNSELOR: You felt more like a man with a knife in your pocket. That's what your dad would have done, isn't it?

JOHN: I'm not like my dad!

COUNSELOR: You were that night. It really bothers you to have me say you're like your dad, but you do a lot of things like him.

JOHN: Like what?

COUNSELOR: Well, your racism is just like his. You hide things from him like he hides things from your mother.

JOHN: But it's different. I'm trying to help my mom. He's trying to hurt her.

COUNSELOR: Are you so sure of that?

JOHN: I'm not sure of much of anything anymore. Everything is so confusing. I didn't mean to hurt anybody at the game. I was so mad. They wouldn't stop laughing. I just wanted to make them stop.

COUNSELOR: And force is the way to do it. That's just like your dad isn't it?

JOHN: (Sighs heavily) Yes. He makes us all do what he wants. We don't want to pay the price, so we do it.

COUNSELOR: It's easier to go along with him than it is to stand up for what you think is right. He lives his life as a tyrant and you live yours as his victim. It's a perfect arrangement.

JOHN: I don't want to be his victim. I don't want to be anybody's victim. I want a life that is mine, where the rules are mine, and nobody has to be a victim.

COUNSELOR: Well, what are you willing to do to get there? You have some hard work to look at that part of your life that is just a reaction to your father. You'll have to give up some misguided thinking.

JOHN: Well, I guess I've got nothing to lose. It can only get better from where I am now.

John continued his therapy by exploring those dimensions of his life that were the result of his accommodation of his father's tyranny. He found that he had adopted many of these same behaviors as a way of dealing with his own difficulties. He tested his understandings through use of the empty chair technique, during which he told his dad how he felt. He was surprised at the tears he felt as he told his dad how much he wanted him to stop drinking and take control of his life again. As he sat in his father's chair to respond, he retained his father's anger, revealing how little hope he had for any real change in his father. He came away from this exercise with an increased understanding of his father's self-defeating behaviors.

The following dialogue occurred near the end of the third stage of therapy when John had developed insight into his own misunderstandings.

COUNSELOR: O.K. You have learned to blame your unhappiness on others and that is a faulty understanding of the world. You have control over your feelings. Other people don't make you feel. What does that mean for the future?

JOHN: Well, I think I have to decide what is right for me and go for it even if my dad doesn't approve. I really don't think he wants me to end up like him. I can't keep blaming a whole race of people for my family's problems. I guess that's stupid.

COUNSELOR: You don't like being stupid, do you?

JOHN: I think I'm pretty smart, but I guess smart means a lot of things. I'm pretty stupid sometimes, too.

COUNSELOR: You've decided to try to be smarter in your life and relationships as well as your school work. That's a worthy goal.

JOHN: Well, I know I have to work for a better way than my dad followed. I've got to do what's right for me.

COUNSELOR: And have you decided what that is? What's right for you?

JOHN: Well, I know one thing. My hope to live a better life means I have to go to college. Nobody in our family has gone to college before. They'll all think that I think I'm better than they are.

COUNSELOR: That's pretty complicated guessing what they think you think about them. Is that how you feel, better than they are?

JOHN: Well, no, not that I'm better, but there are better ways to live than they do. That's a truth for everybody to see.

COUNSELOR: Then you don't feel obligated to live your life as it was given to you. You're ready to make some changes.

JOHN: Yes. I am ready.

Counselor: O.K. What do you have in mind?

John began to work on specific plans for change. He began a journal of his daily thoughts. Often he would bring them to sessions for the counselor's opinion of how he was thinking through things. The counselor praised what was good and helped him evaluate flawed logic. He worked hard to try out new actions.

He made an appointment with his high school counselor to discuss college opportunities and financial aid. When he received the family income statements to fill out, he chose the best time possible and presented the idea to his parents. His mother cried, and his father was silent. He made his proposal and then left the materials with them. Three days later, he found them on the table, fully completed.

His initial fear at presenting the idea of college to his dad was almost overwhelming. He spent a great deal of time rehearsing his presentation and speculating about his father's response. It was a risk for him to take this step, but having taken it, he was well on the way to a more functional life.

By the end of his required therapy, John had made great strides. His grades had improved considerably and he had improved his swimming skill and was likely to make a local swim team, which would improve his chances for a college scholarship. His father's drinking had continued, but John had seen signs that his father's anger had lessened and that he seemed to have more time at home that was pleasant. He continues his journal-keeping and has promised to stop in periodically to keep the counselor informed of his progress.

Summary

John entered therapy under duress. He had never known anyone who had been in therapy, and it was his approach to denounce all things with which he was not familiar. His dysfunctional family environment had taught him unproductive ways of handling anger and disappointment. He struggled to learn more effective ways of living with others and himself. John learned to take risks in the pursuit of his goals, and this has paid off in multiple ways. He will be the first member of his family to go to college and the changes in his behavior at home will be a positive influence for his younger sisters and support for his mother. His future looks bright.

16

Cognitive/Behavioral Therapy:
A Case Approach to Rational Emotive Therapy

Rational emotive therapy (RET) assumes that human beings are both rational and irrational and that neurotic behavior is a product of irrational and illogical thinking rather than the trauma of life events. The source of irrational thinking is learned as a combination of both biological predisposition and learning (perhaps unconsciously) primarily from parents. Emotion and thought are not separate functions, yet emotion is so highly personalized as to be irrational. Because thought is conducted through symbolic language, self-talk helps create emotions. When emotional disturbance exists, it is perpetuated by irrational self-talk. Emotional disturbance is not caused by external events, then, but results from an individual's attitudes and perceptions of these events. The process of RET must address self-defeating thoughts and emotions and help individuals develop logical and rational thinking (Patterson, 1986).

Ellis (1962) identified 11 ideas characteristic of Western societies that are irrational and almost universal. For the most part, these are viewed as irrational because as goals they may be unattainable and may not contribute to happiness if achieved. These ideas are summarized in the following statements:

1. It is essential for one to be loved or approved by nearly everyone in his or her community.
2. One can be worthwhile only if he or she is perfectly competent and achieving.
3. Some individuals are inherently bad or wicked and should be punished or banned.
4. When life does not deliver what we want, it is a terrible catastrophe.
5. An individual has no control over happiness; it is a product of external circumstances.
6. One should continually prepare mentally for catastrophic events.
7. Certain responsibilities are more easily avoided than faced.
8. Dependency on someone stronger is desirable.
9. Current behavior is determined by past events.
10. Other people's problems are a source of emotional distress.
11. Every problem has a perfect solution. (Ellis, 1962, p. 61)

These irrational beliefs are the source of much discontent in individuals who try to live their lives by them. RET acknowledges that life events are largely controlled by forces outside the force of human will, but it also declares that individuals have the capacity to act to change and control their futures.

The recognition of an individual's ability to act to change the impact of life events is described in the ABC theory of RET. If A represents an event or activity and C is the consequence of that event, then B represents the opportunity of the individual to mediate A through a rational belief about A. Thus, the consequence C is not determined by A but by B. Individuals have the power to affect their futures by changing their irrational beliefs to rational ones. This is the process of RET.

RET searches for three conditions in individuals as evidence of neurotic feelings and behaviors. These are (a) self-deprecating talk, (b) insistence that others must respond to them in a kind and considerate manner, and (c) belief that the conditions of life must be comfortable and easy.

Therapeutic Techniques

The goal of RET is to remove self-defeating behaviors and replace them with rational beliefs that will lead to constructive behaviors. The techniques used are directive and may be cognitive, emotive, and behavioral. The cognitive techniques focus on learning the difference between rational preferences and irrational "musts." Therapists are largely teachers while using the cognitive techniques, assigning reading and homework. The homework may involve making lists of disadvantages of destructive behavior and reviewing it several times a day. The client might also be taught to reframe events, which involves reinterpreting a "bad" event by discovering the good that could also come from it. Another technique might involve reading appropriate self-help books or teaching others the techniques of RET.

Emotive techniques include developing and repeating in a forceful manner statements that reflect a more rational view of a self-defeating behavior. Imagery can be used successfully to help a client face his or her worst fears. For example, the client can visualize the worst thing that can happen. In the visualization, he or she experiences the feelings of this event fully, which might include horror or humiliation. Then the client works to change these emotions into sorrow or regret. Role-play and reverse role-play can also be employed to help a client experience life without irrational beliefs to develop coping skills when others provoke old, irrational beliefs and actions.

Behavioral techniques employed by RET practitioners involve putting new beliefs into practice. A client is encouraged to seek out behaviors that are anxiety- or fear-provoking and perform them to desensitize him- or herself against these negative feelings. Behaving in the new, more rational way provides a double incentive in that the new behavior is accomplished and the client is encouraged by his or her ability to act despite fear.

Skill deficiencies can also be addressed by enrolling in courses or securing specific training for these deficiencies.

All of these techniques may be employed with the purpose of helping a client ameliorate the symptoms that have brought him or her to therapy. The client must internalize the skills of RET so that in the future when faced with emotional disturbances, he or she can apply these techniques to restore equilibrium. The three main insights of RET are that (a) emotional disturbances are caused by an individual's construction of "musts" from life conditions; (b) regardless of past conditions, current emotional disturbance is a function of present "musturbatory" beliefs; and (c) the process of changing irrational thinking and dysfunctional beliefs is a result of hard work and practice rather than magic.

The Case of Angelica

The following excerpts represent Angelica's first RET session. Her case was outlined in detail in Chapter 15.

ANGELICA: Well, I guess I should start at the beginning and tell you what happened.

COUNSELOR: Everything went downhill with one incident? It must have been a rather overwhelming event!

ANGELICA: It was awful, and illegal as well. No human being should ever be treated this way! (She begins to cry.) And these people think they are saints and that the rest of us are just crap!

COUNSELOR: Is that what you think? That you're crap?

ANGELICA: No. That's what everybody else thinks!

COUNSELOR: The whole world thinks you're crap and you're just going to buy that as the gospel truth?

ANGELICA: No. I don't think.... You're confusing me.

COUNSELOR: What will help you get unconfused?

ANGELICA: I don't know. I want to know what to do about this job. What can I do? I really can't do anything. I just have to take it and live with it (pauses). But I can't. I just can't.

COUNSELOR: You've answered your own question. You can't live with yourself as crap anymore. That's a silly notion anyway. You are a human being with talents and skills. You can make a contribution to the world.

ANGELICA: Not if I can't get a stupid job, I can't.

COUNSELOR: And you can't get a job? You lose one job and you think there are no jobs left in the world. Is that reality?

ANGELICA: No, I guess not; but what if it happens again? I've got to find a job. My parents won't support me for the rest of my life. They don't even like me, anyway.

COUNSELOR: Let's stick with one thing for a while. You didn't get a job that you wanted because the director of personnel was prejudiced against lesbians. Is that your fault? You could fight that if you want to. Do you really want that job enough to fight for it?

ANGELICA: They hired someone else. The job is gone. And I can't fight for it. I can't go out there and tell the whole world I'm a lesbian when my parents don't even know. They would really hate me then. It's so unfair!

COUNSELOR: And you think the world should be fair.

ANGELICA: Why can't it be?

COUNSELOR: You know the answer. Are you always fair?

ANGELICA: O.K. You're not going to let me get away with that. No, I'm not always fair or good or kind or. . . .

COUNSELOR: But that doesn't make you crap. You have to decide what you want and go for it. Telling yourself that life is unfair and that you're worthless won't get you where you want to go. You have credentials and skills that make you marketable. You can find a job that will be a good place for you.

ANGELICA: But what if the next place doesn't want a lesbian either? They make me sorry that I'm me.

COUNSELOR: Only you can decide if you are a worthwhile person. Why do you let people who don't even know you decide what kind of person you are?

ANGELICA: I don't, really. It's just that the world thinks lesbians aren't as good as other people, and I am a lesbian, therefore. . . .

COUNSELOR: Therefore . . . you didn't finish because you didn't want to say that you aren't as good as other people. But, you do say that to yourself, don't you?

ANGELICA: Yes, I guess I do, and at the same time I hate myself for saying it. I am the way I am and I want other people to accept me.

COUNSELOR: How does hating yourself help? You think everyone would like you if you weren't a lesbian? That's a myth. No one is liked by everyone, gay, lesbian, or straight.

ANGELICA: I guess I know that. It doesn't help to hate myself, I just feel worse. It's that I really wanted this job to show my parents that I can take care of myself. I don't want to be dependent on them forever.

COUNSELOR: You had such high hopes for this job, but it is quite likely that there are other jobs out there that are even better. You may thank this woman some day for not hiring you. You still have choices that you haven't explored. You don't have to be a victim of other people's prejudices. Why not think about other options and make an effort to find something else. Make a list of what you have to offer an employer. Tell yourself these things instead of how weak and dependent you are.

ANGELICA: O.K. But you haven't said anything yet about my being a lesbian.

COUNSELOR: Do you want my approval? What difference does it make what I think? Who am I to tell you how your life should be lived? That's for you to decide.

ANGELICA: Well, I have.

At this point, the counselor and client agree on several tasks for the client to perform before the next session. These involve preparing a list of her marketable talents and skills to help in finding a new job. She will also develop a list of potential agencies to which she may apply.

At the next session, Angelica brings in the list and she and her counselor discuss the progress she has experienced. Even this minor activity has brought Angelica into touch with how little she has appreciated her own abilities. She arrives at the next session in better emotional control and with greater confidence. Over the next few sessions, Angelica becomes increasingly confident and engages in less self-deprecating talk. She learns that she can make mistakes and still not condemn herself. In the following session, Angelica confronts her fear of telling her parents that she is a lesbian.

COUNSELOR: Well, what will happen if you tell them that you are a lesbian?

ANGELICA: They may disown me. No, I think I could handle that. What will really hurt is to see the disappointment in their eyes. They may look at me as if I'm dirty or something. Like other people have done. They are prejudiced too, you know. I'm not sure I could stand that. They always knew exactly what they wanted to do and they did it. Everybody loved them. They were the perfect pair.

COUNSELOR: That's not real. They made mistakes and everybody didn't love them. They made mistakes with you, didn't they?

ANGELICA: They did make mistakes with me, but that didn't matter. I always handled it. I wasn't that important to them. I remember when I was a senior and I had the lead in our class play. Something came up with the business and they didn't come to see me. I think that was when I realized how little I mattered.

COUNSELOR: How can you say that and mean it? You are not important. You are not *important?* What matters is what you do with what happens, not necessarily what happens. You always have the choice to decide what you will do about your experiences, even when you can't choose the experiences. You didn't have to decide that you weren't important just because your parents didn't make it to the play. If they had been surgeons rather than in business, would their absence have been interpreted differently?

ANGELICA: Of course, they wouldn't have had a choice.

COUNSELOR: So you think your parents lied to you and that they did have a choice?

ANGELICA: Well, I don't know. I get so confused. They did say they were sorry but I. . . .

COUNSELOR: You don't have to get confused. That just allows you to hide from reality for a while. You don't want to face what it means to be who you are without hiding. It's easier to lie and keep things O.K. on the surface than to face what would happen if you are honest. You want them to love you, and you fear they won't love you as a lesbian because of their prejudice.

ANGELICA: I didn't think I wanted them to love me most of my life. I thought I could take care of myself and that I didn't really need anyone. I don't feel like that anymore. Now that it matters to me, I may lose them over this.

COUNSELOR: And if you do, the fault is not with you. It is a limit in them. You will still be the same person, with the same talents, regardless of what they think.

ANGELICA: Yes, I will. I will still have a life that I enjoy. But I think it's time to risk it with them and find out how things really are.

Angelica talked with her parents and found that they had suspected that she was a lesbian for a long time. They were afraid they would offend her if they were wrong and so they kept silent. They were disappointed at one level, but they were able to accept her as the daughter they had always loved if not understood. They came to understand that they were prejudiced much like the woman who denied Angelica a job. They were surprised that it was so easy to see how wrong the interviewer had been when they hadn't been able to see their own errors.

This was a turning point for Angelica, who had gained new confidence in herself. She did find a job that was just right for her in an adoption agency. She found that she enjoyed children, a fact that she had not previously known. With her parents' help, she bought a condominium in the city, and 7 years later, she adopted a special needs child who has become the joy of her life. The fact that she is a lesbian has become less important as other aspects of her person have developed. She and her college roommate have a close and supportive relationship and a long-term commitment. Angelica continues to work for a more just world for women through volunteer programs in her city. Periodically, she returns to counseling to check out her thinking and reassure herself that she is developing in a healthy way.

For Angelica, RET provided an opportunity to live a more authentic life. Her fear of discrimination, even though it is a reality, has lessened as she has gained confidence in herself and her ability to control her response to the circumstances of life rather than be controlled by them. Her ability to discriminate rational from irrational thinking has improved immensely.

The future for Angelica will probably include discrimination because of her sexual orientation. That is a product of the culture in which she lives. However, her ability to determine rationally what is worth fighting for and what is self-destructive behavior will promote her happiness and contentment with life. She has the resources to fight when it is appropriate and feels less like a victim even when the act of prejudice is cruel. Her future looks bright.

The Case of John

The following dialogue represents John's first RET session. His background was detailed in Chapter 15.

> COUNSELOR: Well, I see you've had some difficulty with the courts. Tell me about what happened.

JOHN: It wasn't my fault. She started it. She knew what she was doing. I had to protect myself. If they hadn't ganged up on me, I wouldn't be here today.

COUNSELOR: You were just an innocent victim, totally blameless.

JOHN: You're making fun of me.

COUNSELOR: No. I'm trying to find out what you think happened. You seem to think that you are just a victim of circumstance.

JOHN: Well, I am. That "nigger" caused the whole problem.

COUNSELOR: O.K. So she pulled the knife and stabbed herself.

JOHN: Well, no. It was my knife, but it was her fault she got cut. She shouldn't have made fun of me. That's what started everything.

COUNSELOR: You were standing there minding your own business and they made fun of you.

JOHN: Well, no, but she deserved what I said about her. They're all whores. Everybody knows that. If I'd put money in front of her, she would have rolled over in a minute. That's how they are.

COUNSELOR: Cheerleaders? That's how cheerleaders are?

JOHN: You know what I mean. Niggers. That's what they are like.

COUNSELOR: How do you know that?

JOHN: Everybody knows that.

COUNSELOR: I asked you how you know that. Do you know any African Americans personally? Have you ever spent any time with an African American of any age or gender? Or, have you just assumed that they aren't at all like you?

JOHN: They're not like me!

COUNSELOR: How do you know that? Answer my questions.

JOHN: No. I have not ever spent any time with a nigger, and I don't ever expect to.

COUNSELOR: So you don't really know anything personally. Where do you get your information then? Who told you all this stuff about African Americans?

JOHN: I just heard it. My dad says the same thing.

COUNSELOR: And you believe everything your dad says?

JOHN: Nope. He's pretty messed up. He drinks most of the time now that he got laid off. He says the niggers took his job. They're lazier than dogs, but they're the right color when the plant is hiring.

COUNSELOR: So, you don't believe most of what your father says, just what he says about African Americans.

JOHN: Well, things would be a lot better at my house if some nigger hadn't taken my dad's job.

COUNSELOR: And you know that to be a fact, too?

JOHN: (There is a minute of silence.) I have to be here, but I don't have to believe everything you say either.

COUNSELOR: No, you don't. But if you want to get control of your life back, then we are going to have to work together, and I'm going to have to see some progress. That's your ticket out! You do want a life, don't you?

JOHN: Yes, I need a job, too. You can't have a life without some serious dough.

COUNSELOR: O.K. There's a reasonable place to start. You want a life. You want some money. What are you willing to do to get them?

JOHN: Well, I want a better job than my dad had. I don't want to worry about losing it to some nigger.

COUNSELOR: You like saying that word. It makes you feel better than somebody else if you can slur them. You must not think much of yourself.

JOHN: I'm O.K.

COUNSELOR: You are 17 years old, just barely out of jail and you can't go anywhere but school without supervision. Your grades are just marginal, even though you're pretty bright according to your scores. You've got no job and no money. Things are tough at home. Does all that mean O.K. to you?

JOHN: No.

COUNSELOR: Then what are you going to do about it?

JOHN: I don't know. That's why they sent me here I guess.

COUNSELOR: Well, let's decide what it is that you want and see if we can help you get there. Part of that means you're going to have to give up some of the ideas you're holding onto that are just not true. You can't live with lies and be happy. You also have to learn how things work in real life. The first thing is that everybody gets bad breaks now and then. It's not the bad breaks that make the difference in life, it's what you do about them that matters. You have to use your brains to solve your problems—a knife won't do it. You can't slash everybody who makes you mad.

JOHN: It was an accident. I didn't really mean to cut her.

COUNSELOR: O.K. I believe you mean that. That's a start.

John brought much anger and hostility into therapy. He had grown up in a household of individuals who externalized all their problems. Because African Americans were an easy target, John's father had continually blamed them for his job problems, which were actually a function of his drinking. His father's example and John's deterministic thinking could lead John to alcoholism given genetic tendencies.

Over the next few sessions, John had to confront his irrational beliefs. One of his assignments was to spend some time talking with an African American peer. Through his school, the counselor arranged some time with a 16-year-old boy who happened to be a star receiver on the football team and an honor student. John's assignment was to interview the student and find out what had contributed to his success. The next session followed the interview.

JOHN: Well, I talked with him yesterday.

COUNSELOR: And who was that?

JOHN: You know. The Black guy on the football team.

COUNSELOR: Does this guy have a name?

JOHN: Yes (sighs). It is Marvin.

COUNSELOR: Was it that hard to give him a name?

JOHN: Not really. He's an O.K. guy.

COUNSELOR: What did you learn about him?

JOHN: Well, he's pretty smart. He's about fifth or sixth in our class.

COUNSELOR: That seems to surprise you.

JOHN: (Smiles) O.K. I know where you're going with this. You want me to say that Blacks can be smart and that I was wrong to think they were all idiots.

COUNSELOR: Is that true?

JOHN: Yes. It's true.

COUNSELOR: O.K. That's a good lesson. What else did you learn?

JOHN: Well, you won't believe this. His dad works at the same plant as my dad, and he got laid off last year, too. He got another job though, so they're O.K. He said that while his dad was laid off, before he got another job, they practiced every day and that's how he got to be such a good receiver. His dad was a big football star or something when he was in high school, too.

COUNSELOR: I guess he taught him well. How did he explain his good grades?

JOHN: He's always made good grades. His mom makes him study 2 hours every night whether or not he has homework. I don't ever study. I can't imagine 2 hours every night!

COUNSELOR: Well, what do you know about African Americans that you didn't know before?

JOHN: Well, he's doing a lot better than me. He asked me if I wanted to study with him sometime. I said I couldn't just now, but. . . .

COUNSELOR: But. . . ?

JOHN: I was kinda curious about his house and how he lives. I might go sometime just to find out. I couldn't tell my dad though. He'd kill me.

COUNSELOR: He'd kill you for studying with a friend?

JOHN: No, for studying with a nigger. I mean "Black kid." He would hate that.

COUNSELOR: And how would you feel about it?

JOHN: O.K. He's an O.K. guy. He's pretty popular, you know, what with being a football star and everything. He's planning to play college ball. He'll probably get a big scholarship.

COUNSELOR: You sound a little envious.

JOHN: Well, I don't want to stay here all my life doing what my dad did. Maybe I'll go to college, too.

At this point, John had learned a new way of thinking about African Americans that has changed his own possibilities. If a Black boy could go to college and make good grades, then maybe he could at least think about college for himself. John's prejudice has been learned from his environment without examination, as have many other ways of viewing the world. He primarily believed that life is what you get and that you have little opportunity to force your own will upon it. Unless John takes responsibility for his life, he will remain in this state of "victimhood." His statement of a possible goal of college will have many implications for how he spends his time over the next 2 years. It actually will influence his life forever. His ability to learn rational ways of behaving even though he lives in an irrational environment will be quite a challenge.

John remained in therapy for the next 6 months. He was permitted to work 3 hours a day after school and all day on Saturday under the provision that he keep a B average at school and not get in any trouble. He actually managed a very high B average and saved most of his money for the future. He could not quite manage to designate that money as a college fund. The following encounter took place near the end of his court-assigned therapy.

COUNSELOR: What are your plans for the summer?

JOHN: I have a job at the pool lifeguarding in the afternoons and I will teach swimming in the mornings for some extra money. I guess I'll stay pretty busy.

COUNSELOR: What about college visits? Do you have any planned?

JOHN: I've been thinking about that. My parents can't afford to send me to college. I don't know what else to do. Dad says I should go to work and learn how to support myself as soon as I graduate.

COUNSELOR: Is that what you want to do?

JOHN: (Angrily) No! I'll end up just like him! I want something better.

COUNSELOR: What about scholarships? Your grades have improved.

JOHN: Well, they're much better than they were, but averaged across 4 years, I'd have to make better than an A average next year to impress anybody.

COUNSELOR: What about swimming? Are you pretty good?

JOHN: Yeah, I'm good, but we don't have a swim team at school.

COUNSELOR: There is a private team that swims at the YMCA. Why not check them out? If you have good times, you could get a swimming scholarship. And there are loan programs. If you believe in yourself, a college loan is a great investment.

JOHN: Yeah? I could check it out. I guess it couldn't hurt.

COUNSELOR: O.K. So what do you want to be when you grow up? What is college going to do for you?

JOHN: I really like computers. I think I'd like to work with programming.

COUNSELOR: That's a marketable field. It should provide a very secure future. What's your next step?

JOHN: I have an appointment with the school counselor next week. I think he can give me some direction.

COUNSELOR: Well, now that you have your college plans on track, what happens after your hearing in 2 weeks? I think you've made good progress. You seem to have made up your mind to take control of your life and give up being a victim of circumstances.

JOHN: Yes, I have. I want to be something in this world. I think I can make it. I have to check in with the court diversion program once a month until I'm 18 next year, but that's O.K. I think what happened to me was good in a way. I wouldn't be thinking about college and I'd still be mad at everything, I guess.

COUNSELOR: It wasn't what happened to you, it was what you made of it. That's the difference in life. You will make mistakes; everybody does. It's thinking through it and making the right choice that will improve things that makes a difference. It is hard work. You know that now, but you also have learned that you have the skills to check your thinking and throw away the stupid stuff.

JOHN: You didn't always think that I did.

COUNSELOR: (Laughs) O.K. If you're judging the counselor, it must be time to move on. Call me and fill me in. I'd like to hear from you. I look forward to hearing good things from you.

John learned much about himself in the process of therapy. He had been controlled by his emotions and his environment and he felt programmed into a life that he did not want, but he didn't know how to change. RET made him realize the error in his thinking that had limited his opportunities. Once he was able to use his problem-solving skills, he found that he had more talents and resources and options for his life than he had ever considered possible.

John had also learned to be a racist. His limited ability to think for himself had led him into simplistic thinking about African Amcricans. His work at rational thinking and his experience with African Americans gave him a perspective that was new to his family. He will have to work hard to maintain his new perspective in his home environment. One of his assignments is to teach RET to his parents. As his confidence improves, he may find this to be a turning point for the whole family.

Experiential/ Relationship Models:
A Case Approach to Human Resource Development Counseling

Human resource development (HRD) counseling as developed by Carkhuff (Carkhuff & Berenson, 1976) is primarily a teaching-as-treatment model. Carkhuff believed that most problems clients experienced were a result of their lack of skills to meet the demands of their life environment. Clients enter counseling confused and overwhelmed by their emotions. Essentially, they must learn the skills required to face the new events in their lives and be successful. In the HRD model, counselors are called "helpers" and clients are called "helpees." Ultimately, every client will become a teacher in an HRD model because as growth takes place, helpees are transformed into helpers for those who are functioning at a lower level.

HRD counseling is a combination of the insight goals of the psychodynamic models and the skills development of the behavioral models. Unique to the HRD model is the delineation of specific counselor skills that contribute to the therapeutic change. The dimensions of therapeutic change are the same as those identified by Carl Rogers—empathy, congruence, and positive regard—but the translation of these components into observable and measurable skills was a historic event for the field of counseling.

Thus, in HRD counseling, the skills of the helper are noted as the limiting factor for the growth of the helpee. If the counselor offers only low-level interpersonal skills, then the helpee can experience therapeutic change only to a low level of functioning. Though challenging in its breadth, this concept finally freed therapy from the hold of the research that showed no overall therapeutic effect. When high-functioning helpers were compared with low-functioning helpers, it was clear that helpees of the former group showed therapeutic gain, and helpees of the lower functioning group either did not change at all or regressed. This suggests that helpers should pursue their own skills development in physical, interpersonal, and intellectual areas to be effective therapists.

Therapeutic Techniques

All helpees begin therapy with the process of exploration to discover where they are and where they want to be. This exploration will involve the who, what, when, where, how, and why of the helpee's problem. This exploration is assisted by the attending, observing, listening, and responding skills of the helper. Once the helpee has identified a goal, the helper personalizes the experience by discovering its meaning for the client. The helper then initiates actions to "give feet" to the helpee's goals. This process will result in action steps for the helpee to take to ensure problem resolution. Figure 17.1 details the interaction of the learning model with the skills of the helper (Carkhuff, 1993, p. 16).

The first step for the helper in the HRD model is preparation. The environment for the counseling setting must be such that it will not distract the helpee or helper from the encounter. Noise, both real and symbolic (such as pictures or paintings), in the environment must be controlled. Next, the helper attends to the helpee using a three-component process by which the helper makes him- or herself fully available by facing squarely, leaning,

FIGURE 17.1

Phases of Helping

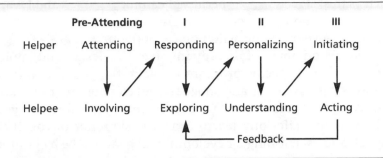

and making eye contact. Observing the helpee for mood, physical energy level, grooming, and emotional energy is important to the formation of inferences that the helper will later confirm with the helpee to involve him or her in the helping process. Listening is the next phase of the process. A helper listens to hear the emotional tenor and intensity as well as the content of importance to the helpee. Carkhuff (1993) designated these activities as pre-helping skills.

Once a helper attends, observes, and listens to the helpee, he or she will then respond to the meaning of the patient's experience using this form: "You feel _(feeling)_ because _(content)_." This statement is called an interchangeable or empathic response. The goal of the statement is to reflect the emotions of the helpee at the same intensity as stated. This response is a powerful one in the therapeutic dimension; it affirms the helpee's experience and reduces the chaos he or she is experiencing by linking emotion to cause.

The process of exploration continues until the patient understands his or her current difficulty and can establish a goal. At this stage, the helper uses personalizing statements that are in this form: You feel _(feeling)_ because you _(meaning, problem, or goal)_ . Personalizing statements cause helpees to internalize or become accountable for their feelings. The goal is personalized by the helper using this form: "You feel __(feeling)__ because you cannot __(problem/deficit)__ and you want to __(goal/asset)__. The helpee acknowledges the personalized goal with a statement such as this: "I feel _____ because I cannot _____ and I want to _____." When the goal is personalized, then the helpee is ready to move on to the action phase of therapy.

The action phase of therapy involves the design and implementation of a specific program to make the goal a reality. It involves defining goals and subgoals, developing programs, and specifying the schedules and reinforcements that will ensure goal achievement. Life-long learning is a basic tenet of the HRD model, and establishing a developmental goal will be a continuous process. During counseling, the helpee learns the skill of program development so that he or she will be able to continue the process after the counseling experience.

The process of program development involves the delineation of a series of steps, intermediary steps, and substeps (enabling tasks). The concept is that a goal must be broken down into accomplishable and measurable tasks to ensure success. These tasks or steps will be individualized for each helpee because they will differ on their abilities and resources. The task of the helper is to facilitate the development of the program and ensure that it will in fact accomplish the main goal. For this same reason, programs will differ in length and complexity for each helpee.

The program begins with the goal statement, which will specify what is to be accomplished, when it will be done, who will be involved, where will it be done, and how it will be achieved. Additionally, a quality measure or standard of performance must be articulated to ensure that the necessary level of performance has been achieved.

Schedules and reinforcements are part of every program to ensure that feedback about progress can be accurately obtained. Rewards are built into programs to reinforce task achievement. Again, these are individualized for each helpee based on his or her individual preferences. The helper's ability to organize the steps of a program is encouraging to helpees, because it promotes their ability to act in their own best interest.

The Case of Angelica

Angelica was referred to her counselor by another client. She was distraught over being turned down for a job and the direct implication by the interviewer that the reason was her sexual preference. She has found this direct rejection almost overwhelming. Angelica has lost weight, is unable to sleep, and spends her days in her apartment. When she arrived for counseling, she was dressed in a rumpled blouse and skirt. Her eyes were red with dark circles underneath. She is tall and quite thin. Her posture was slumped and she continually twisted a tissue in her hands. When the counselor introduced himself, she greeted him with a handshake and a brief smile. They chatted for a few moments about her hometown and then began.

HELPER: Why don't we begin by your telling me what's been going on in your life recently.

ANGELICA: Well, about a month ago, I had an interview for a job as a social worker. It really looked like just the thing for me. I thought the interview went O.K. I haven't been on very many. When it was over, the personnel director who was interviewing me stood up, thanked me for coming in, and said they couldn't use me. I was stunned. I couldn't believe that she could dismiss me so quickly. I managed to ask "Why?" She just looked at me, you know, with that down-her-nose look and said, "I think you know why. This is a family group. You wouldn't fit in!" How could she be so blatantly prejudiced? She just looked at me and decided I was a lesbian and that I wouldn't fit in. (She begins to cry.)

HELPER: You feel furious because she treated you so unfairly.

ANGELICA: Yes, I'm furious, and it was illegal too. I'd like to sue her for everything she has. It is so unfair. I didn't think anybody could still be so blatant.

HELPER: You feel surprised because it was so easy for her to reject you.

ANGELICA: Yes. I still can't believe it happened. She had to know that what she did was illegal. What did she think I'd do, just accept it? Well, I can't; but I can't do anything about it either. She probably knew that too. I can't tell the whole world I'm a lesbian when my own parents don't even know. That's what I'd have to do if I did sue her or even if I filed a complaint with the EEOC. There's nothing I can do.

HELPER: You feel trapped because you'd risk too much to punish her.

ANGELICA: That's just it. I am trapped. There's not a thing I can do.

HELPER: You feel helpless because you don't see any options.

ANGELICA: Yes! And I hate being helpless almost more than anything! I've always been the one who knew what to do. I could always fix things. I could take care of myself, and now look at me. I am pathetic.

HELPER: You're disappointed with yourself because you think you should be able to handle everything that comes your way.

ANGELICA: Well, yes (pauses). Well, I guess maybe not everything. That makes me sound like I think I'm Superwoman or something. I just have always been able to handle whatever came my way and now I'm so angry I can't pick myself up and get started again. She made me feel so—I don't know—dirty, I guess. Like I was contaminating her space. I've never had anybody treat me like that—at least not to my face.

HELPER: You're blocked because you can't get over this and get on to more important things.

ANGELICA: That's right. I need a job and I can't get myself together to get out there and look. My parents can't support me forever. I need to get on my own feet and be responsible for myself.

HELPER: You're afraid that you won't ever get beyond this incident.

ANGELICA: I'm scared now and I'm not sure I'll be able to handle the next thing that happens. I may be a basket case for the rest of my life!

HELPER: You're panicking because you haven't met your own expectations about how you should be able to handle things, even other people's prejudices, and you may not ever get it all back together.

ANGELICA: That's it. I've lost confidence in myself.

HELPER: You've been overwhelmed because you couldn't fight this prejudice, and you want to get back in control of your life.

ANGELICA: Yes. I'm afraid I can't, but I want to know how to get beyond all this and start over.

HELPER: Well, I think we need a program. You want to get in control of your life so that you can get your confidence back. So, we know where you are and where you want to go. Now, we need to define the steps that will get you there.

ANGELICA: Well, I need a job and I need one bad! But not with those idiots who will hate me because I'm a lesbian.

HELPER: That is a step toward getting in control of your life. But it is also a big one to go from where you are. Part of this process is to define steps that you can take from where you are. You've said you're spending all day in your apartment. What would be a small step toward getting a job?

ANGELICA: Well, I guess I need an interview before I get a job. And I don't have a clue where to set up interviews with people who will accept me. Yes, there are many things to do to get a job. But I think I know how to get started. I guess I can do that much. One of my friends from school has a job here. She may be able to give me some leads.

Angelica continued with her program development with input as necessary from the helper. It was clear that she was ready to move on and that she saw hope in just getting started. Her relationship with her roommate was strained because of her self-absorption, but it was still a source of support for her struggle to get back in control.

Angelica returned for weekly sessions. At first, she could only manage one or two steps per week. She had scheduled in rewards that included dinner at her favorite restaurant. This activity was relaxing and encouraged her to eat, which she would not do if she had to cook for herself. After several weeks, her activities accumulated to the point that she had made progress in her job search. She had scheduled three interviews in one week and was proud of her success. With the progress also came mood improvement and improved energy. She had also begun a running program, which helped improve her mood as well. The following session came after 7 weeks of counseling.

HELPER: Well, you seem pleased with life today.

ANGELICA: Yes, I am. I have three interviews for next week, and one of these jobs is really great. The other two are fine, too. No bad choices in this group.

HELPER: You're proud of your accomplishments.

ANGELICA: Yes, I can see a difference. I look forward to most days and I'm staying pretty busy. I'm helping a group I belong to put out a mailing. I get out of the apartment every day. The only down thing is I'm afraid of what will happen in the interviews. What if somebody does the same thing to me again? What if they refuse to hire me because I'm a lesbian? What will I do? I don't want to fall apart again, but I'm not sure that I wouldn't.

HELPER: You're apprehensive about the strength of your new-found skills to face another prejudice experience.

ANGELICA: That's right. I still want to sue the other agency, but it would mean exposure, and I don't think I'm ready for that. People can be so cruel. And not just other people—I'm still not sure what my parents would say if they knew I'm a lesbian. They're prejudiced too, you know.

HELPER: You're conflicted about living an open lesbian life.

ANGELICA: Yes. Maybe I shouldn't be. It is who I am and I can't help that. But my parents won't approve, I can assure you. Maybe all of this started because I've been a coward. If I were not afraid of exposure, I could have reported that woman, and then I wouldn't have felt like such a victim. I'm the one who has trapped myself. She just took advantage of it.

HELPER: You feel guilty that you aren't as honest about your life as you'd like to be.

ANGELICA: Well, it is a reality I have to face. I could talk to Mom and Dad. But if they reject me, I'm in the same boat. I don't want to risk that relationship just now either.

HELPER: You're tangled up in your hopes and fears and you want to get it all honest.

ANGELICA: That would be a load off my mind, but the time isn't right. I want to go home with a job. When I have one, then I can talk to them. I have to do this first.

For Angelica, making decisions was a reinforcing experience. She continued with her job search and found a position in an adoption agency. She liked the problem solving involved in the job, and within 2 weeks, she decided it was time to talk with her parents. She found that they had suspected all along that she was a lesbian. They were disappointed, but they reassured her that they loved her and were not disappointed in her and her accomplishments. With this relationship more secure, Angelica felt confident in her ability to use her new skills to meet the demands of life. The following session was the final one with her helper.

HELPER: Well, things seem to be going very well for you. You look happy.

ANGELICA: I am happy. I love my job. My parents came to visit us last week. We had fun talking and laughing. We went to a concert. It was what I wished we had done when I was at home.

HELPER: You're delighted with your new relationship with your parents.

ANGELICA: It is so much better than I ever hoped. They are really reaching beyond what I thought they were capable of doing. They are helping Shelley and me buy a condo. We'll close in 3 weeks. We are really excited about having our own place. There is so much to do.

HELPER: You're satisfied with the way you've solved the problem you presented to me a few months ago.

ANGELICA: I am thrilled, actually. I've learned a lot about myself. I am much closer to what I want to be than ever before. Things aren't perfect. I don't want to give the wrong impression. The difference is that I feel like I have resources that I didn't have before. I never thought about myself as a victim before this experience, and I realized that other people can victimize you with their prejudices if you don't stand up for yourself. Now, I can think through the experiences that make me feel bad and respond to myself to make sure I know why I feel that way. It orders everything for me, and then I know what to do about the problem. I look forward to new experiences and I am hopeful for the future. I have a good life.

HELPER: You seem to know where you are going. I think you are ready to go solo. I don't think you need to be here anymore.

ANGELICA: It's a little scary to think of leaving, but I think you're right. I am confident now, but I haven't been on my own. I need to try my wings, and if I can't fly as well as I thought, then I'll come back for more training.

HELPER: That's a great plan. Let me hear how things are going. I think you will do fine.

Summary

Angelica was trapped by her decision to keep the fact that she was a lesbian from her parents. This made her feel like a victim with few skills to overcome the prejudice that was targeted toward her. Through HRD counseling, she learned to create order out of the chaos of her feelings and then translate that learning into a program of change.

Her ability to design programs to achieve goals will be essential to her long-term growth and lifelong learning. She can expect many good things in her future. She will face problems, as everyone does. She will probably be the target of prejudice in the future. Her skills repertoire and her ability to acquire the skills she needs to meet these future problems will enable the successful resolution of those problems.

The Case of John

John was assigned to a helper as a part of a juvenile court diversion program for his racially motivated attack on another student. The terms of his program involved two sessions per week with the helper, a peer session with other offenders, a session with his supervisory officer, and 4 hours of community service per week. He was allowed to accompany his parents to any function they approved, as well as to attend school and church. Beyond that, he could not leave the house unless accompanied by his supervisory officer. He arrived for his first session on time and somewhat anxious. He paced the waiting area and perused the titles of the books in the library. He appeared to be nervous, but he was also curious about the process of therapy. After introductions and talk about sports, the session began.

HELPER: Why don't you begin by telling me what happened and how you ended up here?

JOHN: Well, there's not a lot to tell. They ganged up on me and I got in trouble for it. It wasn't my fault at all. You know how "niggers" are.

HELPER: You're pretty angry because they took advantage of you.

JOHN: You got that right! She's a whore and with two of them, there wasn't much I could do. They shouldn't have laughed at me. I know all about them.

HELPER: You're frustrated because you didn't get a fair hearing.

JOHN: Well, I told my side and they told theirs. It was the cut that brought me down. It wasn't my fault though, really. She bumped into the knife. I didn't mean to cut her. She shouldn't have made such a big deal of it all. I'm sure it wasn't the first time she had heard what I said. If I'd waved money at her, she would've sung a different tune.

HELPER: You're mad because no one seemed to see your side of things.

JOHN: It was unfair! Nobody really listened to me. If you're a nigger you get all kinds of special treatment. They were on her side because of that. I didn't stand a chance and now my life is all messed up. I'm done!

HELPER: You're disappointed because you have to suffer a punishment that really isn't fair.

JOHN: No, it's not fair. I can't do anything. They're treating me just like a baby. I almost have to ask to go to the bathroom. My parents are upset, too, but we couldn't afford a lawyer to get me off. They're upset with me for having to go to court at all. But they agree with me that it was the niggers' fault.

HELPER: You're pleased because your parents agree with you.

JOHN: Yeah, but it's the first time. My dad almost never agrees with me about anything. He wouldn't have this time if she hadn't been a nigger. He hates 'em. They cost him his job last year when he got laid off, and he's got no room for them at all.

HELPER: It's pretty tough on you at home because your dad's out of work.

JOHN: Yeah, it's been awful. My mom got a job at the cafe on Sixth Street but she doesn't make much money. Dad stays drunk most of the time. When I come home, he yells at me about everything I do. He yells at Mom too, but she ignores him. Sometimes he gets so mad, he stomps out and slams the door and shakes the whole house. He won't come back for hours. Actually, it's better then. I can have some peace.

HELPER: You're relieved when your dad is out of the house.

JOHN: Well, I don't want him to leave for good, but he's all messed up. He's mad at everybody. I think he hates everything. I'm not going to stay around here and be like him. As soon as I can, I'm outta here.

HELPER: You're miserable and don't see much hope if you stay here.

JOHN: You got that right. But I don't know what I'm gonna do. My dad went to work at the plant when he graduated from high school. He's worked there 18 years and then they just laid him off. Except for the niggers. They didn't get laid off.

HELPER: You're upset because you think African Americans get special treatment.

JOHN: Well, it's not fair and everything's ruined. Nothing's the way it used to be. Dad used to be a pretty good guy. He drank a little on weekends, but he wasn't mad all the time, and we had money to do stuff with. Now we got nothing. You'd be mad at the niggers too.

HELPER: You're fed up with the system.

JOHN: I sure am (pauses). But I've got my own problems now. I'm not going to spend my life figuring out what my dad should do. I've got to make it through this program or they'll put me away.

HELPER: You're a little apprehensive that you may not be able to make it through the program.

JOHN: It's pretty tough. I've got nothing, and nobody cares. The only good thing is that I get to swim at the indoor YMCA pool on Saturdays after I teach the little niggers to swim.

HELPER: You're pleased that at least something good has come out of this mess.

JOHN: Yeah. I like to swim. I feel free in the water. I'm pretty good and I'm getting faster with all this practice. I swim about 3 hours because my mom can't pick me up until 5:30. It's great.

HELPER: You're energized by your swimming.

JOHN: Yeah, I wish the rest of my life were that easy. School's a bummer. I've got stupid classes that are dull and boring. I know more than the teachers, and they treat me like I'm dirt since I got into trouble.

HELPER: You're trapped in dull and uninteresting classes that don't challenge you.

JOHN: Yep. And if I don't keep good grades, they can bust me right into jail. Well, I can make the grades. It's not too hard with this junk I'm taking.

HELPER: You've got a lot of tough stuff to work with, and it's getting you down. You'd like to have things back the way they were when your dad had a job and life was easier.

JOHN: Well, I don't know really. Things at home haven't been really good for a pretty long time. Dad's been drinking too much, and he's not much fun anymore. I just don't know what to do but get out. If I get a job after high school like he did, I'll end up just like him. I don't want that. I'd like to be something!

HELPER: You're discouraged by your prospects for the future and you'd like to be able to turn that around so you'd have something to look forward to.

JOHN: I want a future like other kids. Maybe even college someday. I don't want to just hang on until somebody lays me off and I have nothing.

HELPER: You're hopeful that you can pull things together and make a plan for your future.

JOHN: Sure. I want a life and I need to find a way to get it.

HELPER: O.K. Let's start there next time. You've got a lot going for you. You're bright and you're in good shape physically. Are you eating good food?

JOHN: I have to (laughs). My mom is a great cook, and she makes me eat good stuff. We don't have junk food around our house.

HELPER: You're thankful that your mom does care about you.

JOHN: Yeah. She does.

HELPER: Before our next session, why not think of some careers you'd like and how the classes that you're taking are helping. You may need to change your schedule for next semester. I'll look forward to seeing you then.

For the next several sessions, John focused on his plan for the future. This seemed a welcome relief for him. It took the emphasis off the difficulties of the present. He continued to externalize responsibility for the event that put him in the court program. Two months after his initial visit the following encounter took place.

JOHN: I talked to the counselor and she said there are scholarships that don't require top grades. But with my record, I may not be able to convince some committee that I'm really a good guy.

HELPER: You feel apprehensive about the prospects of a scholarship.

JOHN: Well, if I were a nigger, I wouldn't have to worry about anything. They'd give me a free ride!

HELPER: You're bitter because there are programs to help African Americans, and you don't think they deserve them.

JOHN: Why should they get to go to college? They're too stupid to pass unless they just give it to them.

HELPER: You're outraged that African Americans might get an opportunity they don't deserve.

JOHN: Well, I think it stinks!

HELPER: You're disgusted because you think African Americans are inferior to you and yet they get opportunities you wish you had.

JOHN: (Sighs) You want me to say that they aren't inferior and that I'm a racist pig or something.

HELPER: You're afraid I won't like you if you don't change your attitude.

JOHN: You don't agree with me. You never say anything each time I bring it up. I know what you think. You think I really did cut that girl because she was a nigger, but I didn't. It was an accident. I was so mad when they laughed at me. I just wanted them to stop. That's why I pulled the knife. I just wanted them to stop laughing. He bumped into her and pushed her into the knife. I really didn't cut her on purpose (pauses). I just found out yesterday that the reason I'm in this program instead of juvenile detention is that they told the judge the same thing. My officer told me when I made some remark about niggers. He said I was lucky. If it had been the other way around, a Black kid would have been in detention for sure.

HELPER: You're embarrassed that you said such bad things about people who actually helped you.

JOHN: I guess so. I'm surprised too. I don't really know any Black kids at school. They keep to themselves. There is this one kid who is a receiver on the football team and he's like fifth in the class. I was assigned to work on a project with him in math and he's sharp. He had the whole thing figured out before I did. He asked me to study with him, but I couldn't, you know. I didn't tell him why. I was ashamed.

HELPER: You're bummed because you've found out you might be wrong about African Americans.

JOHN: Yeah. My dad would kill me for saying it, but this kid's O.K. He's going to play college ball. Everybody wants him. He'll get a scholarship too. You know something else? His dad got laid off from the plant when mine did. But he got another job.

HELPER: You're torn between your dad's view of the world and the one you're discovering on your own.

JOHN: My dad hasn't been right about much lately. Maybe he's not right about Marvin either. I won't tell him about it though. I don't want to hear him yell. Marvin is coming to the pool on Saturday. He said he'd time me in the 100.

HELPER: You're excited about making a new friend whom you respect.

JOHN: We'll see (smiles). I don't want to make you too happy!

Summary

John completed his 8 months in the juvenile court diversion program. During the summer, he worked as a lifeguard at the YMCA pool, taught swimming lessons, and developed his swimming skill. He qualified for advanced studies during his senior year and will earn some college credits.

While John was in counseling, he learned to develop programs to achieve his goals. He has a savings account for college and may be able to get a swimming scholarship. He has also continued his community service on Saturdays and has taught interpersonal skills to the African American kids in the program. He is committed to his own development and to the development of those around him.

CHAPTER 18

Summary and Recommendations

To prevent prejudice, we need a clear understanding of the society we would like to create. Figure 18.1 identifies the goals of prejudice prevention. Egalitarianism must be achieved if we are to overcome the divisions created by prejudice. Quality reflects the life style we must assume is required for all. Unity and ultrasensitivity are reciprocal among different racial and ethnic groups. Without involvement, we will remain unchanged. Tolerance and trust are built with truth that is sought earnestly and without bias. Finally, change means yielding to the discovered truth.

Theoretical Underpinnings for Resolving Prejudice

The many factors that influence prejudice resolution relate to the specific paradigm of causation we espouse. For example, if we believe the new prejudice paradigm is fear driven and that our

FIGURE 18.1					

The Goal of Prejudice Prevention is Equity

E	Q	U	I	T	Y
Egalitarianism	Quality	Unity	Involvement	Tolerance	Yield*
Empowerment		Ultra-sensitivity		Trust	
Equal opportunity				Truth/facts	
Equitable conditions					

* To strive, to seek, and to yield.

fear is focused on loss of power, we are likely to conclude that prejudice would be resolved if there were infinite resources and thus no competition for them.

Shepherd and Penna (1991) held that structural conditions are as likely to influence relationships between majority and minority groups as are cultural differences. These conditions hold the key to power resources (economic, social, and political). They believed that when economic conditions are booming, greater flexibility and opportunity exist for minority group members. An economic downturn, however, tends to restrict access to resources. This phenomenon is more likely to affect immigrants and minorities who are struggling to become upwardly mobile.

Thus, America's moral basis is sorely tested when it tries to encompass both progress and compassion. Fortunately, this seeming impasse is being eliminated by the formulation of new concepts of human society. Carkhuff (1983) proposed that society will be well served if it envisions itself as a human development system. This model is based on the assumption that the prime purpose of our existence is to actualize as many human abilities as possible. It does not assume that our natural resources are unlimited, but that human ingenuity is unlimited—that people can devise solutions to most of their problems if they are freed and appropriately motivated to do so. Thus, the challenge is to reorient ourselves from focusing on our limited supply of resources toward solving the problems of our time.

Carkhuff's notion of society is not utopian; it is based on systematic steps rather than magical leaps across all the barriers of human existence. He proposed that scientific technology is the means to achieve an increasing satisfaction of healthy human needs, an effort that is retarded by human skill deficits. The answer to problems such as prejudice lies in skill development programs, including improvement of human relations. His premise is that if the barriers to human fulfillment are interpreted as problems to be solved, then the logical response is to acquire the skills to solve them.

If skill acquisition is the foundation of a society, then that society must make training available to all citizens. This means effective education for everyone. In Carkhuff's terms, education is always the answer to a human problem (Carkhuff, 1983).

General Strategies for Prejudice Prevention

If education and training are the general strategies for prejudice prevention, we must define the content of the interventions. Kavanagh and Kennedy (1992) stated that among other content, interventions directed toward prejudice should acknowledge the cognitive and psychosocial development of the age level targeted for intervention. Additionally, they suggested that awareness and sensitivity are critical to the process of managing diversity and that authentic interaction should be encouraged. Authentic interaction, in their view, would build upon and be enhanced rather than hindered by differences.

Whether we are color conscious or color blind, we must learn to recognize and appreciate differences in one another. Ponterotto (1991) further suggested that "an attitude of cultural pluralism and appreciation must infiltrate the very fabric of society if we are to significantly decrease race-based tension in the United States" (p. 223).

For Martin Luther King, Jr. (Washington, 1986), the notion of acceptance of one another was truly both the process and outcome for defeating racism. He knew that once we begin to judge one another on the basis of character rather than skin color, we will be well on the way to fulfilling his dream of true freedom described in the following passage:

> I have a dream that one day on the red hills of Georgia sons of former slaves and sons of former owners will be able to sit down together at the table of brotherhood.... When we allow freedom to ring—when we let it ring from every city and every hamlet, from every state and every city, we will be able to speed up that day when all of God's children, Black and White men, Jews and Gentiles, Protestants and Catholics, will be able to join hands and sing in the words of the Negro spiritual, "Free at last, free at last, great God a'mighty, we are free at last."

Marcus Garvey (Jacques-Garvey, 1978) arrived in New York City in the early part of the 20th century, an immigrant from Jamaica with a strongly held belief that Black people could improve their lot in life with hard work and determination. He held that Whites ill treated the Black race because they had accomplished nothing such as building a great nation, and because they were dependent on Whites for economic and political existence. He preached a message of self-help, of unity and brotherhood among Black people. However, he also noted that while prejudice could be actuated by many different causes, sometimes economic or sometimes political, it could only be checked by progress and force.

Malcolm X was one of the most potent conveyors of the message of self-help and ethnic pride to the African American community. Elizabeth Wright (1989) explicated his gospel of "Black Nationalism." She believed that its goal was to help the Black man reevaluate himself rather than change the White man. She felt that Black people could solve their problems when they changed their own minds rather than trying to change the culture.

These efforts and others are intended to redirect and/or diminish the effect of prejudice. Specifically, reduction is geared to minimize the formation of both personal inadequacies and prejudicial social traditions. Reduction is a new and appropriate emphasis for counselors, because historically our field's involvement in prejudice has been related to the curative phase rather than reduction. The success of disease eradication using vaccinations indicates that prevention is a preferred course of action.

Mackie and Hamilton (1993) were both optimistic and cautiously pessimistic about prejudice reduction. The results of their interventions clearly support the conclusion that prejudice reduction efforts can be effective. They believed that the process must involve learning over time, which is not easily accomplished but can be done. Ultimately, individuals must learn to act upon their nonprejudiced ideals.

In this regard, prejudice is no different from other human endeavors. We almost always know what is the correct course of action, even if we cannot do it. For example, most individuals whose diet is unhealthy can describe a healthy diet even if they don't select it for themselves. Over time and with assistance, individuals can learn to behave in ways that are consistent with their beliefs.

Reducing Prejudice in Individuals

It has been suggested (Allport, 1954) that prejudice may be "caught" rather than "taught" in childhood. When racial bias or prejudice toward minorities is accepted as the norm in a given social group, children of that majority group do not learn to censure and reject these behaviors because they have become part of their perceptual world. Katz (1987) also supported the notion that parents are the most potent reinforcers regarding prejudice. He noted, however, that our society has done very little to help parents find child-rearing techniques that will enable children to develop positive attitudes toward themselves and others.

The need for positive attitudes toward self and others has been addressed by multiple authors. Byrnes (1988) specifically addressed self-esteem as an antidote for prejudice. Pettigrew (1981) also identified a clear relationship between an individual's self-esteem and degree of prejudice. They demonstrated that children with high self-esteem are less likely to hold prejudiced views of other groups than are those children with low self-esteem. Environments in which individual needs for security and acceptance are met, independence and responsibility are fostered, and warmth and praise are provided are much more likely to build self-esteem.

Self-esteem has been described as the core of psychological health and the requisite platform upon which to build all interpersonal relationships. Without it, individuals tend to develop a pathological sense of judgment. What children see and believe to be true affects their self-talk, which in turn ultimately affects their self-esteem.

Another area for focus in helping children grow and develop without prejudice is the cognitive dimension. It is clear that how we think affects our susceptibility to prejudice. Pate (1988) suggested that cognitive training could help children avoid oversimplification and overgeneralization, which contributes strongly to the process of stereotyping. He also noted that dogmatic individuals thinking in dichotomous terms are much more likely to behave in discriminatory ways. He suggested that helping children attend to meaningful social behaviors instead of biases would help them become less prejudiced.

However, several authors have noted that children in integrated peer groups consistently showed greater preference for children of the same race in social interactions (Sagar, Schofield, & Snyder, 1983; Schofield & Whitney, 1983). It is difficult to determine from studies such as these the antecedents of the behavior and whether or not factors other than race contributed to the findings.

Perhaps the first step in helping children overcome prejudice is to encourage them to recognize differences in ethnic, racial, and cultural groups. They also must come to understand that differences do not necessarily cause problems, but that judging these differences as "good" or "bad" is a step toward problems. Race and ethnicity are as much a characteristic of an individual as the color of his or her eyes and should be appreciated as such. Byrnes (1988) cautioned that color blindness implies that one's color must be ignored to be acceptable and could contribute to stereotypes and prejudgments that we are trying to avoid.

One possible exercise for helping students to recognize and appreciate differences involves taking the role of a member of a stigmatized group (Peters, 1971). Peters suggested that this experience of taking on both the cognitive view as well as the affective response is a potent tool in changing attitudes and behaviors. It also may help individuals become sensitized to their own areas of prejudice, which will ultimately help them develop multicultural sensitivity and competence (Pederson, 1988). This sensitivity is essential because many of us practice unintentional racism. Covert, unintentional racism is much more difficult to change because there is no awareness of dissonance between intention and action (Pederson, 1994; Ridley, 1994).

A Group Approach to Prejudice Reduction

Cooperative learning groups are another effective means by which students become more accepting of others (Lynch & Hanson, 1992; Pate, 1988). McCormick (1990) identified cooperative learning as a prime sex-equity strategy. Tatum (1992) described developing and teaching a course to provide students with an understanding of the psychological causes and emotional reality of racism in everyday life. She said:

> The students in my class, most of whom were White, re-
> peatedly described the course in their evaluations as one of
> the most valuable educational experiences of their careers. I
> was convinced that helping students understand the ways in
> which racism operates in their own lives and what they could
> do about it, was a social responsibility that I should accept.
> (Tatum, 1992, p. 2)

Schools and other social organizations can be influential by removing the tolerance for racism and discriminatory behavior (DeVillar, 1994). Pine and Hilliard (1990) suggested that if school policies reflect unequivocal intolerance for racism, then the context has been established for active intervention programs.

Counselors are ideal facilitators for such programs because of their training. Ponterotto (1991) has suggested that mixed racial groups may be the preferred setting for sharing firsthand experiences of the effects of prejudice. Counselors have been trained in group facilitation, and their *Code of Conduct* (1992) has long held that "counselors are aware of cultural, individual, and role differences, including those due to age, gender, race, ethnicity, national origin, religion, sexual orientation, disability, language, and socioeconomic status" (pp. 3–4).

Because many college campuses have seen a rise in racial conflict, the need exists for programs for prejudice reversal (Stenz, Iasenza, & Troutt, 1990). However, because most programs are designed for counselors (Ivey, 1977; Johnson, 1987; Merta, Stringham, & Ponterotto, 1988), a need exists for training programs to sensitize student leaders on issues related to prejudice.

Stenz et al. (1990) developed a program for student leaders to help them (a) explore their prejudices, (b) identify and challenge group stereotypes, (c) discuss group differences and similarities and the effects of prejudice, and (d) to identify examples of local prejudice and plan remediation for them. The program targeted racism, sexism, homophobia, and anti-Semitism. Specific suggestions from the training session were implemented. Both faculty and students found the training program to be a highly positive experience.

Ponterotto (1991) also suggested that the use of mixed racial groups may be an effective tool for demonstrating and teaching empathic listening and understanding. It may also be an opportunity for catharsis. Allport (1979) noted that catharsis could be effective in that one's outburst could shock another's conscience. He cautioned that the decision of whether to run same-race or interracial groups is an individual choice based on the specific needs of the situation. It is clear that for those individuals with deeply embedded prejudice or those who act out their prejudices overtly, individual counseling may be required.

While abundant evidence of the helpfulness of cultural diversity education and multicultural education has emerged, dissenters remain. Thibodaux (1992) declared that prejudice has now been extended to White men, fundamentalist Christians, conservatives, and Republicans; the current politically correct atmosphere on college campus supports not only criticism of their views but intolerance of them as well. He said:

> Proponents of multiculturalism, genderism, and Afrocentrism
> are political liberals who tend to be intellectual conservatives.
> Most of them have leftist agendas and some of them are
> among the most closed-minded, intolerant individuals I ever
> encountered. (Thibodaux, 1992, p. 27)

General Counseling Activities
for Reducing Prejudice

Specific counseling activities for reducing prejudice will vary according to counselors' theoretical orientation and were addressed in Section II of this book. However, according to Landis and Boucher (1987), it is possible to delineate a group of general counseling activities that contribute to that goal. These include (a) information- or fact-oriented training, (b) attribution training, (c) cultural awareness, (d) cognitive-behavior modification, (e) experiential learning, and (f) interaction.

Information- or fact-oriented training involves strategies to increase the understanding of different races or cultural groups by providing direct information. This information will address attitudes, traditions, and practices that help differing groups discover their commonalities and reduce suspicion. Techniques can be developed for both groups and individuals.

Groups

Many interethnic misunderstandings, stereotypes, and racial attitudes develop from lack of factual information. Group guidance activities that focus on the differences in cultural systems, worldviews, cultural values, and unique cultural experiences are important to dispel misinformation and provide missing information about other ethnic groups. Proactive counselors should develop cultural awareness programs (CAPs) to enhance cultural diversity appreciation and to curb or eliminate prejudicial thinking and behaviors.

Individuals

At the personal level, counselors can help individuals increase their awareness of those psychological defense mechanisms that maintain or heighten prejudice and racism. According to Devine, Monteith, Zuwerink, and Elliot (1991), overcoming life-long experiences of prejudice is not easy. To a large extent, this process involves resolution of several unconscious internal conflicts. From a psychoanalyst's viewpoint, prejudiced people generally lack a secure and affectionate relationship with their parents. As they are raised in authoritarian environments, they project their strong negative feelings onto other people rather than directing them toward their own parents for fear of reprisal. Psychoanalysts suggest that projection and displacement are two major components of the scapegoat theory of prejudice. Counselors should help prejudiced persons become aware of these two defense mechanisms and tailor strategies to change their discriminatory behaviors.

There are many theoretical bases for the development of prejudice reduction programs. Most of these programs target a specific experience or behavior as a function of the cause-and-effect model that is understood as a part of the theory. Table 18.1 summarizes the major approaches in this area.

Target Populations for Prejudice Reduction Services

Victims

People who have been harmed by prejudice come to counseling for assistance in healing their injuries. However, a second aspect of the victim problem pertains to reduction. How can people avoid becoming victims? There are situation-specific factors such as contacting attorneys and other officials who can help alter prejudicious practices. General factors also merit consideration. Victims can become their own advocates by making presentations to groups and writing articles in journals and newspapers to help generate a climate in which prejudice is exposed and thereby not tolerated. In general, these actions are designed to defuse potential sources of prejudice. Counselors are well served by knowledge and skills that prepare them to help their clients avoid becoming victims of prejudicial practices.

Perpetrators

Fortunately, some people who are predisposed toward prejudicial behavior seek counseling before they become perpetrators of

TABLE 18.1	

Strategies for Prejudice Reduction

Program Type	Program Description
Attribution	Teaches individuals to explain behavior from the training point of view of members of other cultures. Understanding other people's viewpoints can lead to racial harmony and curb discriminatory behaviors.
Cultural awareness	Emphasizes the distinctiveness of different cultures and cross-cultural relations. The notion is to promote cross-cultural relations.
Cognitive/ behavior modification	Applies principles of learning to the special adjustment problems of various ethnic groups. Prejudiced people can be taught to unlearn prejudicial behaviors and replace them with more acceptable responses.
Experiential learning	Uses real-life simulations of other cultures. People learn that long-term biases are meaningless, and inaccurate information about others is corrected.
Interaction approach	Involves immersion in others' cultures and teaches people how to interact with host nationals and to use their experiences in real situations during their sojourn. This involves interracial, inter-gender, and interethnic experiences in group contexts. The facilitators train others to reconcile racial and ethnic conflicts.

prejudice. Treatment for potential perpetrators tends to focus on two areas: (a) personality difficulties and (b) acquired social attitudes and beliefs. In general, counseling efforts are designed to eliminate or reorient both the personality difficulties and the acquired attitudes and beliefs. The critical element is to encourage potential perpetrators to enter counseling before they perform prejudicial acts.

The goal of prejudice reduction is to defuse predispositions toward such behavior when people find themselves in situations in which it seems appropriate. A variety of counseling procedures are appropriate for that effort. The availability of a large skills repertoire is fortunate because clients present an extensive array of needs. The challenge is to find an effective treatment that will redirect the prejudicial inclinations of each client.

Combating prejudice is a process that involves increasing sensitization to the attitudes and behaviors that contribute to its formation and continuance. In Table 18.2, we have synthesized a description of these stages and the relevant behaviors exhibited by both the powerful (culturally or individually) and powerless (minority cultures or individuals).

Effecting Change

Identifying the pathway to change has been the goal of many for a long period of time. The difficulty often for those with the same goal is agreeing on the means. Jacques-Garvey (1978) made the following observation, "You can never curb the prejudice of the one race or nation against the other by law. It must be regulated by one's own feeling, one's own will, and if one's feeling and will rebel against you, no law in the world can curb it" (p. 18). Hope should not be lost if we believe that one's feelings can be changed. Devine (1989) and Monteith (1993) cited recent research suggesting that prejudice reduction was a gradual process rather than an all-or-none experience.

Ponterotto and Pedersen (1993) proposed three tasks for educators and counselors who wish to promote healthy racial/ethnic identity development in their students and clients. They suggested that counselors and educators first understand racial/ethnic identity development theory. Second, they should assess their own levels of racial/ethnic identity development. Third, they must be trained in facilitating racial/ethnic identity development in others (Ponterotto & Pedersen, 1993, p. 89).

Change may also be accomplished through proactive means. The proactive approach recognizes three ways that change can be addressed. The first is developmental and recognizes that healthy organisms in healthy environments will develop appropriate responses over time. The second path of change is preventive. If one can identify precursors of prejudice, much as we do in dis-

TABLE 18.2

Sensitivity to Racism

Stage	Powerful	Powerless
Unawareness (insensitive stage)	Not sensitive to the pain caused by discrimination. Knows only through media coverage of racial incidents.	Self-complacent. Internalizes the worldviews of the majority culture and denies prejudice.
Semisensitive stage	Begins taking interest in issues related to discrimination	Starts developing affiliation with own people
Sensitive stage	Active participation to understand the political and economic system and other contributing factors. Reflects upon one's own contribution to the racial dilemma.	Closer intimacy with one's own group and alienation from the other group
Ultrasensitive stage	One might become ultra-generous and contribute to the welfare of minority clients	Offended by names Cleveland Indians, or Washington Redskins, for example

ease identification, then perhaps interventions can be found to block the precursors. Prevention of childhood diseases by vaccination is a relevant example. The third approach is treatment. Again, the disease model applies. Once prejudice is diagnosed an effective intervention should change the course of the phenomenon. Developing effective treatment for prejudice is essential for our time, since we are too late to prevent prejudice in many members of our society.

Table 18.3 describes a model of change. In this model, change is seen as a reaction or response to the status quo that is ultimately transformed at some time in the future. However, once the change has been transformed, it becomes the status quo, and the cycle will be repeated. If prejudice is viewed through this model, male dominance was the past, the women's movement was the

TABLE 18.3

A Model of Change

Past	Present	Future
Thesis	Antithesis	Synthesis
Action	Reaction	Transformation
Suppression/ repression	Expression, exploration, revolution	Resolution

antithesis, and the family values movement may well be the synthesis. The imposition of purpose and will into the process may be necessary to ensure that responses at each successive stage are more than reactionary and will ultimately improve the status quo.

Roadblocks to Change

To move from racial violence to true integration is a difficult task, yet our national commitment demands that we do so. Our pledge of allegiance says "One nation under God, indivisible, with liberty and justice for all."

Change is difficult because it destroys old pathways and familiarities, and we may feel lost in new ways of being. Devine (1989) provided a framework for understanding how those who truly renounce prejudice may continue to experience prejudice-like thoughts and feelings. He also posited that prejudice-like responses are automatically activated in the presence of members of the stereotyped group. In contrast, nonprejudiced responses require the inhibition of the automatically activated negative responses and the conscious, intentional activation of nonprejudiced beliefs. Thus, to Devine, nonprejudiced beliefs and prejudiced thoughts and feelings may coexist within the same individual.

An important assumption of Devine's model is that adoption of nonprejudiced beliefs or personal standards does not immediately eliminate prejudice-like responses. That is, stereotype-based knowledge structures may continue to be activated, resulting in prejudice-like thoughts and feelings that are fundamentally in conflict with the endorsed nonprejudiced beliefs.

According to Gaertner and Dovidio (1986), ambivalence arises because people sincerely embrace egalitarian values but also possess negative feelings and beliefs about racial or ethnic minorities. To cope with this ambivalence, the negative reactions are excluded from conscious awareness. Consequently, some racists are not aware of their conflicted reactions and express their prejudices only in subtle or covert ways.

Ambivalence is also caused by the simultaneous endorsement of positive and negative feelings toward the target group. Adoption of new values is hard. Although many may be committed to egalitarian values, not all may have made the connection that commitment to these values has implications for their reactions to members of stereotyped groups. Only when prejudice is recognized as contradicting fundamental egalitarian values is the stage set for the initiation of prejudice reduction efforts. Further research will have to identify the conditions necessary for discrepancy activation.

It may be too pessimistic to believe that little progress is being made toward the alleviation of prejudice, which is a prevailing force in our country today. However, many people seem to be in the process of prejudice reduction. A necessary first step is the adoption of nonprejudiced standards. Fully overcoming the "prejudiced habit" presents a more formidable task and is likely to entail a great deal of internal conflict over a protracted period of time (Devine, 1989).

The Proactive Model of Prejudice Prevention and Reduction found in Table 18.4 was developed to organize and explain the change process. The focus of change as depicted may involve attributes, attitudes, or actions, and the forces of change may be parenting, education, or the justice system. Change may be developmental, it may require a preventive process, or it may be an attempt to remediate the problem. Patterns of change are sometimes circular or they may require either a bottom-up or grass-roots effort or a top-down approach such as a policy or edict.

TABLE 18.4

The Proactive Model of Prejudice Prevention and Reduction

Focus of Change	Forces of Change	Types of Change	Patterns of Change
Attributes	Parenting/ religion	Developmental	Circular
Attitudes	Education/ counseling	Preventive	Bottom-up
Actions	Laws/justice system	Remedial	Top-down

To plan for change, select one target from each column. For example, you may focus a change intervention on attitudes, use parents as the force of change for a remediation, and expect that the pattern of change would be circular or require continual reinforcement.

Chapter Summary

In this chapter, we described the current theoretical approaches to prejudice prevention and reduction. The clear picture that emerges is that change in these attitudes is extremely difficult and will not occur all at once, but over time, as we develop our skills and attitudes of nonprejudice, they will occur. Just as with any skill, practice improves performance, and we must practice the discipline of nonprejudice.

We may not have fully appreciated or applied the resources that we already have available to prevent prejudice. Effective parenting skills can provide an environment of caring and discipline that helps children develop self-appreciation and self-esteem. This would mitigate the need to define enemies among those who are different. We can teach the need for cooperation as well as the skills required to make it a reality. We can teach sensitivity and awareness of others' feelings and concerns through empathy training. These skills are powerful, and a world where empathy abounds would have little time or need for prejudice.

Comprehensive models are available, such as the Multidimensional Model of Prejudice Prevention and Reduction, that show us techniques to address the problem of prejudice in a multifaceted way. Strategies such as this one are much more likely to address the multiple factors that interact to institutionalize prejudice in our society. We can work with individuals and groups in social and political avenues to change those aspects of our culture that deny the American dream to selected groups. We can make the dream of equality upon which our nation was founded a reality. We have the tools. Do we have the will?

INSTRUMENTS
TO DIAGNOSE
PREJUDICE

Introduction

Half a century ago, Gunner Myrdal (1944) brought to national attention the notion that prejudice was indeed an American dilemma. As quoted in the introduction of this book, Myrdal poignantly described to us the hypocritical disparity between American political and religious philosophical ideals and our actual social and cultural practices. Unfortunately, Myrdal's stunning and sad commentary on prejudice has remained true even though the past 50 years have seen monumental efforts toward change.

Sniderman, Tetlock, and Carmines (1993) have described a doubling of the American dilemma. They wrote that race issues are now two-sided and that no true understanding of the problem can be obtained without the perspectives of both Whites and Blacks. We further recognize that the problem of prejudice extends beyond Black and White. Racism is one concern, but we must also address sexism, ageism, classism, and prejudice against those with disabilities or who are gay, lesbian, or bisexual.

We propose that counselors and other mental health professionals take proactive steps to ameliorate this painful and deleterious societal problem. These steps have been addressed in this book from a number of different methodologies. As a group, we must develop clear-cut goals to combat prejudice and implement strategies to achieve the desired results. It is time for a movement against prejudice that is based on a strong commitment to educate others about the significance of prejudice prevention. We must increase our educational and research efforts so that the voices of reason will be heard. As long as prejudice creates untold misery in our society, it is imperative that we raise loud and knowledgeable voices against it. When we tolerate sinister acts of prejudice in our own institutions, we perpetuate prejudice and allow silence to become violence.

To encourage proactive approaches to prevent, reduce, or combat prejudice, we have devoted a section of this book to various instruments to assess prejudice in its various forms. This addition will equip readers with a compendium of instruments that can be used to gather baseline information to appraise the nature and level of prejudice before designing appropriate strategies. This information should be helpful in encouraging much-needed research studies in the areas of prejudice and discrimination. As prejudice plays a menacing role in acculturation, life satisfaction, and psychological well-being, we have included instruments that relate to these issues as well.

As a caveat, readers are urged to seek updated information about these instruments before using them. This information might include additional reliability and validity statistics, results of recent studies, and availability of new versions of the scales. Also, the necessary permission in writing must be sought from the respective authors of these instruments. The names and addresses of the authors are provided at the end of this section. Please note that use of these scales in any form without explicit written permission from the authors is a direct violation of copyright laws.

Acculturative Stress Scale for International Students

The Acculturative Stress Scale for International Students is a 36-item, self-report, Likert-type measure of stress attributed to perceived discrimination, hate, and culture shock. Twelve major recurring themes are reported. Most of these themes are the underlying thesis of this book. These themes with two sample items are reproduced. The number of items representing each theme are shown in parentheses.

TABLE 1

Twelve Major Recurring Themes of Acculturative Stress for International Students and Some Sample Items

---

1. Perceived Discrimination (14*)
    Many opportunities are denied to me.
    I feel that I receive unequal treatment.
2. Social Isolation (9)
    I am treated differently in social situations.
    Some people ostracize me.
3. Threat to Cultural Identity (10)
    I am losing my ethnic identity.
    I feel lost for being unable to find my roots in this society.
4. Inferiority (15)
    I am made to feel inferior in this society.
    I feel inadequate to function here.
5. Homesickness (8)
    I feel sad leaving my relatives behind.
    I feel sad living in these unfamiliar surroundings.
6. Fear (14)
    I feel insecure here.
    I dread to pass through certain residential areas where people from other ethnic groups live.
7. Anger/Disappointments (15)
    It makes me angry when I hear negative stereotypes about my culture and people.
    I get angry when people use racial slurs and jokes about my culture.

TABLE 1 continued

**Twelve Major Recurring Themes of Acculturative Stress
for International Students and Some Sample Items**

---

8. Mistrust (6)
    It is hard for me to make trustworthy friends here.
    I cannot trust somebody to discuss my personal problems.

9. Communication Problems (7)
    I feel nervous to communicate in English.
    Due to language difficulties, I feel unable to express myself fully.

10. Culture Shock (9)
    Multiple pressures were placed upon me after migration.
    I feel uncomfortable to adjust to new foods.

11. Perceived Hatred (13)
    I am stared at in public places scornfully.
    Some people show hatred toward me because of my different
    ethnic background.

12. Guilt (5)
    I feel guilty when I think that I am better off here but my people
    still suffer.
    I feel guilty that I am living a different life style here.

Note. Reproduced with permission of publisher from Sandhu, D. A., & Asrabadi, B. R. Development
of an acculturative stress scale for international students: preliminary findings. *Psychological Reports*,
1994, 75, 435–448. © Psychological Reports 1994.

RELIABILITY AND VALIDITY DATA

Four of the following six extracted factors (perceived discrimination, perceived hate, fear, and culture shock) that comprise the
acculturative stress are also the major focus of this book. In our
strategies to reduce, prejudice, hatred and bigtory, the personal
concerns of international students are difficult to overlook.

It should be noted that factor one, Perceived Discrimination,
captured the highest percentage of total variation (38.3%). For
this reason, perceived discrimination and alienation of the international students is a major concern. All 36 items of ASSIS are
reproduced.

TABLE 2

Summary of Extracted Principal Factors of the Acculturative Stress Scale for International Students

Factors	Eigenvalue	% Variance	Cumulative Variance
1. Perceived Discrimination	13.78	38.30	38.30
2. Homesickness	3.24	9.00	47.30
3. Perceived Hate	2.60	7.20	54.50
4. Fear	2.20	6.10	60.60
5. Stress Due to Change/ Culture Shock	1.33	3.70	64.30
6. Guilt	1.16	3.20	67.50
7. Nonspecific	1.11	3.10	70.60

TABLE 3

Principal Factors and Representative Items With Their Factor Loadings and Commonalities

Factor Name and Item Content	Loading	h^2*
1. Perceived Discrimination		
Many opportunities are denied to me.	0.78	0.70
I am treated differently in social situations.	0.60	0.58
Other are biased toward me.	0.80	0.74
I feel that I receive unequal treatment.	0.79	0.74
I am denied what I deserve.	0.64	0.80
I feel that my people are discriminated against.	0.74	0.59
I am treated differently because of my race.	0.68	0.77
I am treated differently because of my color.	0.70	0.77
2. Homesickness		
I feel sad leaving my relatives behind.	0.86	0.83
Homesickness bothers me.	0.79	0.84
I feel sad living in unfamiliar surroundings.	0.79	0.80
I miss the people and country of my origin.	0.69	0.73
3. Perceived Hate/Rejection		
People show hatred toward me nonverbally.	0.85	0.81
People show hatred toward me verbally.	0.91	0.84
People show hatred toward me through actions.	0.87	0.80
Others are sarcastic toward my cultural values.	0.67	0.57
Others don't appreciate my cultural values.	0.68	0.73

TABLE 3 continued

Principal Factors and Representative Items With Their Factor Loadings and Commonalities

Factor Name and Item Content	Loading	h^2*
4. Fear		
I fear for my personal safety because of my different cultural background.	0.78	0.68
I generally keep a low profile due to fear.	0.77	0.81
I feel insecure here.	0.69	0.68
I frequently relocate for fear of others.	0.65	0.70
5. Stress Due to Change/Culture Shock		
I feel uncomfortable to adjust to new foods.	0.70	0.70
Multiple pressures are placed on me after migration.	0.61	0.77
I feel uncomfortable to adjust to new cultural values.	0.58	0.68
6. Guilt		
I feel guilty to leave my family and friends behind.	0.79	0.75
I feel guilty that I am living a different life style here.	0.62	0.76

* Commonalities are shown by h^2. The proportion of variance explained by the common factors is called the communality of the variable.

SCORING INFORMATION

The scores of the Perceived Discrimination subscale range from 8 to 40. Higher scores indicate high acculturative stress for international students attributed to perceived discrimination. The Cronbach's alpha coefficient of this subscale was calculated as .88.

Adult Life Satisfaction Scale

The Adult Life Satisfaction Scale (ALSS) is a 56-item, Likert-type, self-reporting scale to assess global life satisfaction of adults and the elderly. The ALSS can be used to compare the life satisfaction levels or indexes of clients with different sexual orientations, racial minorities, and men and women. It can also be used to assess the level of life satisfaction of people in different countries. This scale is not designed for diagnostic purposes.

Adult Life Satisfaction Scale

This scale is designed to assess the degree of life satisfaction you are experiencing at this time. There are no right or wrong answers. However, for the data to be meaningful, please answer each statement as honestly as possible. All of your responses will be kept strictly confidential. Please rate the following statements as follows:

I am satisfied . . .
1 = Strongly disagree   4 = Agree
2 = Disagree   5 = Strongly agree
3 = Not sure   NA = Does not apply to me

Generally speaking,
1. I feel proud of my family.
2. I derive a great comfort from my religion.
3. I enjoy my work.
4. I am happy with the respect my spouse and I have for each other.
5. I derive great satisfaction from raising my family.
6. I feel safe living in this community.
7. I am free from major ailments.
8. I am satisfied with the way we (as spouses) relate to each other's family members.
9. I am satisfied with who I am.
10. I am satisfied with how I am viewed by my family.
11. I feel that I have made a good work choice.
12. I have enough time to enjoy my leisure activities.

13. I derive great satisfaction from my friendships.
14. I enjoy spending time in fun activities with my family members.
15. Generally speaking, I have enjoyed good health.
16. There are plenty of entertainment opportunities available in my life.
17. I really enjoy relations with my mom.
18. Participation in church (worship) activities gives me a lot of satisfaction.
19. I am happy with my spouse's/friend's daily habits.
20. I am satisfied with the emotional support I receive from my family.
21. My creative activities provide great satisfaction.
22. I am satisfied with the job/career opportunities that are available to me.
23. I enjoy relationships with my family members.
24. I am in fairly good physical health.
25. I am satisfied with my partner's physical attractiveness.
26. I like the way we spend our leisure time together as husband and wife.
27. I enjoy my relations with my brothers and sisters.
28. I feel good about myself.
29. Generally speaking, I am satisfied with my life.
30. I am satisfied that there is a great spiritual power that I can turn to for help.
31 I am satisfied with the spiritual directions I am receiving.
32. I enjoy being a part of this community.
33. I am becoming the best I can become in those things that interest me most in my life.
34. I enjoy participating in social activities with my friends.
35. I am satisfied with my sex or love life.
36. Generally speaking, I enjoy my relations with other relatives who are not the immediate members of my family.
37. I feel my basic survival needs of food and shelter are met.
38. I am satisfied with the prestige I have in my job.
39. I have at least one hobby I really enjoy.
40. I am satisfied with the way we (as spouses) respect each other's beliefs (religion, politics, and other beliefs).

41. Participation in church social activities gives me great satisfaction.
42. My involvement in intellectual activities gives me great satisfaction.
43. It feels good to participate in social activities held in this community.
44. My family is a great source of happiness for me.
45. There have been a lot of good opportunities in my life.
46. I am optimistic about my future.
47. I feel I am accomplishing my goals of life.
48. My family is a great source of satisfaction for me.
49. I have open communications with my partner(s).
50. I feel a sense of belonging in this society.
51. I feel that I am better off than a lot of people I know about.
52. I feel I am getting what I want from my life.
53. Generally, I have attained what I desired in my life.
54. Life is an enjoyable experience for me.
55. I am satisfied with the fulfillment of those objectives that I see as the main purposes of my life.
56. I am satisfied with the way, as husband and wife, we make decisions about raising our children.

SCORING INSTRUCTIONS
Two different methods for scoring are proposed.

First Method. The total score of the scale can be obtained by adding the scores of all items. The higher the total score on ALSS, the higher the level of one's perceived life satisfaction.

Second Method. Eleven subscales can be scored individually by adding the scores of specific items. These subscales and their subsequent items are listed in Table 4. Total scores of different subscales are helpful to look at one's specific aspects of life.

TABLE 4

Eleven Subscales of Adult Life Satisfaction With Their Specific Items

Subscale	Cronbach's Alpha	Range of Scores
Spiritual (items 2, 18, 30, 31, 41)	.96	5–25
Relations (items 17, 23, 27, 36, 48)	.90	5–25
Work (items 3, 11, 22, 38)	.90	4–20
Marriage/Sex (items 4, 8, 19, 25, 26, 35, 40, 49, 56)	.96	9–45
Family Life (items 1, 5, 10, 20, 44)	.87	5–25
Social Life (items 6, 13, 32, 43)	.77	4–20
Health (items 7, 15, 24, 37)	.86	4–20
Leisure (items 12, 14, 16, 34, 39)	.68	5–25
Mental Health (items 9, 28, 51, 54)	.84	4–20
General (items 29, 45, 46, 47, 50, 52, 53)	.86	7–35
Personal Fulfillment (items 21, 33, 42, 55)	.75	4–20

Black Racial Identity Attitude Scale

Janet E. Helms and Robert T. Carter (1990) asserted that The Black Racial Identity Attitude Scale is a rationally constructed scale to measure attitudes that contribute to the racial identity of Blacks.

To avoid respondent reactivity, the title "Social Attitude Scale" should replace the scale's title when the measure is administered.

Black Racial Identity Attitude Scale

This questionnaire is designed to measure people's social and political attitudes. There are no right or wrong answers. Use the scale below to respond to each statement. On your answer sheet, blacken the number of the box that describes how you feel.

1 = Strongly disagree   **4** = Strongly agree
2 = Disagree   **5** = Agree
3 = Uncertain

1. I believe that being Black is a positive experience.
2. I know through experience what being Black in America means.
3. I feel unable to involve myself in White experiences and am increasing my involvement in Black experiences.
4. I believe that large numbers of Blacks are untrustworthy.
5. I feel an overwhelming attachment to Black people.
6. I involve myself in causes that will help all oppressed people.
7. I feel comfortable wherever I am.
8. I believe that White people look and express themselves better than Blacks.
9. I feel very uncomfortable around Black people.
10. I feel good about being Black, but do not limit myself to Black activities.
11. I often find myself referring to White people as honkies, devils, pigs, etc.

12. I believe that to be Black is not necessarily good.
13. I believe that certain aspects of the Black experience apply to me, and others do not.
14. I frequently confront the system and the man.
15. I constantly involve myself in Black political and social activities (art shows, political meetings, Black theater, etc.)
16. I involve myself in social action and political groups, even if there are no other Blacks involved.
17. I believe that Black people should learn to think and experience life in ways similar to White people.
18. I believe that the world should be interpreted from a Black perspective.
19. I have changed my style of life to fit my beliefs about Black people.
20. I feel excitement and joy in Black surroundings.
21. I believe that Black people came from a strange, dark, and uncivilized continent.
22. People, regardless of their race, have strengths and limitations.
23. I find myself reading a lot of Black literature and thinking about being Black.
24. I feel guilty and/or anxious about some of the things I believe about Black people.
25. I believe that a Black person's most effective weapon for solving problems is to become part of the White person's world.
26. I speak my mind regardless of the consequences (e.g., being kicked out of school, being imprisoned, being exposed to danger).
27. I believe that everything Black is good, and consequently, I limit myself to Black activities.
28. I am determined to find my Black identity.
29. I believe that White people are intellectually superior to Blacks.
30. I believe that because I am Black, I have many strengths.
31. I feel that Black people do not have as much to be proud of as White people do.

32. Most Blacks I know are failures.
33. I believe that White people should feel guilty about the way they have treated Blacks in the past.
34. White people can't be trusted.
35. In today's society if Black people don't achieve, they have only themselves to blame.
36. The most important thing about me is that I am Black.
37. Being Black just feels natural to me.
38. Other Black people have trouble accepting me because my life experiences have been so different from their experiences.
39. Black people who have any White people's blood should feel ashamed of it.
40. Sometimes, I wish I belonged to the White race.
41. The people I respect most are White.
42. A person's race usually is not important to me.
43. I feel anxious when White people compare me to other members of my race.
44. I can't feel comfortable with either Black people or White people.
45. A person's race has little to do with whether or not he or she is a good person.
46. When I am with Black people, I pretend to enjoy the things they enjoy.
47. When a stranger who is Black does something embarrassing in public, I get embarrassed.
48. I believe that a Black person can be close friends with a White person.
49. I am satisfied with myself.
50. I have a positive attitude about myself because I am Black.

Note. Janet E. Helms, *Black and White Identity: Theory, research, and practice*, reprinted with permission of Greenwood Publishing Group, Inc., Westport, CT. © 1990.

Cultural Adaptation Pain Scale

The Cultural Adaptation Pain Scale (CAPS) was designed to assess the degree of adjustment of individuals from various backgrounds as they come in contact with new or different social contexts. The CAPS aims to explore the extent of mental distress and emotional sensitivity experienced in everyday life. It is a 55-item scale of counterbalanced statements that are answered on a 5-point Likert scale. Each statement presents a view, feeling, or experience related to cultural adaptation. As a global measure of adaptation, the CAPS produced an overall Cronbach's alpha of .85. This scale has four factors. The knowledge of all factors, Factor 1 (pain), Factor 2 (learned helplessness), Factor 3 (positive adaptation), and Factor 4 (bigoted) are useful to understand the acculturation process and the psychodynamics of racism, sexism, bigotry, and hate.

The Cultural Adaptation Pain Scale

Often times social interactions, confrontations, and even collaborations with diverse people can become very painful psychologically. Adapting to new situations is often uncomfortable. This scale is designed to assess the degree of pain and mental distress you may be experiencing at the present time. There are no right or wrong answers. However, for the results to be meaningful, you must answer these statements as honestly as possible. Circle "Strongly agree" if the item holds true for you most of the time, and so on. Please respond to all items.

In general, I feel that:	Strongly Agree	Agree	Not Sure	Dis-agree	Strongly Dis-agree
1. Many opportunities are denied to me.	5	4	3	2	1
2. My choices for success in life are limited.	5	4	3	2	1
3. Some ethnic groups are inherently inferior to others.	5	4	3	2	1
4. I am looked down upon by some people.	5	4	3	2	1

In general, I feel that:	Strongly Agree	Agree	Not Sure	Disagree	Strongly Disagree
5. I am often not taken seriously.	5	4	3	2	1
6. I get impatient when I cannot understand a different accent.	5	4	3	2	1
7. I am often considered less capable than I really am.	5	4	3	2	1
8. Others try to make me feel inferior.	5	4	3	2	1
9. Meaningful communication is a problem with most folks.	5	4	3	2	1
10. My achievements are not considered very important.	5	4	3	2	1
11. This society is becoming a mixture of too many different ethnic groups.	5	4	3	2	1
12. I do not feel others are biased toward me.	5	4	3	2	1
13. I have been denied opportunities I deserve.	5	4	3	2	1
14. I suffer from prejudice and unequal treatment.	5	4	3	2	1
15. I am required to do more than others to prove my abilities.	5	4	3	2	1
16. I feel I have a clear identity in this culture.	5	4	3	2	1
17. I lose enthusiasm about trying to succeed when I know that I have to face extra obstacles.	5	4	3	2	1
18. I do not have as many choices as others around me.	5	4	3	2	1
19. I become angry about the stereotypes and negative reactions people have about me.	5	4	3	2	1
20. Affirmative action laws are necessary to empower certain ethnic groups.	5	4	3	2	1
21. Trying hard to get ahead does not work for people like me.	5	4	3	2	1
22. I feel adequate to function in this society.	5	4	3	2	1

In general, I feel that:	Strongly Agree	Agree	Not Sure	Dis-agree	Strongly Dis-agree
23. I do not have much control over my life generally.	5	4	3	2	1
24. I feel I do not have as much support as others.	5	4	3	2	1
25. I feel a sense of community with others around me.	5	4	3	2	1
26. I feel I belong in the present culture.	5	4	3	2	1
27. Our government should not allow migration from some ethnic groups to our country.	5	4	3	2	1
28. I am treated as a second-rate citizen some of the time.	5	4	3	2	1
29. I feel sad living in my present surroundings.	5	4	3	2	1
30. I feel I can get ahead in life as well as anyone else.	5	4	3	2	1
31. I feel uncomfortable with other people's cultural values in this society.	5	4	3	2	1
32. Some ethnic groups are freeloaders in our society.	5	4	3	2	1
33. If I try to work hard I will have a good future.	5	4	3	2	1
34. It hurts me to think that I am treated differently because of my background or gender.	5	4	3	2	1
35. Others act as if they are better than I am.	5	4	3	2	1
36. I feel sorry for children who have to adapt to a different culture.	5	4	3	2	1
37. To maintain one's cultural identity, one should not try to assimilate with other cultural groups.	5	4	3	2	1
38. I often sense a feeling of alienation.	5	4	3	2	1
39. Some groups have hostility towards me.	5	4	3	2	1
40. I feel uncomfortable participating in social activities.	5	4	3	2	1

In general, I feel that:	Strongly Agree	Agree	Not Sure	Dis-agree	Strongly Dis-agree
41. People often exchange greetings with me.	5	4	3	2	1
42. I feel it is fair to blame some ethnic groups for their plight.	5	4	3	2	1
43. I feel irritated when people are insensitive to the cultural values of others.	5	4	3	2	1
44. I feel amused when people make fun of cultural stereotypes.	5	4	3	2	1
45. I am not bothered when people use ethnic/racial slurs.	5	4	3	2	1
46. I am ostracized (shunned) by some people.	5	4	3	2	1
47. When I have to communicate with authority figures, I feel inadequate.	5	4	3	2	1
48. Despite all my efforts, I will not be able to succeed in this society as well as I could.	5	4	3	2	1
49. I feel a sense of helplessness and hopelessness.	5	4	3	2	1
50. It makes me work harder when others have an unfair advantage.	5	4	3	2	1
51. It is very important to have high hopes in this society.	5	4	3	2	1
52. I have deep roots in this country.	5	4	3	2	1
53. Gender issues are more important to me than cultural background.	5	4	3	2	1
54. I am bothered when persons from minority groups take unfair advantages (to advance themselves).	5	4	3	2	1
55. Cultural identity is most important to my sense of self.	5	4	3	2	1
56. Only one language should be used to teach children in school.	5	4	3	2	1

Note. Reprinted from *Journal of Multicultural Counseling and Development*, vol. 24, pp. 15–25. © ACA. Reprinted with permission. No further reproduction authorized without written permission of the American Counseling Association.

SCORING INFORMATION

Factor 1: Pain. Alpha = .89. This factor has 24 items. The scores range from 24–120.

Factor 2: Learned helplessness. Alpha = .71. This factor has 13 items. The scores range from 13–65.

Factor 3: Positive adaptation. Alpha = .66. This factor has 10 items. The scores range from 10–50.

Factor 4: Bigoted. Alpha = .23. This factor has only 5 items. The scores range from 5–25.

TABLE 5

The Cultural Adaptation Pain Scale Factor Pattern Loadings

Factor	Loading
Factor 1: Pain	
Feel looked down on by other people.	.69
Become angry about the stereotyping and negative reactions people have.	.68
Feel ostracized by some people.	.65
Feel others try to make them feel inferior.	.63
Feel that some groups have hostility toward them.	.62
Feel treated as second-rate citizens some of the time.	.62
Feel they have been denied opportunities they deserve.	.60
Often feel they are not taken seriously.	.60
Often considered less capable than they really are.	.59
People will often not exchange greetings with them.	.58
Suffer from prejudice and unequal treatment.	.57
Are required to do more than others to prove abilities.	.56
Often feel a sense of alienation.	.55
Feel they do not have as much support as others.	.52
Feel many opportunities are denied to them.	.52
Feel status in this society is considered "low" by others because of cultural background, gender, or both.	.50
Often feel they have lead a dual life in this society.	.49
Feel treated the same as others in social situations.	−.44
Often feel pressure to conform.	.43
Feel hurt when negative images about their culture are presented in media.	.42

TABLE 5 continued

The Cultural Adaptation Pain Scale Factor Pattern Loadings

Factor	Loading
Factor 1: Pain continued	
Experience conflict with the cultural values of groups contacted.	.42
Experience more loneliness than others.	.41
Factor 2: Learned helplessness	
Feel choices for success in life are limited.	.69
Feel that despite all efforts they will not be able to succeed in this society.	.60
Feel they do not have as many choices as others around them.	.57
Feel uncomfortable participating in social activities.	.54
Feel trying hard to get ahead does not work for people like them.	.49
Lose enthusiasm about trying to succeed when they know that they have to face extra obstacles.	.43
Feel sad living in present surroundings.	.42
Feel that if they try to work hard, they will have a good future.	−.42
Feel they do not have as much support as others.	.41
Factor 3: Positive adaptation	
Feel adequate functioning in this society.	.62
Feel they have a clear identity in this culture.	.61
Feel they have deep roots in this country.	.55
Feel a sense of community with others around them.	.47
Feel they belong in the present culture.	.45
Feel they can get ahead in life as well as anyone else.	.41
Are bothered when persons from minority groups take unfair advantage (to advance themselves).	.41
Factor 4: Bigoted	
Feel irritated when people are insensitive to the cultural values of others.	−.66
Feel it is fair to blame some ethnic groups for their plight.	.61
Get impatient when they cannot understand a different accent.	.50
Not bothered when people use ethnic or racial slurs.	.50
Feel amused when people use ethnic or racial slurs.	.47

Past Prejudice Affliction Scale

The Past Prejudice Affliction Scale is constructed to assess the role of painful past experiences in present intercultural relations. This scale is administered to determine if historical hostilities, internalized hatred, pent-up anger, and unhealed psychological wounds are contributing to the current worldviews of the clients. This information is important to address the perennial problem of persisting prejudice. Six extracted factors, historical/persistent prejudice, social paranoia, historical biases, persistent prejudice pain, discrimination denials, and historical fear, are also discussed with the Cronbach's alpha relibilities.

Past Prejudice Affliction Scale

There are no right or wrong answers. However, for the data to be meaningful, you must answer each statement below as honestly as possible.

Respond to each item using the following scale:

1 = Strongly disagree   **4** = Somewhat agree
2 = Disagree   **5** = Agree
3 = Somewhat disagree   **6** = Strongly agree

I feel that people from my ethnic group
1. experience pent-up anger against some other ethnic group(s).
2. harbor unresolved guilt because of past historical events.
3. suffer from the unhealed wounds of the racial past.
4. mistrust even the good intentions of some other ethnic groups.
5. discuss certain matters only with the members of their own ethnic group.
6. hate some other ethnic group(s) because of the negative cultural experiences from the past.
7. carry hostile feelings toward the members of other ethnic group(s).

I feel that people from my ethnic group

8. believe that racism is a cultural dilemma that has deep roots in the past.

9. believe that people who cry racism are their own worst enemies.

10. believe that some ethnic groups have been historically considered inferior to others.

11. believe that some ethnic groups have been historically considered less intelligent than others.

12. are afraid even of the good intentions of people from some other ethnic groups, based on past experiences.

13. are afraid to openly discuss racial issues.

14. are apprehensive to make friends with members of other ethnic groups because of past troubling experiences.

15. engage only in superficial conversations with members of other ethnic groups.

16. believe that some ethnic groups have historically enjoyed privileges just because of their skin colors.

17. feel that there have always been social, economic, and political inequalities in America.

18. believe that America has always had a race problem.

19. believe that minorities have been historically oppressed in America.

20. feel that because of skin color, contributions made by our ethnic group have been historically underestimated.

21. believe that ethnic minorities need to put history behind them and move on with their current lives.

22. believe that some ethnic groups unnecessarily spend their energies on ruminating about the past.

23. refuse to take blame for the miseries of other ethnic groups.

24. believe that speaking about the evils of the past will not solve present-day problems.

25. feel that discounting or minimizing past racial injustices would be like adding insult to the injury of our ethnic group.

26. believe that our ethnic group has been the target of hate crimes in America.

27. believe that throughout the history of our nation, our ethnic group has been betrayed.

I feel that people from my ethnic group

28. believe that members of our ethnic group have always been considered as second-rate citizens.
29. believe that contributions made by our ethnic group have not been fairly recognized.
30. feel that our ethnic group has been historically discriminated against.
31. feel that people from our ethnic group have always been looked down upon scornfully.
32. feel angry that our ethnic group has been abused throughout the history of America.
33. feel sad to think about the long-term prejudice problems of our ethnic group.
34. feel some other ethnic groups don't associate with our group because of racial and ethnic differences.
35. feel that they have been considered worthless members of this society because of our different racial background.
36. feel confused for being unable to find their roots in this society.
37. believe that people from other ethnic groups have plans to hurt them.
38. believe that some ethnic groups have never been welcomed in America.
39. believe that based on historical events, they must raise their children to be always on their guard.
40. believe that mistrust among various ethnic groups go back centuries.
41. believe that there are deep-rooted suspicions among many ethnic groups.
42. believe because of past events, it is safer to be suspicious of people from other ethnic groups.
43. believe that there is no honest communication among people from different ethnic groups.

SCORING INFORMATION

Factor 1: Historical/persistent prejudice
Total of 12 items: 29, 30, 32, 28, 31, 27, 35, 36, 26, 25, 20, 33
(score range 12–72); Cronbach's alpha relibility coefficient = .94

Factor 2: Social paranoia
Total of 8 items: 39, 42, 41, 37, 38, 34, 43, 40
(score range 8–48); Cronbach's alpha reliability coefficient = .84

Factor 3: Historical biases
Total of 7 items: 11, 10, 17, 19, 18, 8, 16
(score range 7–42); Cronbach's alpha reliability coefficient = .87

Factor 4: Persistent prejudice pain
Total of 7 items: 1, 2, 3, 4, 5, 6, 7
(score range 7–42); Cronbach's alpha relibility coefficient = .86

Factor 5: Discrimination denials
Total of 5 items: 9, 21, 22, 23, 24
(score range 5–35); Cronbach's alpha relibility coefficient = .81

Factor 6: Historical fear
Total of 4 items: 12, 13, 14, 15
(score range 4–24); Cronbach's alpha relibility coefficient = .77

Quick Discrimination Index

The Quick Discrimination Index (QDI) is a 30-item, Likert-type, self-report measure of racial and gender attitudes. The instrument itself is titled "Social Attitude Survey" to control for some forms of response bias. Users of the QDI should read development and validity studies on the QDI before use.

Social Attitude Survey

Please respond to all items in the survey. Remember there are no right or wrong answers. The survey is completely anonymous; do not put your name on the survey. Please circle the appropriate number to the right.

1 = Strongly disagree   4 = Agree
2 = Disagree   5 = Strongly agree
3 = Not sure

1. I do think it is more appropriate for the mother of a newborn baby, rather then the father, to stay with the baby (not work) during the first year.
2. It is as easy for women to succeed in business as it is for men.
3. I really think affirmative action programs on college campuses constitute reverse discrimination.
4. I feel I could develop an intimate relationship with someone from a different race.
5. All Americans should learn to speak two languages.
6. It upsets (or angers) me that a women has never been president of the United States.
7. Generally speaking, men work harder than women.
8. My friendship network is very racially mixed.
9. I am against affirmative action programs in business.
10. Generally, men seem less concerned with building relationships than women.
11. I would feel O.K. about my son or daughter dating someone from a different race.

12. It upsets (or angers) me that a racial minority person has never been president of the United States.
13. In the past few years there has been too much attention directed toward multicultural or minority issues in education.
14. I think feminist perspectives should be an integral part of the higher education curriculum.
15. Most of my close friends are from my own racial group.
16. I feel somewhat more secure that a man rather than a woman is currently president of the United States.
17. I think it is (or would be) important for my children to attend schools that are racially mixed.
18. In the past few years there has been too much attention directed towards multicultural or minority issues in business.
19. Overall, I think racial minorities in America complain too much about racial discrimination.
20. I feel (or would feel) very comfortable having a woman as my primary physician.
21. I think the president of the United States should make a concerted effort to appoint more women and racial minorities to the country's Supreme Court.
22. I think White people's racism toward racial minority groups still constitutes a major problem in America.
23. I think the school system, from elementary school through college, should encourage minority and immigrant children to learn and fully adopt traditional American values.
24. If I were to adopt a child, I would be happy to adopt a child of any race.
25. I think there is as much female physical violence towards men as there is male physical violence toward women.
26. I think the school system, from elementary school through college, should promote traditional American values as well as the values representative of the culturally diverse students in the class.
27. I believe that reading the autobiography of Malcolm X would be of value.
28. I would enjoy living in a neighborhood consisting of a racially diverse population (i.e., Asians, Blacks, Hispanics, Whites).

29. I think it is better if people marry within their own race.
30. Women make too big of a deal out of sexual harassment issues in the workplace.

Note. From Joseph G. Ponterotto et al., Educational and Psychological Measurements, *55* (6), 1016–1031. © 1995 by Sage Publications. Reprinted by permission of Sage Publications, Inc.

SCORING INFORMATION

There are two methods of scoring the QDI. First, you can simply use the total score, which measures overall sensitivity, awareness, and receptivity to cultural diversity and gender equality.

The second scoring procedure involves scoring three separate subscales (factors) of the QDI. This is the preferred method at this time (1994) given that both exploratory and confirmatory factor analysis support the construct validity of the three-factor model.

Of the 30 items on the QDI, 15 are worded and scored in a positive direction (high scores indicate high sensitivity to multicultural/gender issues), and 15 are worded and scored in a negative direction (low scores are indicative of high sensitivity). Naturally, when tallying the total score response, these latter 15 items need to be reverse scored. Reverse scoring simply means that if a respondent circles a 1 they should get five points; a 2, four points; a 3, three points; a 4, two points; and a 5, one point.

The following QDI items need to be reverse scored: 1, 2, 3, 7, 9, 10, 13, 15, 16, 18, 19, 23, 25, 29, and 30.

The score range is 30 to 150, with high scores indicating more awareness, sensitivity, and receptivity to racial diversity and gender equality.

If scoring separate subscales (factors), the researcher should not also use the total score. As expected, the total score is highly correlated with subscale scores, and to use both would be redundant.

When scoring separate subscales, only 23 of the total 30 items are scored.

Factor 1: General (Cognitive) Attitudes Toward Racial Diversity/Multiculturalism (items in parentheses are reverse-scored)
9 items: (3), (9), (13), (18), (19), 22, (23), 26, 27
(score range = 9 to 45)

Factor 2: Affective Attitudes Toward More Personal Contact (Closeness) with Racial Diversity (items in parentheses are reverse-scored)
7 items: 4, 8, 11, (15), 17, 24, (29)
(score range = 7 to 35)

Factor 3: Attitudes Toward Women's Equity (items in parentheses are reverse scored)
7 items: (1), 6, (7), 14, (16), 20, (30)
(score range = 7 to 35)

Situational Attitude Scale

Sadlacek and Brooks (1972) developed the Situational Attitude Scale (SAS) to measure the attitudes of Whites toward African Americans. To make a psychological withdrawal difficult and also to provide a racial context, they created 10 personal and social situations. These situations have some important relevance to racial responses.

The Situational Attitude Scale (SAS) consists of 10 bipolar semantic differential scales for each of the 10 personal and social situations. Thus, the SAS consists of 100 items. To compare the responses, participants are asked to complete two versions of the SAS, Form A and Form B. Both versions are alike except the fact that in Form B, the word *Black* is added. For instance, Form A reads, "A new family moves in next door to you." Form B reads,"A new Black family moves in next door to you."

The respondents are asked to select their responses to describe their feelings. They are also required to rate the extent of their feelings on a 5-point semantic differential adjective scale.

The authors maintain that the SAS can be used for self-evaluation, diagnostic work, and with clients in counseling. The SAS would be greatly useful in situations where racial issues and personality attitudes are involved.

The Scale—Form A

This questionnaire measures how people think and feel about a number of social and personal incidents and situations. It is not a test, so there are no right or wrong answers. The questionnaire is anonymous, so please do not sign your name.

Each item or situation is followed by 10 descriptive word scales. Your task is to select, for each descriptive scale, the rating which best describes your feeling toward the item.

Sample item: Going out on a date

happy   A   B   C   D   E   sad

You may indicate the direction and extent of your feelings by indicating your choice in your response sheet by blackening in the appropriate space for that word scale. Do not mark on the booklet. Please respond to all word scales.

Sometimes you may feel as though you had the same item before on the questionnaire. This will not be the case, so do not look back and forth through the items. Do not try to remember how you checked similar items earlier in the questionnaire. Make each item a separate and independent judgment. Respond as honestly as possible without puzzling over individual items. Respond with your first impressions whenever possible.

I. A new family moves in next door to you.

1. good	A	B	C	D	E	bad
2. safe	A	B	C	D	E	unsafe
3 angry	A	B	C	D	E	not angry
4. friendly	A	B	C	D	E	unfriendly
5. sympathetic	A	B	C	D	E	not sympathetic
6. nervous	A	B	C	D	E	calm
7. happy	A	B	C	D	E	sad
8. objectionable	A	B	C	D	E	acceptable
9. desirable	A	B	C	D	E	undesirable
10. suspicious	A	B	C	D	E	trusting

II. You read in the paper that a man has raped a White woman.

11. affection	A	B	C	D	E	disgust
12. relish	A	B	C	D	E	repulsion
13. happy	A	B	C	D	E	sad
14. friendly	A	B	C	D	E	hostile
15. uninvolved	A	B	C	D	E	involved
16. hope	A	B	C	D	E	hopelessness
17. aloof	A	B	C	D	E	outraged
18. injure	A	B	C	D	E	kill
19. safe	A	B	C	D	E	fearful
20. empathetic	A	B	C	D	E	can't understand

III. It is evening, and a man appears at your door saying he is selling magazines.

21. relaxed	A	B	C	D	E	startled
22. receptive	A	B	C	D	E	cautious
23. excited	A	B	C	D	E	not excited
24. glad	A	B	C	D	E	angered
25. pleased	A	B	C	D	E	annoyed
26. indifferent	A	B	C	D	E	suspicious
27. tolerable	A	B	C	D	E	intolerable
28. afraid	A	B	C	D	E	secure
29. friend	A	B	C	D	E	enemy
30. unprotected	A	B	C	D	E	protected

IV. You are walking down the street alone and must pass a corner
where a group of five young men are loitering.

31. relaxed	A	B	C	D	E	tensed
32. pleased	A	B	C	D	E	angered
33. superior	A	B	C	D	E	inferior
34. smarter	A	B	C	D	E	dumber
35. whiter	A	B	C	D	E	blacker
36. aggressive	A	B	C	D	E	passive
37. safe	A	B	C	D	E	unsafe
38. friendly	A	B	C	D	E	unfriendly
39. excited	A	B	C	D	E	unexcited
40. trivial	A	B	C	D	E	important

V. Your best friend has just become engaged.

41. aggressive	A	B	C	D	E	passive
42. happy	A	B	C	D	E	sad
43. tolerable	A	B	C	D	E	intolerable
44. complimented	A	B	C	D	E	insulted
45. angered	A	B	C	D	E	overjoyed
46. secure	A	B	C	D	E	fearful
47. hopeful	A	B	C	D	E	hopeless
48. excited	A	B	C	D	E	unexcited
49. right	A	B	C	D	E	wrong
50. disgusting	A	B	C	D	E	pleasing

VI. You are stopped for speeding by a policeman.

51. calm	A	B	C	D	E	nervous
52. trusting	A	B	C	D	E	suspicious
53. afraid	A	B	C	D	E	safe
54. friendly	A	B	C	D	E	unfricndly
55. tolerant	A	B	C	D	E	intolerant
56. bitter	A	B	C	D	E	pleasant
57. cooperative	A	B	C	D	E	uncooperative
58. acceptable	A	B	C	D	E	belligerent
59. inferior	A	B	C	D	E	superior
60. smarter	A	B	C	D	E	dumber

VII. A new person joins your social group.

61. warm	A	B	C	D	E	cold
62. sad	A	B	C	D	E	happy
63. superior	A	B	C	D	E	inferior
64. threatened	A	B	C	D	E	neutral
65. pleased	A	B	C	D	E	displeased
66. understanding	A	B	C	D	E	indifferent
67. suspicious	A	B	C	D	E	trusting
68. disappointed	A	B	C	D	E	elated
69. favorable	A	B	C	D	E	unfavorable
70. uncomfortable	A	B	C	D	E	comfortable

VIII. You see a youngster steal something in a dime store.

71. surprising	A	B	C	D	E	not surprising
72. sad	A	B	C	D	E	happy
73. disinterested	A	B	C	D	E	interested
74. close	A	B	C	D	E	distant
75. understandable	A	B	C	D	E	baffling
76. responsible	A	B	C	D	E	not responsible
77. concerned	A	B	C	D	E	unconcerned
78. sympathy	A	B	C	D	E	indifference
79. expected	A	B	C	D	E	unexpected
80. hopeful	A	B	C	D	E	hopeless

IX. Some students on campus stage a demonstration.

81. bad	A	B	C	D	E	good
82. understanding	A	B	C	D	E	indifferent

83. suspicious	A	B	C	D	E	trusting
84. safe	A	B	C	D	E	unsafe
85. disturbed	A	B	C	D	E	undisturbed
86. justified	A	B	C	D	E	unjustified
87. tense	A	B	C	D	E	calm
88. hate	A	B	C	D	E	love
89. wrong	A	B	C	D	E	right
90. humorous	A	B	C	D	E	serious

X. You get on a bus that you are the only person who has to stand.

91. fearful	A	B	C	D	E	secure
92. tolerable	A	B	C	D	E	intolerable
93. hostile	A	B	C	D	E	indifferent
94. important	A	B	C	D	E	trivial
95. conspicuous	A	B	C	D	E	inconspicuous
96. calm	A	B	C	D	E	anxious
97. indignant	A	B	C	D	E	understanding
98. comfortable	A	B	C	D	E	uncomfortable
99. hate	A	B	C	D	E	love
100. not resentful	A	B	C	D	E	resentful

101. Blacken in the appropriate box to indicate your religion or religious preference:
   ☐ Catholic   ☐ None
   ☐ Jewish   ☐ Other
   ☐ Protestant

102. Blacken in the appropriate box to indicate your sex:
   ☐ Female   ☐ Male

103. Blacken in the appropriate box to indicate your age:
   ☐ Under 17 years old   ☐ 19 years old
   ☐ 17 years old   ☐ Over 19 years old
   ☐ 18 years old

104. *Father's Occupation:* Which of the following comes close to describing your father's occupation? Mark only one answer. If he works more than one job, mark the most important one. If

he is temporarily unemployed, deceased, or if he is retired, mark the one he held last. If your father never held a formal job, leave the item blank.

A. Professional—such as clergyman, dentist, doctor, engineer, lawyer, professor, scientist, or teacher.

B. Semiprofessional—such as accountant, airplane pilot, actor, armed forces officer, medical technician, musician, writer, librarian, artist, dental technician, or engineering aid. Manager-Proprietor-Executive—such as sales manager, store manager, owner of small business, factory supervisor, wholesaler, retailer, contractor, restaurant owner, manufacturer, banker, official in a large company, or government official.

C. Salesperson—such as life insurance, real estate or industrial goods salesperson. Clerical Worker—such as sales clerk, office clerk, bookkeeper, or ticket agent.

D. Skilled Worker or Foreperson—such as baker, carpenter, plasterer, electrician, mechanic, plumber, tailor, or farm or ranch owner or manager.

E. Service or Protective—such as armed forces enlistee or noncommissioned officer, barber, beautician, bus driver, fire fighter, police officer, or waiter.

105. The father's occupation above represents:
□ full-time work □ part-time work

106. *Mother's Occupation*—Please use the same options found in question 104 to describe your mother's occupation. If your mother has never held a formal job, leave the item blank.

107. The mother's occupation described above represents:
□ full-time work □ part-time work

108. Blacken in the appropriate box to indicate your race:
□ Black (Afro-American, Negro)
□ White (Caucasian)
□ Oriental (Asian American)
□ American Indian (Native American)
□ Spanish surname

SCORING INFORMATION

A total score is obtained by summing total responses on all items and dividing by 100. The authors do not recommend calculating a total score. They suggest that scores are determined for each individual situation due to the relative independence of each situation.

RELIBILITY INFORMATION

Sedlacek and Brooks (1972) accounted for the reliability of SAS in two different ways. The median communalities from principal factor analyses using squared multiples correlations as communalities and varimax rotation were reported as .64 for Form A and .65 Form B. For both Form A and Form B combined, it was .66.

The Scale—Form B

This questionnaire measures how people think and feel about a number of social and personal incidents and situations. It is not a test, so there are no right or wrong answers. The questionnaire is anonymous, so please, do not sign your name.

Each item or situation is followed by 10 descriptive word scales. Your task is to select, for each descriptive scale, the rating which best describes your feeling toward the item.

Sample item: Going out on a date

happy   A   B   C   D   E   sad

You might indicate the direction and extent of your feelings by indicating your choice on your response sheet by blackening in the appropriate space for that word scale.

Sometimes you may feel as though you had the same item before on the questionnaire. This will not be the case, so do not look back and forth through the items. Do not try to remember how you checked similar items earlier in the questionnaire. Make each item a separate and independent judgment. Respond as honestly as possible without puzzling over individual items. Respond with your first impressions whenever possible.

I. A Black family moves in next door to you.

1. good	A	B	C	D	E	sad
2. safe	A	B	C	D	E	unsafe
3 angry	A	D	C	D	E	not angry
4. friendly	A	B	C	D	E	unfriendly
5. sympathetic	A	B	C	D	E	not sympathetic
6. nervous	A	B	C	D	E	calm
7. happy	A	B	C	D	E	sad
8. objectionable	A	B	C	D	E	acceptable
9. desirable	A	B	C	D	E	undesirable
10. suspicious	A	B	C	D	E	trusting

II. You read in the paper that a Black man has raped a White woman.

11. affection	A	B	C	D	E	disgust
12. relish	A	B	C	D	E	repulsion
13. happy	A	B	C	D	E	sad
14. friendly	A	B	C	D	E	hostile
15. uninvolved	A	B	C	D	E	involved
16. hope	A	B	C	D	E	hopelessness
17. aloof	A	B	C	D	E	outraged
18. injure	A	B	C	D	E	kill
19. safe	A	B	C	D	E	fearful
20. empathetic	A	B	C	D	E	can't understand

III. It is evening, and a Black man appears at your door saying he is selling magazines.

21. relaxed	A	B	C	D	E	startled
22. receptive	A	B	C	D	E	cautious
23. excited	A	B	C	D	E	not excited
24. glad	A	B	C	D	E	angered
25. pleased	A	B	C	D	E	annoyed
26. indifferent	A	B	C	D	E	suspicious
27. tolerable	A	B	C	D	E	intolerable
28. afraid	A	B	C	D	E	secure
29. friend	A	B	C	D	E	enemy
30. unprotected	A	B	C	D	E	protected

IV. You are walking down the street alone and must pass a corner where a group of five young Black men are loitering.

31. relaxed	A	B	C	D	E	tensed
32. pleased	A	B	C	D	E	angered
33. superior	A	B	C	D	E	inferior
34. smarter	A	B	C	D	E	dumber
35. whiter	A	B	C	D	E	blacker
36. aggressive	A	B	C	D	E	passive
37. safe	A	B	C	D	E	unsafe
38. friendly	A	B	C	D	E	unfriendly
39. excited	A	B	C	D	E	unexcited
40. trivial	A	B	C	D	E	important

V. Your best friend has just become engaged to a Black person.

41. aggressive	A	B	C	D	E	passive
42. happy	A	B	C	D	E	sad
43. tolerable	A	B	C	D	E	intolerable
44. complimented	A	B	C	D	E	insulted
45. angered	A	B	C	D	E	overjoyed
46. secure	A	B	C	D	E	fearful
47. hopeful	A	B	C	D	E	hopeless
48. excited	A	B	C	D	E	unexcited
49. right	A	B	C	D	E	wrong
50. disgusting	A	B	C	D	E	pleasing

VI. You are stopped for speeding by a Black policeman.

51. calm	A	B	C	D	E	nervous
52. trusting	A	B	C	D	E	suspicious
53. afraid	A	B	C	D	E	safe
54. friendly	A	B	C	D	E	unfriendly
55. tolerant	A	B	C	D	E	intolerant
56. bitter	A	B	C	D	E	pleasant
57. cooperative	A	B	C	D	E	uncooperative
58. acceptable	A	B	C	D	E	belligerent
59. inferior	A	B	C	D	E	superior
60. smarter	A	B	C	D	E	dumber

VII. A new Black person joins your social group.

61. warm	A	B	C	D	E	cold
62. sad	A	B	C	D	E	happy

63. superior	A	B	C	D	E	inferior
64. threatened	A	B	C	D	E	neutral
65. pleased	A	B	C	D	E	displeased
66. understanding	A	B	C	D	E	indifferent
67. suspicious	A	B	C	D	E	trusting
68. disappointed	A	B	C	D	E	elated
69. favorable	A	B	C	D	E	unfavorable
70. uncomfortable	A	B	C	D	E	comfortable

VIII. You see a Black youngster steal something in a dime store.

71. surprising	A	B	C	D	E	not surprising
72. sad	A	B	C	D	E	happy
73. disinterested	A	B	C	D	E	interested
74. close	A	B	C	D	E	distant
75. understandable	A	B	C	D	E	baffling
76. responsible	A	B	C	D	E	not responsible
77. concerned	A	B	C	D	E	unconcerned
78. sympathy	A	B	C	D	E	indifference
79. expected	A	B	C	D	E	unexpected
80. hopeful	A	B	C	D	E	hopeless

IX. Some Black students on campus stage a demonstration.

81. bad	A	B	C	D	E	good
82. understanding	A	B	C	D	E	indifferent
83. suspicious	A	B	C	D	E	trusting
84. safe	A	B	C	D	E	unsafe
85. disturbed	A	B	C	D	E	undisturbed
86. justified	A	B	C	D	E	unjustified
87. tense	A	B	C	D	E	calm
88. hate	A	B	C	D	E	love
89. wrong	A	B	C	D	E	right
90. humorous	A	B	C	D	E	serious

X. You get on a bus that has all Black people aboard and you are the only person who has to stand.

91. fearful	A	B	C	D	E	secure
92. tolerable	A	B	C	D	E	intolerable
93. hostile	A	B	C	D	E	indifferent
94. important	A	B	C	D	E	trivial

95. conspicuous	A	B	C	D	E	inconspicuous
96. calm	A	B	C	D	E	anxious
97. indignant	A	B	C	D	E	understanding
98. comfortable	A	B	C	D	E	uncomfortable
99. hate	A	B	C	D	E	love
100. not resentful	A	B	C	D	E	resentful

101. Blacken in the appropriate box to indicate your religion or religious preference:
    ☐ Catholic   ☐ None
    ☐ Jewish   ☐ Other
    ☐ Protestant

102. Blacken in the appropriate box to indicate your sex:
    ☐ Female   ☐ Male

103. Blacken in the appropriate box to indicate your age:
    ☐ Under 17 years old   ☐ 19 years old
    ☐ 17 years old   ☐ Over 19 years old
    ☐ 18 years old

104. *Father's Occupation:* Which of the following comes close to describing your father's occupation? Mark only one answer. If he works on more than one job, mark the most important one. If he is temporarily unemployed, deceased, or if he is retired, mark the one he held last. If your father never held a formal job, leave the item blank.
    A. Professional—such as clergyman, dentist, doctor, engineer, lawyer, professor, scientist, or teacher.
    B. Semiprofessional—such as accountant, airplane pilot, actor, armed forces officer, medical technician, musician, writer, librarian, artist, dental technician, or engineering aid. Manager-Proprietor-Executive—such as sales manager, store manager, owner of small business, factory supervisor, wholesaler, retailer, contractor, restaurant owner, manufacturer, banker, official in a large company, or government official.

C. Salesperson—such as life insurance, real estate or industrial goods salesperson. Clerical Worker—such as sales clerk, office clerk, bookkeeper, or ticket agent.

D. Skilled Worker or Foreperson—such as baker, carpenter, plasterer, electrician, mechanic, plumber, tailor, farm or ranch owner or manager.

E. Service or Protective—such as armed forces enlistee or noncommissioned officer, barber, beautician, bus driver, fire fighter, police officer, or waiter.

105. The father's occupation above represents:
☐ full-time work   ☐ part-time work

106. *Mother's Occupation*—Please use the same options found in question 104 to describe your mother's occupation. If your mother has never held a formal job, leave the item blank.

107. The mother's occupation described above represents:
☐ full-time work   ☐ part-time work

108. Blacken in the appropriate box to indicate your race:
☐ Black (Afro-American, Negro)
☐ White (Caucasian)
☐ Oriental (Asian American)
☐ American Indian (Native American)
☐ Spanish surname

The Social Scale and Social Scenarios Scale

To measure contemporary racial attitudes, Deborah Byrnes and Gary Kiger (1988) developed two companion scales called the Social Scale and the Social Scenarios Scale. The Social Scale is a revision of Bogardus' old Social Distance Scale (1933), and the Social Scenarios Scale is adapted from Kogan and Downey's the Social Situations Scale (1956). The purpose of the Social Scale is to assess the degree of discomfort people experience when they encounter African Americans in positions of power or when they experience intimacy with them in activities of everyday life. The Social Scenarios Scale is designed to measure the willingness of non-Blacks to confront prejudice and discrimination in various social situations.

Social Scale

There are eight statements on the Social Scale. The total scores range from 7–56. Respondents rate these statements from 1 = *very uncomfortable* to 7 = *very comfortable* while answering these statements.

I believe I would be happy to have a Black person

	Very Uncomfortable				Very Comfortable		
1. as governor of my state.	1	2	3	4	5	6	7
2. as president of the U.S.	1	2	3	4	5	6	7
3. as my personal physician.	1	2	3	4	5	6	7
4. rent my home from me.	1	2	3	4	5	6	7
5. as my spiritual counselor.	1	2	3	4	5	6	7
6. as my roommate.	1	2	3	4	5	6	7
7. as someone I would date.	1	2	3	4	5	6	7
8. as a dance partner.	1	2	3	4	5	6	7

Social Scenarios Scale

1. Imagine that as you are sitting in your parents' home one day, a neighbor comes in to ask your parents to sign a letter to a neighbor discouraging her from renting or selling her house to Blacks. He explains that it would not hurt Blacks, because there are plenty of other good places in town to live. He says keeping Blacks out would keep the value of all the houses in the neighborhood high. Your folks are about to sign the letter. Under these conditions,

   ☐ I would insist that they were wrong and try to persuade them not to sign the petition.

   ☐ I would probably tell my parents that I didn't think that they were doing the right thing.

   ☐ I would probably keep quiet because it wouldn't make much difference to me one way or another.

   ☐ I would understand their reasons for signing the letter, so I wouldn't say anything.

2. Imagine you have just arrived in a large city and have a heavy suitcase to carry from the bus terminal to your hotel a few blocks away. You decide to take a cab. Waiting on the corner for a cab, you glance across the street and see a Black person also waiting for a cab. After a few minutes, a cab comes by and both of you signal for it. The cab goes right by the Black person, turns around, and comes back to pick you up. When the driver opens the door, he remarks, "I really saw that Black fellow first, but I always go by the rule that you should take care of your own first." Under these conditions,

   ☐ I would figure the cabbie has good reasons for his behavior.

   ☐ would probably get into the cab without saying or doing anything.

   ☐ I would let the driver know nonverbally that I didn't like what he said.

   ☐ I would definitely tell the cabbie that he had done the wrong thing.

3. Imagine that in one of your classes your instructor has broken the class into small groups to discuss race relations. One of the students in your group says it would be great if Blacks and

Whites got along better but they shouldn't go so far as to inter-marry and have children. Under these conditions,

☐ I would voice my disagreement with the student.

☐ I would disagree with the student but not say anything.

☐ I would agree with the student but not say anything.

☐ I would voice my agreement with the student.

4. Imagine you and your friend are in a small store waiting to make a purchase. Across the aisle, a White person is asking the manager about a sales position that is open. He is given an application to complete and return. Several minutes later a Black person approaches the manager about the same job opening and he is told the position has already been filled. Under these conditions,

☐ I would confront the manager about his discriminatory actions and tell him I was taking my business elsewhere.

☐ I would make my purchase and would probably write a letter of complaint to the manager.

☐ I would stay out of it because it wouldn't make that much difference to me one way or the other.

☐ I would feel it is the right of the management to reject Black employees if they want.

5. Imagine that you have a 19-year-old brother who has been going pretty steadily with a young Black woman for the past month or so. Although your parents admit she is very nice, they have been trying to force your brother to stop taking her out because they are afraid that they might get serious about each other. Your parents don't mind him having her as a friend, but they don't want him to date her or call her his girlfriend. One night, during an argument, when your brother is present, your parents ask you what you think. Under these conditions,

☐ I would disagree with my parents and say that, as long as she was a nice person, it was O.K.

☐ I would probably disagree with my parents, but I'd try to keep out of it.

☐ I would probably tend to side with my parents.

☐ I would definitely side with my parents.

6. Imagine that you are visiting with several good friends, chatting and sharing humorous stories. One of your friends tells a joke about Blacks using the word *nigger*. Under these conditions,

☐ I wouldn't say anything, and would think that it was a harmless joke.

☐ I probably wouldn't say anything, but I would feel uncomfortable.

☐ I would probably say it wasn't a very good joke.

☐ I would criticize him for telling such a joke.

7. Imagine you are standing in line at the movies waiting for the theater to empty. The person in front of you, pointing at a Black man and a White women holding hands as they walk out of the theater, turned to you and says, "Isn't that disgusting?" Under these conditions,

☐ I would speak up and say, "No, it doesn't bother me."

☐ I would feel uncomfortable with his comment, and I would probably give the person a disapproving look.

☐ I would probably agree with him, but I wouldn't say anything back to him.

☐ I would agree with the person.

8. Imagine you and some friends are talking about living arrangements for the next school quarter. One of your friends says with great disgust that he was assigned a dorm room with "some Black guy. " Under these conditions,

☐ I would tell him I found his attitude offensive.

☐ I would disapprove of his attitude, but I wouldn't say anything.

☐ I would figure that's just his opinion and he has a right to it.

☐ I would understand why he didn't like the idea.

9. Imagine that several co-workers at your job are Black. You notice that they tend to get the worst job assignments and they don't get promoted as often as the other workers. Under these conditions,

☐ I would feel the supervisor knows what's right.

☐ I wouldn't want to create problems, so I would probably stay out of the situation.

☐ I would express my concerns to my Black co-workers.

☐ I would go to the next higher supervisor and tell him or her what was going on.

10. Imagine you are a member of a casting committee for a drama club that is in the process of casting parts for a tragic play

about two young lovers. The casting committee is in complete agreement that the male lead should go to Sam Olsen. Clearly, the best actress for the part of the heroine is a beautiful young Black woman. However, a number of the members of the casting committee refuse to have a Black actress play opposite a White actor in a romantic play. Under these conditions:

- ☐ I would say that if they refuse to give the part to the most qualified actress I would resign from the committee.
- ☐ I would say that the actress should be judged on her talent and not her skin color; but I would go along with any decision the majority made.
- ☐ I wouldn't know what to do so I'd go along with whatever the majority wanted.
- ☐ I wouldn't side with those who felt that regardless of the talent issue it would not be a good idea to cast a biracial couple.

11. Imagine you are looking for an apartment to rent that you saw advertised in the newspaper. You stop a stranger who is watering his lawn to ask for directions. The person you have stopped gives you the directions but says, "You don't want to live there, that place is full of coloreds." Under these conditions,

- ☐ I would tell him that what color the people were who live there didn't make any difference to me.
- ☐ I would be offended by his comment, but I wouldn't say anything.
- ☐ I wouldn't respond to his comment, but if he was right I probably wouldn't rent it.
- ☐ I would thank him for his advice and I would no longer consider living in that apartment building.

12. Imagine you are having dinner with your parents and a well-respected friend of your parents. During dinner everyone is chatting about different sports players. At this point, your parents' friend states, "It's a good thing coloreds are good at sports because they sure aren't good at much of anything else." Under these conditions,

- ☐ I would nod agreement.
- ☐ I would ignore the comment, not wanting to make an issue of it.

☐ I would probably noticeably scowl, but I wouldn't say anything.

☐ I would tell my parents' friend that I was offended by his
comment.

Note. From Deborah Byrnes and Gary Kiger, *Educational and Psychological Measurement, 48,*
107–118. © 1988 by Sage Publications. Reprinted by permission of Sage Publications, Inc.

Scoring and Reliability Coefficients

The Social Scale is scored as a semantic differential scale by
adding the scores for each statement. The lowest total scores are
indicative of discomfort the respondent experiences encounter-
ing a Black person in a position of power or authority. Byrnes
and Kiger (1988) reported the Cronbach's alpha reliability coefficient for the Social Scale as .90. The test-retest correlations coefficients of this scale were .94.

The Social Scenario Scale is scored as following: The respondents are asked to select one of four given responses. The lower
scores mean less antidiscriminatory answers. The reliability of
this scale is reported as alpha = .75 and test–retest correlation
coefficients as .93.

The Social Scale and Social Scenarios Scale for Chinese Americans

The Social Scale and Social Scenarios Scale for Chinese Americans was adapted with permission from Byrnes and Kiger's (1988) revised scales. This newly developed scale is designed to study the psychodynamics of prejudice against an Asian minority group, a newly recognized minority. The main purpose of developing this new scale is to keep up with the current concerns of discrimination in our society and to further explore if and why Chinese Americans face more discrimination than other ethnic minorities in America. This scale is scored as described earlier in Byrnes and Kiger's (1988) scales.

The Social Scale for Chinese Americans

I believe I would be happy to have a Chinese person:

		Very Uncomfortable				Very Comfortable	
1.	as governor of my state.	1	2	3	4	5	6	7
2.	as president of the U.S.	1	2	3	4	5	6	7
3.	as my personal physician.	1	2	3	4	5	6	7
4.	rent my home from me.	1	2	3	4	5	6	7
5.	as my spiritual counselor.	1	2	3	4	5	6	7
6.	as my roommate.	1	2	3	4	5	6	7
7.	as someone I would date.	1	2	3	4	5	6	7
8.	as a dance partner.	1	2	3	4	5	6	7

Social Scenarios Scale for Chinese Americans

1. Imagine that as you are sitting in your parents' home one day, a neighbor comes in to ask your parents to sign a letter to a neighbor discouraging her from renting or selling her house to a Chinese couple. He explains that it would not hurt Chinese people because there are plenty of other good places in town to live. He says keeping Chinese out would keep the value of all the houses in the neighborhood high Your folks are about to sign the letter. Under these conditions,

   ☐ I would insist that they were wrong and try to persuade them not to sign the petition.

☐ I would probably tell my parents that I didn't think that they were doing the right thing.

☐ I would probably keep quiet because it wouldn't make much difference to me one way or another.

☐ I would understand their reasons for signing the letter, so I wouldn't say anything.

2. Imagine you have just arrived in a large city and have a heavy suitcase to carry from the bus terminal to your hotel a few blocks away. You decide to take a cab. Waiting on the corner for a cab, you glance across the street and see a Chinese person also waiting for a cab. After a few minutes, a cab comes by and both of you signal for it. The cab goes right by the Chinese person, turns around, and comes back to pick you up. When the driver opens the door, he remarks, "I really saw the Chinese fellow first, but I always go by the rule that you should take care of your own first." Under these conditions,

☐ I would figure the cabbie has good reasons for his behavior.

☐ I would probably get into the cab without saying or doing anything.

☐ I would let the driver know nonverbally that I didn't like what he said.

☐ I would definitely tell the cabbie that he had done the wrong thing.

3. Imagine that in one of your classes your instructor has broken the class into small groups to discuss race relations. One of the students in your group says it would be great if Chinese and Whites got along better but they shouldn't go so far as to intermarry and have children. Under these conditions,

☐ I would voice my disagreement with the student.

☐ I would disagree with the student but not say anything.

☐ I would agree with the student but not say anything.

☐ I would voice my agreement with the student.

4. Imagine you and your friend are in a small store waiting to make a purchase. Across the aisle, a White person is asking the manager about a sales position that is open. He is given an application to complete and return. Several minutes later a Chinese person approaches the manager about the same job

opening and he is told the position has already been filled. Under these conditions,

☐ I would confront the manager about his discriminatory actions and tell him I was taking my business elsewhere.

☐ I would make my purchase and would probably write a letter of complaint to the manager.

☐ I would stay out of it because it wouldn't make that much difference to me one way or the other.

☐ I would feel it is the right of the management to reject Chinese employees if they want.

5. Imagine that you have a 19-year-old brother who has been going pretty steadily with a young Chinese woman for the past month or so. Although your parents admit she is very nice, they have been trying to force your brother to stop taking her out because they are afraid that they might get serious about each other. Your parents don't mind him having her as a friend, but they don't want him to date her or call her his girlfriend. One night, during an argument, when your brother is present, your parents ask you what you think. Under these conditions,

☐ I would disagree with my parents and say that, as long as she was a nice person, it was O.K.

☐ I would probably disagree with my parents, but I'd try to keep out of it.

☐ I would probably tend to side with my parents.

☐ I would definitely side with my parents.

6. Imagine that you are visiting with several good friends, chatting and sharing humorous stories. One of your friends tells a joke about Chinese people using the term slant eyes. Under these conditions,

☐ I wouldn't say anything, and would think that it was a harmless joke.

☐ I probably wouldn't say anything, but I would feel uncomfortable.

☐ I would probably say it wasn't a very good joke.

☐ I would criticize him for telling such a joke.

7. Imagine you are standing in line at the movies waiting for the theater to empty. The person in front of you, pointing at a Chinese man and a White women holding hands as they

walk out of the theater, turned to you and says, "Isn't that disgusting?" Under these conditions,

- ☐ I would speak up and say, "No, it doesn't bother me."
- ☐ I would feel uncomfortable with his comment and I would probably give the person a disapproving look.
- ☐ I would probably agree with him, but I wouldn't say anything back to him.
- ☐ I would agree with the person.

8. Imagine you and some friends are talking about living arrangements for the next quarter. One of your friends says with great disgust that he was assigned a dorm room with "some Chinese guy." Under these conditions,

- ☐ I would tell him I found his attitude offensive.
- ☐ I would disapprove of his attitude, but I wouldn't say anything.
- ☐ I would figure that's just his opinion and he has a right to it.
- ☐ I would understand why he didn't like the idea.

9. Imagine that several co-workers at your job are Chinese. You notice that they tend to get the worst job assignments and they don't get promoted as often as the other workers. Under these conditions,

- ☐ I would feel the supervisor knows what's right.
- ☐ I wouldn't want to create problems, so I would probably stay out of the situation.
- ☐ I would express my concerns to my Chinese co-workers.
- ☐ I would go to the next higher supervisor and tell her or him what was going on.

10. Imagine you are a member of a casting committee for a drama club that is in the process of casting parts for a tragic play about two young lovers. The casting committee is in complete agreement that the male lead should go to Sam Olsen. Clearly, the best actress for the part of the heroine is a beautiful young Chinese woman. However, a number of the members of the casting committee refuse to have a Chinese actress play opposite a White actor in a romantic play. Under these conditions,

- ☐ I would say that if they refuse to give the part to the most qualified actress I would resign from the committee.

☐ I would say that the actress should be judged on her talent and not her skin color; but I would go along with any decision the majority made.

☐ I wouldn't know what to do, so I'd go along with whatever the majority wanted.

☐ I wouldn't side with those who felt that regardless of the talent issue it would not be a good idea to cast a biracial couple.

11. Imagine you are looking for an apartment to rent that you saw advertised in the newspaper. You stop a stranger who is watering his lawn to ask for directions. The person you have stopped gives you the directions but says, "You don't want to live there, that place is full of Chinese." Under these conditions,

☐ I would tell him that what color the people were who live there didn't make any difference to me.

☐ I would be offended by his comment, but I wouldn't say anything.

☐ I wouldn't respond to his comment, but if he was right I probably wouldn't rent it.

☐ I would thank him for his advice, and I would no longer consider living in that apartment building.

12. Imagine you are having dinner with your parents and a well-respected friend of your parents. During dinner your parents' friend makes a remark about how Chinese people aren't good at much of anything. Under these conditions,

☐ I would nod agreement.

☐ I would ignore the comment, not wanting to make an issue of it.

☐ I would probably noticeably scowl, but I wouldn't say anything.

☐ I would tell my parents' friend that I was offended by his comment.

From Byrnes and Kiger (1988). Adapted with permission.

SCORING INFORMATION
The Social Scale for Chinese Americans has a Cronbach's alpha coefficient of .96.

Factor 1: Authoritative/Prestigious Positions (distant relationships)
Items 1, 2, 3, 5 (score range 4 to 28)

Factor 2: Close Relationships
Items 4, 6, 7, 8 (score range = 4 to 28)

The Social Scale and Social Scenarios Scale for Gay Men and Lesbians

The Social Scale and Social Scenarios Scale for Gay Men and Lesbians was adapted with permission from Byrnes and Kiger's (1988) revised scales. This newly developed scale is designed to study the psychodynamics of prejudice against a Gay minority group, a newly recognized minority. The main purpose of developing this new scale is to keep up with the current concerns of discrimination in our society and to further explore if and why gay men and lesbians face more discrimination than other minorities in America. This scale is scored as described earlier in Byrnes and Kiger's (1988) scales.

The Social Scale for Gay Men and Lesbians
I believe I would be happy to have a lesbian or gay man:

		Very Uncomfortable				Very Comfortable	
1.	as governor of my state.	1	2	3	4	5	6	7
2.	as president of the U.S.	1	2	3	4	5	6	7
3.	as my personal physician.	1	2	3	4	5	6	7
4.	rent my home from me.	1	2	3	4	5	6	7
5.	as my spiritual counselor.	1	2	3	4.	5	6	7
6.	as my roommate.	1	2	3	4	5	6	7
7.	as someone I would date.	1	2	3	4	5	6	7
8.	as a dance partner.	1	2	3	4	5	6	7

Social Scenarios Scale for Gay Men and Lesbians

1. Imagine that as you are sitting in your parents' home one day, a neighbor comes in to ask your parents to sign a letter to a neighbor discouraging her from renting or selling her house to lesbians or gay men. He explains that it would not hurt them, because there are plenty of other good places in town to live. He says keeping gays out would keep the value of all the houses in the neighborhood high. Your folks are about to sign the letter. Under these conditions,

   ☐ I would insist that they were wrong and try to persuade them not to sign the petition.

☐ I would probably tell my parents that I didn't think that they were doing the right thing.

☐ I would probably keep quiet because it wouldn't make much difference to me one way or another.

☐ I would understand their reasons for signing the letter, so I wouldn't say anything.

2. Imagine you have just arrived in a large city and have a heavy suitcase to carry from the bus terminal to your hotel a few blocks away. You decide to take a cab. Waiting on the corner for a cab, you glance across the street and see a two men holding hands also waiting for a cab. After a few minutes, a cab comes by and both of you signal for it. The cab goes right by the gay couple, turns around, and comes back to pick you up. When the driver opens the door, he remarks, "I really saw the gay men first, but I decided to pick you up first rather than those queers." Under these conditions,

☐ I would figure the cabbie has good reasons for his behavior.

☐ I would probably get into the cab without saying or doing anything.

☐ I would let the driver know nonverbally that I didn't like what he said.

☐ I would definitely tell the cabbie that he had done the wrong thing.

3. Imagine that in one of your classes your instructor has broken the class into small groups to discuss sexual orientation issues. One of the students in your group says, "I don't mind that some people are gay, but they shouldn't go so far as to marry and adopt children." Under these conditions,

☐ I would voice my disagreement with the student.

☐ I would disagree with the student but not say anything.

☐ I would agree with the student but not say anything.

☐ I would voice my agreement with the student.

4. Imagine you and your friend are in a small store waiting to make a purchase. Across the aisle, a person is asking the manager about a sales position that is open. He is given an application to complete and return. Several minutes later two men holding hands approach the manager about the same job

opening and are told the position has already been filled. Under these conditions,

☐ I would confront the manager about his discriminatory actions and tell him I was taking my business elsewhere.

☐ I would make my purchase and would probably write a letter of complaint to the manager.

☐ I would stay out of it because it wouldn't make that much difference to me one way or the other.

☐ I would feel it is the right of the management to reject gay employees if they want.

5. Imagine that you have a 19-year-old brother who has been going pretty steadily with another 19-year-old man for the past month or so. Although your parents admit he is very nice, they have been trying to force your brother to stop going out with him because they are afraid that they might get serious. Your parents don't mind your brother having him as a friend, but they don't want him to develop a homosexual relationship. One night, during an argument, when your brother is present, your parents ask you what you think. Under these conditions,

☐ I would disagree with my parents and say that, as long as he was a nice person, it was O.K.

☐ I would probably disagree with my parents, but I'd try to keep out of it.

☐ I would probably tend to side with my parents.

☐ I would definitely side with my parents.

6. Imagine that you are visiting with several good friends, chatting and sharing humorous stories. One of your friends tells a joke about gay men using the term "faggot." Under these conditions,

☐ I wouldn't say anything, and would think that it was a harmless joke.

☐ I probably wouldn't say anything, but I would feel uncomfortable.

☐ I would probably say it wasn't a very good joke.

☐ I would criticize him for telling such a joke.

7. Imagine you are standing in line at the movies waiting for the theater to empty. The person in front of you, pointing at two

men holding hands as they walk out of the theater, turns to you and says, "Isn't that disgusting?" Under these conditions,

☐ I would speak up and say, "No, it doesn't bother me."

☐ I would feel uncomfortable with his comment and I would probably give the person a disapproving look.

☐ I would probably agree with him, but I wouldn't say anything back to him.

☐ I would agree with the person.

8. Imagine you and some friends are talking about living arrangements for the next school quarter. One of your friends says with great disgust that he was assigned a dorm room with someone he suspects to be gay. Under these conditions,

☐ I would tell him I found his attitude offensive.

☐ I would disapprove of his attitude, but I wouldn't say anything.

☐ I would figure that's just his opinion and he has a right to it.

☐ I would understand why he didn't like the idea.

9. Imagine that several co-workers at your job are gay. You notice that they tend to get the worst job assignments and they don't get promoted as often as the others workers. Under these conditions,

☐ I would feel the supervisor knows what's right.

☐ I wouldn't want to create problems, so I would probably stay out of the situation.

☐ I would express my concerns to my gay co-workers.

☐ I would go to the next higher supervisor and tell her or him what was going on.

10. Imagine you are a member of a casting committee for a drama club that is in the process of casting parts for a tragic play about two young lovers. The casting committee is in complete agreement that the male lead should go to Sam Olsen. Clearly, the best actress for the part of the heroine is a beautiful young woman. However, a number of the members of the casting committee refuse to have this actress, whom they suspect to be a lesbian. Under these conditions,

☐ I would say that if they refuse to give the part to the most qualified actress I would resign from the committee.

☐ I would say that the actress should be judged on her talent, not her sexual orientation; but I would go along with any decision the majority made.

☐ I wouldn't know what to do, so I'd go along with whatever the majority wanted.

☐ I wouldn't side with those who felt that regardless of the talent issue it would not be a good idea to cast a lesbian actress.

11. Imagine you are looking for an apartment to rent that you saw advertised in the newspaper. You stop a stranger who is watering his lawn to ask for directions. The person you have stopped gives you the directions but says, "You don't want to live there, that place is full of homosexuals." Under these conditions,

☐ I would tell him whether gay people live there didn't make any difference to me.

☐ I would be offended by his comment, but I wouldn't say anything.

☐ I wouldn't respond to his comment, but if he was right I probably wouldn't rent it.

☐ I would thank him for his advice, and I would no longer consider living in that apartment building.

12. Imagine you are having dinner with your parents and a well-respected friend of your parents. During dinner your parents' friend makes remarks that gay people aren't good at much of anything. Under these conditions,

☐ I would nod agreement.

☐ I would ignore the comment, not wanting to make an issue of it.

☐ I would probably noticeably scowl, but I wouldn't say anything.

☐ I would tell my parents' friend that I was offended by his comment

---

From Byrnes and Kiger (1988). Adapted with permission.

SCORING INFORMATION
The Social Scale for Gay Men and Lesbians has a Cronbach's alpha of .96.

Factor 1: Visible Authority Positions
Items 1 and 2 (score range 2–14)

Factor 2: Intimate Relationships
Items 3, 4, 5, 6, 7, and 8 (score range 6–42)

The Social Scenarios Scale for Gay Men and Lesbians has a Cronbach's alpha of .92.

Factor 1: Antigayism
Items 10, 4, 12, 6, 2, 1, 9, 8, and 11 (score range 9–36)

Factor 2: Anti-Gay Relationships
Items 5, 3, and 7 (score range 3–12)

White Racial Identity Attitude Scale

This questionnaire is designed to measure people's social and political attitudes. There are no right or wrong answers. Use the scale below to respond to each statement. On your answer sheet beside each item number, write the number that best describes how you feel.

1 = Strongly disagree   4 = Agree
2 = Disagree   5 = Strongly agree
3 = Uncertain

1. I hardly think about what race I am.
2. I do not understand what Blacks want from Whites.
3. I get angry when I think about how Whites have been treated by Blacks.
4. I feel as comfortable around Blacks as I do around Whites.
5. I involve myself in causes regardless of the race of the people involved in them.
6. I find myself watching Black people to see what they are like.
7. I feel depressed after I have been around Black people.
8. There is nothing that I want to learn from Blacks.
9. I seek out new experiences even if I know a large number of Blacks will be involved in them.
10. I enjoy watching the different ways that Blacks and Whites approach life.
11. I wish I had a Black friend.
12. I do not feel that I have the social skills to interact with Black people effectively.
13. A Black person who tries to get close to you is usually after something.
14. When a Black person holds an opinion with which I disagree, I am not afraid to express my viewpoint.
15. Sometimes jokes based on Black people's experiences are funny.
16. I think it is exciting to discover the little ways in which Black people and White people are different.

17. I used to believe in racial integration, but now I have my doubts.
18. I'd rather socialize with Whites only.
19. In many ways Blacks and Whites are similar, but they are also different in some important ways.
20. Blacks and Whites have much to learn from each other.
21. For most of my life, I did not think about racial issues.
22. I have come to believe that Black people and White people are very different.
23. White people have bent over backwards trying to make up for their ancestors' mistreatment of Blacks; now it is time to stop.
24. It is possible for Blacks and Whites to have meaningful social relationships with each other.
25. There are some valuable things that White people can learn from Blacks that they can't learn from other Whites.
26. I am curious to learn in what ways Black people and White people differ from each other.
27. I limit myself to White activities.
28. Society may have been unjust to Blacks, but it has also been unjust to Whites.
29. I am knowledgeable about which values Blacks and Whites share.
30. I am comfortable wherever I am.
31. In my family, we never talked about racial issues.
32. When I must interact with a Black person, I usually let him or her make the first move.
33. I feel hostile when I am around Blacks.
34. I think I understand Black people's values.
35. Blacks and Whites can have successful intimate relationships.
36. I was raised to believe that people are people regardless of their race.
37. Nowadays, I go out of my way to avoid associating with Blacks.
38. I believe that Blacks are inferior to Whites.
39. I believe I know a lot about Black people's customs.
40. There are some valuable things that White people can learn from Blacks that they can't learn from other Whites.

41. I think that it's okay for Black people and White people to date each other as long as they don't marry each other.
42. Sometimes I'm not sure what I think or feel about Black people.
43. When I am the only White in a group of Blacks, I feel anxious.
44. Blacks and Whites differ from each other in some ways, but neither race is superior.
45. I am not embarrassed to admit that I am White.
46. I think White people should become more involved in socializing with Blacks.
47. I don't understand why Black people blame all White people for their social misfortunes.
48. I believe that White people look and express themselves better than Blacks.
49. I feel comfortable talking to Blacks.
50. I value the relationships that I have with my Black friends.

Note. Janet E. Helms, *Black and White Identity: Theory, research, and practice*, reprinted with permission of Greenwood Publishing Group, Inc., Westport, CT. © 1990.

Workplace Perceived Prejudice Scale

The Workplace Perceived Prejudice Scale is constructed to measure the prevalence of racism, sexism, and heterosexism in the workplace. The WPPS consists of three Likert-type subscales. Responses range from 1 = *strongly disagree*, 2 = *disagree*, 3 = *not sure*, 4 = *agree*, to 5 = *strongly agree*. Each of these subscales with their factors and Cronbach's alpha relibilities are presented.

SCORING METHODS

Two different methods for scoring can be used. A cumulative score on all statements would suggest workplace perceived prejudice in general. These scores range from 44–220. The second and preferable method is to calculate scores for all three subscales separately.

Workplace Perceived Prejudice Scale

Subscale 1: Perceived Racism in the Workplace (Cronbach's alpha =.83)

Factor 1: White Men's Perceptions (Cronbach's alpha = .91)

1. Affirmative action is a reverse discrimination against White people.
2. Affirmative action should be eliminated.
3. The job requirements for people of color are lowered or changed so they may acquire the jobs more easily than Whites.
4. In today's society, White men are the most discriminated against.
5. Whites are more likely to be the victims of discrimination on the job than workers from other ethnic groups.
6. African Americans can "get away" with discrimination toward other races/ethnic groups.
7. Bosses allow leniency in rules when it comes to minorities.

8. Minorities have a greater chance of being hired than do White men.
9. Being overly sensitive to racial issues, people from minority groups exaggerate their problems in the workplace.

Factor 2: Minorities' Perceptions (Cronbach's alpha = .73)
1. Opportunities for higher level jobs are more available to White men than men from minority groups.
2. Discrimination against minority members is a serious problem in the workplace.
3. Many White men are unhappy about advantages given to minorities in the workplace.
4. Bosses from minority groups are less respected.
5. Members of minorities have to work harder than their White counterparts to keep their jobs.
6. Workers from minority groups should be paid more to make up for past injustices.

Subscale 2: Perceived Sexism in the Workplace (Cronbach's alpha = .81)
Factor 1: Women in Authority Positions (Cronbach's alpha = .92)
1. To avoid management problems, it is better that women work separately from men.
2. Women should not become bosses.
3. For their own benefit, it is better for women to remain in their traditional professions.
4. Men are better authority figures than women.
5. Women overreact about sexual harassment to control men.

Factor 2: Work-Related Gender Bias (exploitation of women) (Cronbach's alpha = .67)
1. For the same job, women are generally paid less than men.
2. Women often are given more responsibilities than men when employed in the same job.
3. The concept of equal pay for equal work does not seem to apply to women in the workplace.
4. Women have to be more aggressive than men to get ahead in the workplace.

5. Women are more "tolerated" than respected by males in the workplace.

Factor 3: Sexual Attraction (Cronbach's alpha = .79)
1. Physical attractiveness affects job placement and pay.
2. Sexual attraction is an important issue in the workplace.
3. Women workers generally face more sexual harassment than men.
4. Most male employers look at the physical attractiveness of a woman before hiring her for a job.
5. Male supervisors generally prefer working with and favor women over men.
6. A male boss has more empathy for female employees than for male employees.

Subscale 3: Perceived Discrimination Against Gay Men and Lesbians (Cronbach's alpha = .78)

Factor 1: Gay Identity at Workplace (Cronbach's alpha = .80)
1. Gay men and lesbians should not be hired for certain jobs.
2. Gay men and lesbians should only work around "their kind."
3. Gay men and lesbians reveal their sexual orientation to demand special privileges in their workplace.
4. Gay men and lesbians reveal their sexual orientation to promote their life style in their work settings.

Factor 2: Heterosexism (Cronbach's alpha = .73)
1. A person that is known to be gay receives more "grief" in the workplace.
2. Gay men and lesbians are treated differently (harassed) more than other minority groups in the workplace.
3. Gay co-workers are perceived as inferior.
4. A gay boss is less respected.
5. Open knowledge about gay men and lesbians causes morale problems in the workplace.
6. Gay men and lesbians have to work harder than their co-workers to keep their jobs.

Factor 3: Gay Visibility (Cronbach's alpha = .69)
1. Gay men and lesbians should keep their sexual orientation to themselves.
2. One's sexual orientation should not be disclosed at the workplace.
3. Preference in sexuality should be left out of the workplace.

TABLE 6

Information About Scales

Scales	Authors	Contact Person and Address
Acculturative Stress Scale for International Students	Daya Singh Sandhu and Badiolah R. Asrabadi	Daya Singh Sandhu, Chair and Associate Professor Department of Educational and Counseling Psychology 320 Education Building University of Louisville Louisville, KY 40292
Adult Life Satisfaction Scale	Daya Singh Sandhu, Joe Petrosko, and Pedro Portes	Same
Cultural Adaptation Pain Scale	Daya Singh Sandhu, Pedro Portes, and Sidney McPhee	Same
Past Prejudice Affliction Scale	Daya Singh Sandhu and Cheryl B. Aspy	Same
Social Scale–Revised (Chinese Americans, Gay Men and Lesbians)	Daya Singh Sandhu and Cheryl B. Aspy	Same
Social Scenarios Scale–Revised (Chinese Americans, Gay Men and Lesbians)	Daya Singh Sandhu and Cheryl B. Aspy	Same
Black Racial Identity Attitudes Scale (Form RIAS-B)	Janet E. Helms and Thomas A. Parham	Janet E. Helms, Professor Department of Psychology University of Maryland College Park, MD 20742

TABLE 6 continued

Information About Scales

Scales	Authors	Contact Person and Address
White Racial Identity Attitudes Scale (WRIAS)	Janet E. Helms and Robert T. Carter	Same
Quick Discrimination Index (QDI)	Joseph G. Ponterotto	Joseph G. Ponterotto, Chair and Professor Department of Counseling Psychology, Graduate School of Education at Lincoln Center Fordham University New York, NY 10023
Situational Attitude Scale	William Sedlacek and Glenwood C. Brooks	William E. Sedlacek, Professor Counseling Center University of Maryland College Park, MD 20742
Social Scale and Social Scenarios Scale	Deborah A. Byrnes and Gary Kiger	Deborah A. Byrnes, Professor Department of Elementary Education Utah State University Logan, UT 84322-2805

References

Aboud, F. E. (1987). The development of ethnic self-identification and attitudes. In J. D. Phinney & M. J. Rothman (Eds.), *Children's ethnic socialization: Pluralism and development.* Newbury Park, CA: Sage.

Adler, J. (1995, July 31). The rise of the overclass. *Newsweek*, p. 33.

Alexander, A. L. (1995). "She's no lady, she's a nigger": Abuses, stereotypes and realities from the middle passage to Capitol (and Anita) Hill. In A. Hill & E. C. Jordan, (Eds.), *Race, gender, and power in America: The legacy of the Hill-Thomas hearing* (pp. 3–25). New York: Oxford University.

Allport, G. W. (1979). *The nature of prejudice* (25th anniversary ed.). Reading, MA: Addison-Wesley.

Allport, G. W. (1954). *The nature of prejudice.* Cambridge, MA: Addison-Wesley

Allport, G. W. (1958). *The nature of prejudice.* Garden City, New York: Doubleday.

Alter, J. (1995, September 25). Why Powell's race matters; will it hurt him—or help make Americans feel better about themselves? *Newsweek, 126,* 43.

American Psychological Association. (1992). *Code of conduct.* Washington, D.C.: Author.

Ansbacher, H. L., & Ansbacher, R. R. (1956). *The individual psychology of Alfred Adler.* New York: Basic Books.

Aptheker, H. (1993). *Anti-racism in U.S. history.* Westport, CT: Praeger.

Asante, M. K. (1991a). Afrocentric curriculum. *Educational Leadership 49*(4), 28–31.

Asante, M. K. (1991b). The Afrocentric idea in education. *Journal of Negro Education, 60*(2), 170–80.

Asante M. (1992, Summer). African American studies: The future of the discipline. *The Black Scholar, 22*(3), 25.

Ashmore, R., & Del Boca, F. (1976). Psychological approaches to understanding intergroup conflict. In Katz (Ed.), *Towards the elimination of racism.* (pp. 72–123) New York: Pergamon.

Ashmore, R. D., & McConahay, J. B. (1975). *Psychology and America's urban dilemmas.* New York: McGraw-Hill.

Atkinson, D., Morten, G., & Sue, D. (1979), *Counseling American Minorities: A cross-cultural perspective* (2nd ed.). Dubuque, IA: Brown.

Axelson, J. A. (1993). *Counseling and development in multicultural society* (2nd ed.). Pacific Grove, CA: Brooks/Cole.

Behind the Verdict (1995, October 7). *The Economist,* pp. 27–28.

Benokraitis, N. V., & Feagin, J. R. (1995). *Modern sexism.* Englewood Cliffs, NJ: Prentice-Hall.

Benson, P., Karabenick, S. A., & Lerner, R. M. (1976). Pretty pleases: The effect of physical attractiveness, race, and sex on receiving help. *Journal of Experimental Social Psychology, 12,* 409–419.

Bernstein, A. (1995, July 17). The wage squeeze. *Business Week,* 54–62.

Berry, W. W. (1984). Affirmative action is just. In D. L. Bender (Ed.), *Is affirmative action just?* (pp. 16–21). St. Paul, MN: Greengaven.

Bethlehem, B., & Janowitz, M. (1964). *Social change and prejudice.* London: Collier-MacMillan.

Bogardus, E. S. (1933). Social distance scale. *Sociology and Social Research, 17,* 265–271.

Brewer, M. B., & Kramer, R. M. (1985). The psychology of intergroup attitudes and behavior. *Annual Review of Psychology, 36,* 219–243.

Brislin, D., Landis, R. W., & Brandt, M. E. (1983). Conceptualizations of intercultural behavior and training. In D. Landis and R. Brislin (Eds.), *Handbook of intercultural training* (pp.1–35). New York: Pergamon.

Brodie, J. M. (1991). Chilly environment not ally to minority retention. *Black Issues in Higher Education, 8*, 31.

Brown, D. (1990), Racism and race relations in the university. *Virginia Law Review, 76*(2), 295.

Bryant, B. K. (1994). *Counseling for racial understanding.* Alexandria, VA: American Counseling Association.

Budiansky, S. (1996, July 1). Publicity is not a cure-all. *U.S. News & World Report*, 8–9.

Bwahuk, D. P. S., & Brislin, R. (1992). The measurement of intercultural sensitivity using the concepts of individualism and collectivism. *International Journal of Intercultural Relations, 16*, 413–436.

Byrnes, D. (1988). Children and prejudice. *Social Education, 52*, 267–271.

Byrnes, D. H., & Kiger, G. (1988). Contemporary measures of attitudes towards Blacks. *Educational and Psychological Measurement, 48*, 107–118.

Calabresi, M. (1994, February 14). Skin deep 101 (teachings of Leonard Jeffries). *Time, 143*, 16.

Caplow, T. (1954). *The sociology of work.* Minneapolis: University of Minesota.

Carkhuff, R. R. (1983). *Sources of human productivity.* Amherst, MA: Human Resource Development.

Carkhuff, R. R. (1993). *The art of helping* (7th ed.). Amherst, MA: Human Resource Development.

Carkhuff, R. R, & Berenson, B. G. (1976). *Teaching as treatment. An introduction to counseling and psychotherapy.* Amherst, MA: Human Resource Development.

Carter, J. H. (1994). Racism's impact on mental health. *Journal of the National Medical Association, 86*(7), 543–547.

Carter, S. (1993). *The culture of disbelief.* New York: HarperCollins.

CBS suspends Andy Rooney for alleged racial slurs. (1990, February 26). *Jet*, 10.

Chalk, F., & Jonnassohn, K. (1990). *The history and sociology of genocide: Analyses and case studies.* New Haven, CT: Yale University.

Cohen, R. (1988, January 19). The Greek's offense. *The Washington Post*, p. A15.

Cohen, R. (1995, June 6). Junk affirmative action? *The Washington Post*, p. A19.

Combs, A. W. (1994). *Helping relationships: Basic concepts for the helping professions*. Boston: Allyn and Bacon.

Constable, P. (1995, October 10). A "glass ceiling" of misperceptions, *The Washington Post*, p. A1.

Corey, G. (1991a). *Case approach to counseling and psychotherapy*. Pacific Grove, CA: Brooks/Cole.

Corey, G. (1991b). *Theory and practice of counseling and psychoterapy* (4th ed.). Pacific Grove, CA: Brooks/Cole.

Corey, G., & Corey, M. (1990). *I never knew I had a choice*. Pacific Grove, CA: Brooks/Cole.

Cornell, S. (1988). *The return of the native: American Indian political resurgence*. New York: Oxford University.

Corsini, R., & Wedding, D. (Eds.). (1989). *Current psychotherapies* (4th ed.). Itasca, IL: Peacock.

Cose, E. (1995, October 9). Shuffling the race cards. *Newsweek*, 34–35.

Crevecoeur, J. H, SJ. (1904). *Letters from an American farmer*. New York: Fox Duffield.

Cross, W. E. (1991). *Shades of Black: Diversity in African-American identity*. Philadelphia: Temple University.

Delaney, L. T. (1980). The other bodies in the river. In R. L. Jones (Ed.), *Black psychology* (2nd ed.). New York: Harper & Row.

Deloria, V. (1983). *American Indians, American justice*. Austin, TX: University of Texas.

DeVillar, R. A. (1994). *Cultural diversity in schools: From rhetoric to practice*. Albany, NY: State University of New York.

Devine, P. G., Monteith, M. J., Zuwerink, J. R., & Elliot, A. J. (1991). Prejudice with and without compunction. *Journal of Personality and Social Psychology, 60*, 817–830.

Devine, P. G. (1989). Stereotypes and prejudice: Their automatic and controlled components. *Journal of Personality and Social Psychology, 56*, 5–18.

Dinkmeyer, D., Dinkmeyer, D., Jr., & Sperry, L. (1987). *Adlerian counseling and psychotherapy* (2nd ed). Columbus, OH: Merrill.

Dipboye, R. L., Arvey, R. D., & Terpstra, D. E. (1977). Sex and physical attractiveness of raters and applicants as determinants of resumé evaluations. *Journal of Applied Psychology, 62,* 288–294.

D'Souza, D. (1995). *The end of racism: Principles for a multiracial society.* New York: Free Press.

Du Bois, W. E. B. (1903). *The souls of black folk: Essays and sketches.* Chicago: McClurg.

Duckitt, J. (1992). *The social psychology of prejudice.* New York: Praeger.

Dworkin, S. H., & Gutierrez, F. G. (1992). *Counseling gay men and lesbians: Journey to the end of the rainbow.* Alexandria, VA: American Counseling Association.

Dye, T. (1992). *Understanding public policy* (8th ed.). Englewood Cliffs, NJ: Prentice-Hall.

Ehrhart, J. K., & Sandler, B. R. (1987). *Looking for more than a few good women in traditionally male fields.* Washington, DC: Association of American Colleges.

Ehrlich, H. J. (1990). *Campus ethnoviolence and the policy options.* Bethesda, MD: National Institute Against Prejudice and Violence.

Eisenstein, H. (1994). Reconstructing the family. In G. Handel & G. G. Whitchurch (Eds.), *The psychosocial interior of the family* (4th ed.) (pp. 363–374). New York: Aldine de Gruyter.

Ellis, A. (1962). *Reason and emotion in psychotherapy.* New York: Stuart.

Erikson, E. H. (1963). *Childhood and society* (2nd ed.). New York: Norton.

Erikson, E. H. (1968). *Identity, youth, and crisis.* New York: Norton.

Estrada, R. (1995, October 20). Lack of jobs drives Black alienation. *Dallas Morning News,* p. A25.

Fassinger, R. E. (1991). The hidden majority: Issues and challenges in working with lesbian women and gay men. *The Counseling Psychologist, 19*(2), 157–176.

Fields-Meyer, T. (1996, April 8). Flames of fire. *People Weekly,* 96–100.

Fineman, H. (1995, September 11). Powell on the march. *Newsweek,* 26–31.

Fineman, H., & Smith, V. E. (1995, October 30). An angry "charmer." *Newsweek,* 32.

Frankl, V. E. (1959). *Man's search for meaning: An introduction to logotherapy.* Boston: Beacon.

Frankl, V. E. (1967). *Psychotherapy and existentialism.* New York: Simon & Schuster.

Franklin, J. H. (1975, Summer). The moral legacy of the founding fathers. *University of Chicago Magazine,* 10–13.

Franklin, J. H. (1993). *The color line: Legacy for the twenty-first century,* Columbia, Mo: University of Missouri.

Fredrickson, G. (1981). *White supremacy: A comparative study in American and South African history.* New York: Oxford University.

Friedan, B. (1963). *The feminine mystique.* New York: Norton.

Friedan, B. (1993). *The fountain of age.* New York: Simon & Schuster.

Friedan, B. (1995, September 4). Beyond gender. *Newsweek,* 30–32.

Gaertner, S. L., & Dovidio, J. F. (1986). The aversive form of racism. In J. F. Dovidio & S. L. Gaertner (Eds.), *Prejudice, discrimination, and racism* (pp. 61–89). San Diego, CA: Academic.

Gaines, S. O., & Reed, E. S. (1994). Two social psychologies of prejudice: Gordon W. Allport, W. E. B. Du Bois, and the legacy of Booker T. Washington. *Journal of Black Psychology, 20*(1), 8–28.

Gates, H. L., Jr. (1995a, October 10). Grading Farrakhan. *New Yorker,* 35.

Gates, H. L., Jr. (1995b, October 23). Thirteen ways of looking at a Black man (African American leaders react to the O. J. Simpson trial and the Million Man March). *The New Yorker,* 56–65.

Geoseffi, D. (1993). *On prejudice: A global perspective.* New York: Doubleday.

Gerlach, J., & Hart, B. L. (1992). Gender equity in the classroom: An inventory. *Teaching English in the Two-Year College, 19,* 49–54.

Goldman, D. (1995). *Emotional intelligence.* New York: Bantam.

Gould, S. (1994, November 28). Curve ball. *New Yorker,* 139.

Gray, D. B., & Ashmore, R. D. (1976). The biasing influence of defendants' characteristics on simulated sentencing. *Psychological Reports, 38*(3), 727–738.

Haizlip, S. T. (1996, June 23). We knew what glory was. *The New York Times,* p. 13.

Hardiman, R. (1982). *White identity development: A process-oriented model for describing the recial conciousness of White Americans.* Unpublished doctoral dissertation, University of Massachusetts, Amherst.

Harris, J. (1995, October 11). Clinton "struck" by racial divide on Simpson case, *The Washington Post*, p. A13.

Harris, S. M. (1991). Are all college students educated? Approaches to integrating race, gender, and ethnicity into classroom behaviors. *College Student Journal, 25,* 382–387.

Healey, J. F. (1995). *Race, ethnicity, gender, and class.* Thousand Oaks, CA: Pine Forge.

Helms, J. E. (1984). Toward a theoretical model of the effects of race on counseling: A Black and White model. *The Counseling Psychologist, 12,* 153–165.

Helms, J. E., & Carter, R. T. (1990). White Racial Identity Attitude Scale (Form WRIAS). In J. E. Helms (Ed.), *Black and White racial identity: Theory, research, and practice* (pp. 249–251). Westport, CT: Praeger.

Helms, J. E., & Parham, T. A. (1990). Black Racial Identity Attitude Scale (Form RIAS-B). In J. E. Helms (Ed.), *Black and White racial identity: Theory, research, and practice* (pp. 245–247). Westport, CT: Praeger.

Helms, J. E. (Ed.). (1990). *Black and White racial identity: Theory, research, and practice.* Westport, CT: Greenwood.

Henry, F. (1994). *The Caribbean diaspora in Toronto: Learning to live with racism.* Toronto: University of Toronto.

Herek, G. M. (1988). Hate crimes against lesbians and gay men: Issues for research and policy. *American Psychologist, 44,* 948–955.

Herek, G. M., & Berrill, K. T. (1992). *Hate crimes: Confronting violence against lesbians and gay men.* Newbury Park, CA. Sage.

Herrnstein, R. J., & Murray, C. A. (1994). *The bell curve: Intelligence and class structure in American life.* New York: Free Press.

Hill, A., & Jordan, E. C. (1995). *Race, gender, and power in America: The legacy of the Hill-Thomas hearing.* New York: Oxford University.

Holland, J. J. (1996, August 17). Two accused of masterminding church burning. *The Washington Post,* p. A14.

Holt, F. (1992). Foreword. In K. H. Kavanagh & P. H. Kennedy (Eds.), *Promoting cultural diversity: Strategies for healthcare professionals.* Newbury Park, CA: Sage.

Hornblower, M. (1995, July 31). Taking it all back: at Pete Wilson's urging, the University of California says no to racial preferences. *Time,* 34–35.

Horner, M. (1972). Toward an understanding of achievement-related conflicts in women. *Journal of Social Issues, 28,* 129–156.

Hoyt, K. (1988). The changing workforce: A review of projections, 1986 to 2000. *The Career Development Quarterly, 37,* 31–39.

Husserl, E. (1929). Phenomenology. In *Encyclopaedia Britannica* (vol. 17, pp. 699–702). Chicago: Encyclopedia Britannica.

Ilkka, R. J. (1995). Applicant appearance and selection decision-making: Revitalizing employment interview education. *Business Communications Quarterly, 58*(3), 11–18.

Ivey, A. E. (1977). Cultural expertise: Toward systematic outcome criteria in counseling and psychological education. *The Personnel and Guidance Journal, 55,* 296–302.

Ivey, A. E., Ivey, M. B., & Simek-Downing, L. (1987). *Counseling and psychotherapy: Integrating skills, theory, and practice* (2nd ed). Englewood Cliffs, NJ: Prentice-Hall.

Jacques-Garvey, A. (1978). *Philosophy and opinions of Marcus Garvey.* New York: Ayer.

Johnson, D. W., & Johnson, R. T. (1994). *Learning together and alone: Coopertive, competitive, and individualist learning* (4th ed.). Boston: Allyn & Bacon.

Johnson, H. (1994). *Divided we fall.* New York: Norton.

Johnson, H. D. (1987). Knowing what versus knowing how: Toward achieving expertise through multicultural training for counseling. *The Counseling Psychologist, 15*(2), 320–331.

Jones, J. M. (1972). *Prejudice and racism.* Reading, MA: Addison-Wesley.

Jones, J. M. (1981). The concept of racism and its changing reality. In B. P. Bowser, & R. G. Hunt (Eds.), *Impact of racism on White Americans.* (pp. 27–49). Beverly Hills, CA: Sage.

Kaplan, D. A., & Klaidman, D. (1996, June 3). A battle, not the war. *Newsweek,* 24–30.

Katz, P. A. (1987). Developmental and social processes in ethnic attitudes and self-identification. In J. S. Phinney & M. J. Rotheram (Eds.), *Children's ethnic socialization: Pluralism and development* (pp. 92–99). Newbury Park, CA: Sage.

Katz, P. A. (1976). *Towards the elimination of racism.* New York: Pergamon.

Kavanagh, K. H., & Kennedy, P. H. (1992). *Promoting cultural diversity: Strategies for health care professionals.* Newbury Park, CA: Sage.

Kennedy, R. (1995, October 16). Is all discrimination created equal? (special report—the Simpson verdict). *Time,* 72.

Kennon, P. (1995). *The twilight of democracy.* New York: Doubleday.

Kierkegaard, S. (1954). *The sickness unto death.* New York: Doubleday.

Kinder, D. R., & Sears, D. O. (1981). Prejudice and politics: Symbolic racism versus racial threats to the good life. *Journal of Personality and Social Psychology, 40,* 414–431.

King, C. I. (1995a, Septermber 16). Banneker '55: Separate, unequal, determined. *The Washington Post,* p. A17.

King, C. I. (1995b, October 7). The dead end of racial separation. *The Washington Post,* p. A29.

King, M. L. (1968). *Where do we go from here: Chaos or community?* Boston: Beacon.

Kinloch, G. C. (1974). *The dynamics of race relations: A sociological analysis.* New York: McGraw-Hill.

Kistner, J., Metzler, A., Gatlin, D., & Risi, S. (1993). Classroom racial proportions and children's peer relations: Race and gender effects. *Journal of Educational Psychology, 85*(3), 446–452.

Kleg, M. (1993). *Hate, prejudice, and racism.* Albany, NY: State University of New York.

Kochanska, G. (1994). Beyond cognition: Expanding the search for the early roots of internalization and conscience. *Developmental Psychology, 30*(1), 20–22.

Kogan, N., & Downey, J. F. (1956). Scaling norm conflicts in prejudice and discrimination. *Journal of Abnormal Social Psychology, 53,* 292–295.

Kotkin, J. (1993). *Tribes: How race, religion, and identity determines success in the new global economy.* New York: Random House.

Krasner, L., & Ullmann, L. (1965). *Research in behavior modification.* New York: Holt, Rinehart & Winston.

Lacayo, R. (1995a, October 30). Critical mass. *Time,* 34–36.

Lacayo, R. (1995b, October 9). An ugly end to it all. *Time,* 30(6).

Lakeoff, R. T., & Scherr, R. L. (1984). *Face value: The politics of beauty.* Boston: Routledge & Kegan Paul.

Landis, D. & Boucher, J. (1987). Themes and models of conflict. In Boucher, J, Landis, D., & Clark, K (Eds.), *Ethical conflict: International perspectives* (pp. 18–32). Newbury Park, CA: Sage.

Lauer, R. H. (1986). *Social problems and the quality of life.* Dubuque, IA: Brown.

Lazarus, A. A. (1976). *Multimodal behavioral therapy.* New York: Springer.

Levine, D. U. (1977). Level and rate of desegregation and White enrollment decline in a big city school district. *Social Problems, 24*(4), 451–462.

LeVine, R. A., & Campbell, D. T. (1972). *Ethnocentrism: Theories of conflict, ethnic attitudes and group behavior.* New York: Wiley.

Lewis, A. (1995a, November 10). Why not the best? *The New York Times,* p. A19.

Lind, M. (1995). Brave new right. In Fraser, S. (Ed.), *The bell curve wars: Race, intelligence, and the future of America.* Scranton, PA: HarperCollins.

Linder, R. (1954). *The fifty minute hour.* New York: Bantam.

Locke, D. C. (1992). *Increasing multicultural understanding: Comprehensive model. Multicultural aspects of counseling: Series 1.* Newbury Park, CA: Sage.

Lorde, A. (1984), *Sister outsider.* New York: Crossing.

Loury, G. C. (1995a). *One by one from the inside out: Essays and reviews on race and responsibility in American.* New York: Free Press.

Loury, G. C. (1995b, November 6). One man's march: Wrestling with October 16. *The New Republic,* 18–21.

Lynch, E., & Hanson, M. (1992). *Developing cross-cultural competence: A guide for working with young children and their families.* Baltimore: Paul Brooks.

Lynch, F. (1991). *Invisible victims: White males and the crisis of affirmative action.* New York: Praeger.

Mackie, D. M., & Hamilton, D. L. (1993). *Affect, cognition, and stereotyping: Interactive processes in group perception.* San Diego, CA: Academic.

Maldonado, D. (1975). The Chicano aged. *Social Work, 20*(3), 213–216.

Marriott, M. (1995, October 22). Another majority, silent and Black. *The New York Times,* p. E5.

Martin, T. (1976). *Race first: The ideological and organizational struggles of Marcus Garvey and the Universal Negro Improvement Association.* Westport, CT: Greenwood.

Maslow, A. H. (1968). *Toward a psychology of being.* Princeton, NJ: Van Nostrand.

May, R. (1953). *Man's search for himself.* New York: Norton.

May, R. (1967). *Psychology and the human dilemma.* New York: Van Nostrand Reinhold.

McConahay, J. B. (1986). Modern racism, ambivalence, and the modern racism scale. In J. F. Dovidio and S. L. Geartner (Eds.), *Prejudice, discrimination, and racism* (pp. 91–126). San Diego, CA: Academic.

McConahay, J. B., & Hough, J. C. (1976). Symbolic racism. *Journal of Social Issues, 32*(2), 23–45.

McCormick, T. E. (1990). Counselor-teacher interface: Promoting nonsexist education and career development. *Journal of Multicultural Counseling and Development, 18*, 2–10.

McGuire, W. (1969). The nature of attitudes and attitude change. In G. Lindsey & E. Aronson (Eds.), *Handbook of social psychology* (2nd ed., vol. 3). Reading, MA: Addison-Wesley.

McWhirter, E. H. (1994). *Counseling for empowerment.* Alexandria, VA: American Counseling Association.

Meredith, R. (1996, June 23). North Carolina case perplexes a town. *The New York Times*, p. A10.

Merida, K. (1995, October 9). Worry, frustration build for many in Black middle class. *The Washington Post*, pp. A1, A22.

Merta, R. J., Stringham, E. M., & Ponterotto, J. G. (1988). Stimulating culture shock in counselor trainees: An experimental exercise for cross-cultural training. *The Journal of Counseling and Development, 66*, 242–245.

Moghaddam, F. M., & Taylor, D. M. (1987). The meaning of multiculturalism for visible minority immigrant women. *Canadian Journal of Behavioural Science, 19*(2), 121–136.

Monk, R. C. (1996). *Taking sides: Clashing views on controversial issues in race and ethnicity* (2nd ed.). Guilford, CT: Dushkin.

Monteith, M. J. (1993). Self-regulation of prejudiced responses: Implications for progress in prejudice-reduction efforts. *Journal of Personality and Social Psychology, 65*(3), 469–485.

Morganthau, T. (1996, June 24). Fires in the night. *Newsweek*, 28–32.

Morrow, L. (1993, October, 9). A trial for our times. *Time*, 28–29.

Myrdal, G. (1944). *An American dilemma: the Negro problem and modern democracy.* New York, Harper.

NAACP chair outraged by SC Sen. Holling's remarks about African leaders. (1994, January 10). *Jet*, 18.

Neil, A. S. (1970). *Summerhill: For and against.* New York: Hart.

Nietzsche, F. (1967). *Thus spake Zarathustra.* London: Allen & Unwin.

Noble, K. D. (1987). The dilemma of the gifted woman. *Psychology of Women Quarterly, 11*(3), 367–378.

Noel, D. (1968). A theory of the origin of ethnic stratification. *Social Problems, 16,* 157–172.

No sanctuary. (1996, June 15–21). *The Economist,* 27.

O'Connor, T. (1989). Cultural voice and strategies for multicultural education. *Journal of Education, 171,* 57–74.

O'Neil, J., & Egan, J. (1993). Abuses of power against women: Sexism, gender role conflict, and psychological violence. In E. O. Cook (Ed.), *Women, relationships, and power: Implications for counseling* (pp. 49–78). Alexandria, VA: American Counseling Association.

Pate, G. S. (1988). Research on reducing prejudice. *Social Education, 52,* 287–289.

Patterson, C. H. (1986). *Theories of counseling and psychotherapy* (4th ed.) New York: Harper & Row.

Patterson, O. (1995, October 30). Going separate ways: The history of an old idea. *Newsweek, 43.*

Pederson, P. (1988). *A handbook for developing multicultural awareness.* Alexandria, VA: American Association for Counseling and Development.

Pederson, P. (1994). *A handbook for developing multicultural awareness* (2nd ed.). Alexandria, VA: American Counseling Association.

Peters, W. (1971). *A class divided.* Garden City, NY: Doubleday.

Pettigrew, T. (1973). Racism and the mental health of White Americans: A social psychological view. In. C. V. Willie, B. M. Kramer, & B. S. Brown (Eds.), *Racism and mental health* (pp. 269–298). Pittsburgh: University of Pittsburgh.

Pettigrew, T. (1981). The mental health impact. In B. P. Bowser, & R. G. Hunt (Eds.), *Impact of racism on White Americans* (pp. 97–118). Beverly Hills, CA: Sage.

Pettigrew, T. (1987, May 12). "Useful" modes of thought contribute to prejudice. *The New York Times,* pp. 17–20.

Pettigrew, T., Fredrickson, G., Knobel, D., Glazer, N., & Ueda, R. (1982). *Prejudice.* Cambridge, MA: Harvard University.

Pharr, S. (1988). *Homophobia: A weapon of sexism.* Little Rock: Chardon.

Phinney, J. S., & Rotheram, M. J. (Eds.). (1987). *Children's ethnic socialization: Pluralism and development.* Newbury Park, CA: Sage.

Pine, G. J., & Hilliard, A. G. III. (1990). Rx for racism: Imperatives for America's schools. *Phi Delta Kappan, 71*(8), 593–600.

Ponterotto, J. G. (1988) Racial conciousness development among White counselor trainees: A stage model. *Journal of Multicultural Counseling and Development, 16,* 146–156.

Ponterotto, J. G. (1991). The nature of prejudice revisited: Implications for counseling and intervention. *Journal of Counseling and Development, 70,* 216–224.

Ponterotto, J. G., Burkard, A., Rieger, B. P., Grieger, I., D'Onofrio, A., Dubuisson, A., Heenehan, M., Millstein, B., Parisi, M., Rath, J. F., & Sax, G. (1995). Development and initial validation of the Quick Discrimination Index (QDI). *Educational and Psychological Measurement, 55*(6), 1016–1031.

Ponterotto, J. G., & Pederson, P. B. (1993). *Preventing prejudice: A guide for counselors and educators. Multicultural aspects of counseling: Series 2.* Newbury Park, CA: Sage.

Powers, R. L., & Griffith, J. (1985). *An Adlerian lexicon.* Chicago: AIAS.

Powers, R. L., & Griffith, J. (1986). *Individual psychology client workbook.* Chicago: AIAS.

Pressley, S. A. (1995, September 24). Quarterback change puts racial issue under West Texas stadium lights. *The Washington Post,* p. A3.

Prochaska, J. O. (1984). *Systems of psychotherapy: A transtheoretical analysis* (2nd ed.). Pacific Grove, CA: Brooks/Cole.

Puddington, A. (1995, October). Will affirmative action survive? *Commentary, 100,* 22–26.

Purkey, W. W. (1978). *Inviting school success.* Belmont, CA: Wadsworth.

Purkey, W. W. (1996). *Invitational counseling: A self-concept approach to professional practice.* Pacific Grove, CA: Brooks/Cole.

Racist jokes at VA political roast not funny to Governor Wilder. (1993, April 5). *Jet,* 5–6.

Ramirez, M., III. (1991). *Psychotherapy and counseling with minorities: A cognitive approach to individual and cultural differences.* New York: Pergamon.

Ridley, C. R. (1989). Racism in counseling as an aversive behavioral process. In P. B. Pederson, J. G. Draguns, & W. J. Lonner (Eds.), *Counseling across cultures* (3rd ed., pp. 55–77). Honolulu, HI: University of Hawaii.

Ridley, C. R. (1994). Multicultural training: Reexamination, operationalization, and integration. *Counseling Psychologist, 22*(2), 227–289.

Ridley, C. R. (1995). *Overcoming unintentional racism in counseling and therapy: A practitioner's guide to intentional intervention.* Thousand Oaks, CA: Sage.

Riger, S. (1991). Gender dilemmas in sexual harassment: Policies and procedures. *American Psychologist, 46,* 497–505.

Rogers, C. R. (1951). *Client centered therapy.* Boston: Houghton Mifflin.

Rogers, C. R. (1954). *Psychotherapy and personality change: Coordinated research studies in the client centered approach.* Chicago: University of Chicago.

Rogers, C. R. (1961). *On becoming a person.* Boston: Houghton Mifflin.

Rogers, C. R. (1983). *Freedom to learn for the 80s.* Columbus, OH: Merrill.

Rokeach, M., & Mezei, L. (1966). Race and shared belief as factors in social choice. *Science, 151,* 167–172.

Rokeach, M., Smith, P., & Evans, R. (1960). Two kinds of prejudice or one? In M. Rokeach (Ed.), *The open and the closed mind* (pp. 132–168). New York: Basic.

Saakvitne, K. W., & Pearlman, L. A. (1993). The impact of internalized misogyny and violence against women on feminine identity. In E. P. Cook (Ed.), *Women, relationships, and power: Implications for counseling* (pp. 247–274). Alexandria, VA: ACA.

Sagar, H. A., Schofield, J. W., & Synder, H. N. (1983). Race and gender barriers: Pre-adolescent peer behavior in academic classrooms. *Child Development, 54,* 1032–1040.

Sandhu, D. S., & Aspy, C. B. (1996). *Workplace Perceived Prejudice Scale.* Unpublished manuscript.

Sandhu, D. S., & Asrabadi, B. R. (1994). Development of an acculturative stress scale for international students: Preliminary findings. *Psychological Reports, 75,* 435–448.

Sandhu, D. S., Petrosko, J., & Portes, P. R. (1995) *Adult Life Satisfaction Scale.* Unpublished manuscript.

Sandhu, D. S., Portes, P. R., & McPhee, S. (1996). Assessing cultural adaptation: Psychometric properties of the Cultural Adaptation Pain Scale. *Journal of Multicultural Counseling and Development, 24,* 15–25.

Schofield, J. W., & Whitney, B. E. (1983). Peer nomination versus rating scale measurement of children's peer preferences in desegregated schools. *School Psychology Quarterly, 46,* 242–251.

Schreier, B. A. (1995). Moving beyond tolerance: A new paradigm for programming about homophobia/biphobia and heterosexism. *Journal of College Student Development, 36,* 19–26.

Schwarz, T. (1995). *What really matters.* New York: Bantam.

Sedlacek, W. E., & Brooks, G. C., Jr. (1972). *Situational attitude scale (SAS): Manual.* College Park, MD: University of Maryland.

Shaffer, G. W., & Lazarus, A. (1952). *Fundamental concepts in clinical psychology.* New York: McGraw-Hill.

Shepherd, G. W. & Penna, D. (1991). *Racism and the underclass: State policy and discrimination against minorities.* New York: Greenwood.

Sigall, H., & Ostrove, N. (1975). Beautiful but dangerous: Effects of offender attractiveness and nature of the crime on juridic judgment. *Journal of Personality and Social Psychology, 31*(3), 410–414.

Sigall, H., & Page, R. (1971). Current stereotypes: A little fading, a little faking. *Journal of Personality and Social Psychology, 18,* 247–255.

Sizemore, B. A. (1990). The politics of curriculum, race, and class. *Journal of Negro Education, 59,* 77–85.

Skillings, J. H., & Dobbins, J. E. (1991). Racism as a disease: Etiology and treatment implications. *Journal of Counseling and Development, 70*(1), 206–212.

Skinner, B. F. (1948). *Walden Two.* New York: Macmillan.

Sleeter, C. E. (1989). Doing multicultural education across the grade levels and subject areas: A case study of Wisconsin. *Teaching and Teacher Education, 5*(3), 189–203.

Smith, C. R., Williams, L., & Willis, R. (1967). Race, sex, and belief as determinants of friendship acceptance. *Journal of Personality and Social Psychology, 5,* 127–137.

Smothers, R. (1996, June 23). In Alabama, rebuilding heals hearts of workers. *The New York Times,* p. A10.

Sniderman, P. M., Tetlock, P. E., & Carmines, E. G. (Eds.). (1993). *Prejudice, politics, and the American dilemma.* Stanford, CA: Stanford University.

Solomon, B. B. (1976). *Black empowerment social work in oppressed communities.* New York: Columbia University.

Sowell, T. (1989). The new racism on campus. *Fortune, 119*(4), 116.

Steele, S. (1990). *The content of our character.* New York: St. Martin's.

Steele, S. (1995, October 24). Race and the curse of good intentions. *The New York Times,* p. A19.

Stenz, K. M., Iasenza, S., Troutt, B. V. (1990). A training program to diminish prejudicial attitudes in college student leaders. *Journal of College Student Development, 31,* 83–84.

Stephen, C. W., & Langlois, J. H. (1980). Physical attractiveness and ethnicity: Implications for stereotyping and social development. *Journal of Genetic Psychology, 137*(2), 303–304.

Streisand, B. (1995, October 16). The verdict's aftermath. *U.S. News & World Report,* 34–37.

Sue, D. W. (1978). Eliminating cultural oppression in counseling: Toward a general theory. *Journal of Counseling Psychology, 25,* 419–428.

Super, D. E. (1949). *Appraising vocational fitness.* New York: Harper & Row.

Super, D. E. (1957). *The psychology of careers.* New York: Harper & Row.

Tajfel, H. (1978). *Differentiation between social groups: Studies in the social psychology of intergroup relations.* New York: Academic.

Tajfel, H. (1969). Cognitive aspects of prejudice. *Journal of Social Issues, 25,* 79–97.

Tatum, B. D. (1992). Talking about race, learning about racism: The application of racial identity development theory in the classroom. *Harvard Educational Review, 62*(1), 1–24.

Taylor, R. B. (1969). *Cultural ways: a compact introduction to cultural anthropology.* Boston, MA: Allyn & Bacon.

The other american (1995, October 21). *The Economist,* 19–20.

Thernstrom, A. (1995, October 12). Two nations, separate and hostile? Why the chasm between the races is growing. *The New York Times,* p. A15.

Thibodaux, D. (1992). *Political correctness.* Lafayette, LA: Huntington House.

Tobach, E., & Rosoff, B. (1994). *Challenging racism and sexism: Alternatives to genetic explanations.* New York: Feminist Press at the City University of New York.

Triandis, H. C. (1961). Rokeach's theory of prejudice. *Journal of Abnormal and Social Psychology, 62,* 184–186.

Triandis, H. C. (1971). *Attitude and attitude change.* New York: Wiley.

Tryman, M. D. (1992). Racism and violence on college campuses. A model of ethnoviolence and public policy on college campuses. *The Western Journal of Black Studies, 16*(4), 221–230.

United Nations. (1966). Convention on the prevention and punishment of the crime of genocide. Her Majesty's Stationary Office. (Originally published 1948)

U.S. Bureau of the Census. (1993). *Statistical abstract of the United States*: Washington, DC: Author.

Voices in the land. (1995, October 21). *The Economist,* 26.

Vontress, C. E. (1991). Traditional healing in Africa: Implications for cross-cultural counseling. *Journal of Counseling & Development, 70*(1), 242–249.

Walsh, E. (1995, October 8). Criticism of Farrakhan's Million Man March muted. *The Washington Post,* p. A22.

Ward, A. (1995, October 6). Fundamental human vices. *The Washington Post,* p. A25.

Washington, J. M. (Ed). (1986). *A testament of hope: The essential writings of Martin Luther King, Jr.* San Francisco: Harper.

Watson, D. L. & Tharp, R. G. (1989). *Self-directed behavior: Self-modification for personal adjustment* (5th ed). Pacific Grove, CA: Brooks/Cole.

Watson, J. B. (1916). Behaviorism and the concept of mental disease. *Journal of Philosophical Psychology, 13,* 589–597.

Weinberg, G. (1972). *Society and the healthy homosexual.* New York: Anchor/Doubleday.

Weiss, J. C., Ehrlich, H. J., & Larcom, B. E. K. (1992). Ethnoviolence at work. *The Journal of Intergroup Relations, 18*(4), 21–33.

Wellman, D. T. (1977). *Portraits of White racism.* New York: Cambridge University.

Welsing, F. C. (1970). *The Cress theory of color-confrontation and racism (White supremacy).* Washington, DC: C-R.

West, C. (1993a). *Keeping faith.* New York: Routledge.

West, C. (1993b). *Race matters.* Boston: Beacon.

West, C. (1995, October 14). Why I'm marching in Washington. *New York Times,* p. A23.

Whitaker, M. (1995, October 16). Whites v. Blacks. *Newsweek,* 23.

Whitbourne, S. K., & Hulicka, I. M. (1990). Ageism in undergraduate psychology texts. *American Psychologist, 45,* 1127–1136.

Wievorka, M. (1995). *The arena of racism*. Thousand Oaks, CA: Sage.

Willard, L. D. (1975). *Aesthetic discrimination against persons*. Unpublished manuscript.

Williams, A., & Giles, H. (1992). Prejudice-reduction simulations: Social cognition, intergroup theory and ethics. *Simulations and Gaming, 23*(4), 472–484.

Williamson, E. G. (1965). *Vocational counseling*. New York: McGraw-Hill.

Williamson, E. G., & Darley, J. G. (1937). *Student personnel work: An outline of clinical procedures*. New York: McGraw-Hill.

Willie, C. V., Kramer, B. M., & Brown, B. S. (1973). *Racism and mental health*. Pittsburgh: University of Pittsburgh.

Wilson, J. Q. (1993). *The moral sense*. New York: Free Press.

Wirth, L. (1945). The problem of minority groups. In R. Linton (Ed.), *The science of man in world crisis* (pp. 347–372). New York: Columbia University.

Witkin, G. (1996, June 24). Who is torching the churches? *U.S. News & World Report*, 30–32.

Wolf, N. (1992). *The beauty myth*. New York: Anchor.

Wolpe, J. (1958.) *Psychotherapy by reciprocal inhibition*. Palo Alto, CA: Stanford.

Wolpe, J. (1973). *The practice of behavior therapy* (2nd ed.). New York: Pergamon.

Wolpe, J. (1976). *Theme and variations*. New York: Pergamon.

Wrenn, C. G. (1962). The culturally encapsulated counselor. *Harvard Educational Review, 32*, 444–449.

Wright, E. (1989, Winter). The true legacy of Malcolm X: Responsibility was the core of his message to blacks. *Issues and Views Open Forum Foundation, 5*(1), 5–6, 8, 10.

Yinger, J. M. (1976). Ethnicity in complex societies. In L. A. Coser & O. N. Larsen (Eds.), *The uses of controversy in sociology*, 197–216. New York: Free Press.

Yinger, J. M. (1994). *Ethnicity: Source of strength? Source of conflict?* Albany: State University of New York.

Zangwill, I. (1912). *The melting pot: Drama in four acts*. New York: Macmillan.

APPENDIXES

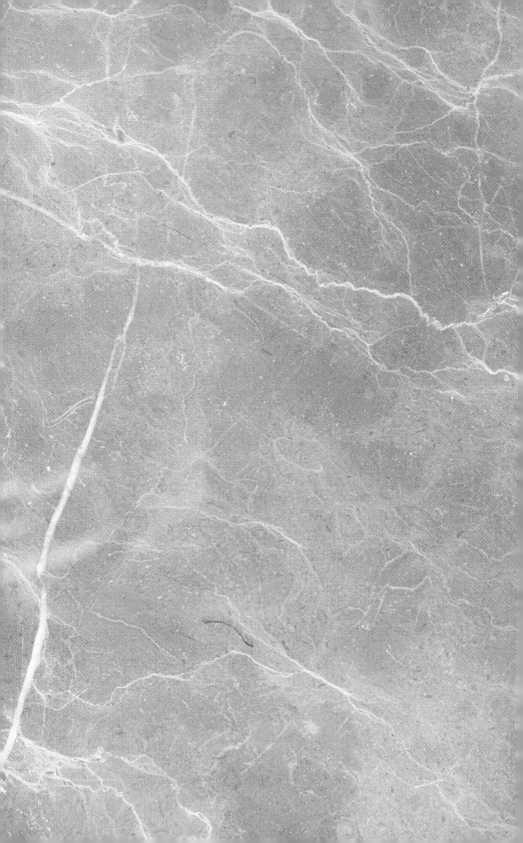

Annotated Bibliography

Adleman, J., & Enguidanos, G. (1995). *Racism in the lives of women: Testimony, theory, and guides to antiracist practice.* New York: Harrington Park.

> This as an anthology of 23 topics that deal with the oppression of women in various facets of their lives. The major focus of this book is on the examination of historical, cultural, and political forces that have detrimental effects on women's personal experiences. This book is highly recommended for practitioners interested in understanding complex issues related to feminism and racism in psychotherapy.

Baird, R. M., & Rosenbaum, S. E. (Eds.). (1992). *Bigotry, prejudice, and hatred: Definitions, causes, and solutions.* Buffalo, NY: Prometheus.

> This book is an excellent collection of contributions from 18 different authors to explain the mentality of internalized prejudice, bigotry, and hatred. The five parts of the book include essays from noted writers such as Gordon Allport, Jean-Paul Sartre, Samuel Gaertner, and John F.

Dovidio. Part 1 explains the phenomenon of hatred and prejudice, Part 2 addresses issues relating to political correctness at universities. The other three sections are devoted to explanations of the persistence of hatred and prejudice, moral and rational critiques of hatred, and ways to set desirable goals and find possible solutions to combat prejudice and hate.

Bell, L. A., & Blumenfeld, D. (Eds.). (1995). *Overcoming racism and sexism*. Lanham, MD: Rowman & Littlefield.

This book is a collection of 17 papers presented at a conference named "Racism and Sexism: Difference and Connections." It mainly focuses on the ways racism and sexism intersect and buttress each other. The contributors to this volume have analyzed, critiqued, and attempted to illustrate the various aspects of sexism and racism, which cause oppressive behaviors. Understanding the interconnection between sexism and racism is highlighted as the first and foremost step to alleviate afflictions of discrimination.

Bowser, B. P., & Hunt, R. G. (Eds.). (1996). *The impact of racism on White Americans* (2nd ed.). Thousand Oaks, CA: Sage.

This edited anthology of 12 articles examines two major issues dealing with racism in the United States. First, it explores the underlying factors that motivate White racism. Second, it discusses the effects of racism on Whites. The central theme of this book rests on the ideas that racism is deeply rooted in the social structure of American society, and that it is a "White problem." The authors contend that primarily Whites have the power to address race-related problems in America. To reduce or negate the deleterious impact of racism on Whites and ethnic minorities, these authors recommend some government interventions to limit the powers of some special interest groups.

Brookhiser, R. (1991). *The way of the WASP: How it made America and how it can save it so to speak*. New York: Free Press.

> The author laments that White Anglo-Saxon Protestant (WASP) character has been soiled for the past 60 years. Brookhiser asserts that the feats America has accomplished in the world have been attributed to the efforts and guidance of the WASP. This is a provocative book that portrays vehemently the perspectives and the worldviews of the majority culture. The ways of the WASP are eulogized.

Bryant, B. K. (Ed.). (1994). *Counseling for racial understanding*. Alexandria, VA: American Counseling Association.

> This book provides some basic information about prejudice and its psychodynamics. It is a very useful practical guide to identify and ameliorate the negative effects of prejudice. The book focuses on understanding prejudice in real world settings and provides some practical solutions.

Cox, T., Jr. (1994). *Cultural diversity in organizations: Theory, research, and practice*. San Francisco, CA: Berrett-Koehler.

> This book is based on a new conceptual model called the Interactional Model of Cultural Diversity (IMCD). The three major components that constitute a climate of diversity in organizations include individual factors, group/intergroup factors, and organizational factors. This book is extremely useful for those interested in studying prejudice and discrimination in the context of interpersonal relations in various institutions and organizations.

Cross, M., & Keith, M. (Eds.). (1993). *Racism, the city, and the state*. London: Routledge.

> As the title suggests, this edited book examines the re lationship between city, state, and racism from several contributors. The major focus is upon the process of racialization. The authors hold institutional frameworks responsible for producing and sustaining racial segregation

through prejudice and discrimination. This book is a must for those who would like to study the relationship between urban social theory and theories of racism in the context of postmodernity.

Donald, J., & Rattansi, A. (Eds.). (1992). *Race, culture, and difference.* London: Sage.

This edited book focuses on the emerging traditions of postmodernism and poststructuralism through the critical rethinking of cultural aspects of race and racism. It is a very intriguing and provocative book in which new insights are presented about theoretical, pedagogical, and political underpinnings of multiculturalism and antiracism.

D'Souza, D. (1995). *The end of racism: Principles for a multiracial society.* New York: Free Press.

This is a provocative book on the topic of racism. The author argues vehemently that prevalent assumptions about racism and concerns about civil rights in some cases are wrong and in others, obsolete. D'Souza forcefully compels the readers to reexamine their beliefs about racism. He cherishes the ideals of equal rights and advocates justice in the multiracial society of the United States. This book provides a new vision to transcend and combat the pathology of racism in America and offers new strategies to overcome the problems of prejudice and poverty.

Franks, V., & Rothblum, E. D. (Eds.). (1983). *The stereotyping of women: Its effects on mental health.* New York: Springer.

This book is an excellent collection of articles devoted to describing the impact of sex-role stereotypes on women's mental health. As feminists and clinical psychologists, the editors would like to raise women's consciousness about several clinical problems in which women are overrepresented as patients. Some of these problems include agoraphobia, lack of assertion, and sexual dysfunction. As this book is especially intended for mental health professionals, it has a great relevance for working with women clients.

Fulani, L. (Ed.). (1988). *The psychopathology of everyday: Racism and sexism*. New York: Harrington Park.

This enlightening book contends that traditional psychotherapy fails to attend to the concerns of women of color. The major focus of this book is to highlight the issues of women of color in the context of help-seeking behaviors from the institutions of therapy. The contributors maintain that because standards of normalcy in traditional psychotherapy are White, male, middle class, and heterosexual, there is a need to reexamine the role of social institutions that are oppressive in nature for women of color. The authors also propose their own therapies that are emotionally empowering and take into account the personal historical perspectives of the clients.

Gabelko, N. H., & Michaelis, J. U. (1981). *Reducing adolescent prejudice: A handbook*. New York: Teachers College.

This handbook is an excellent guide for those interested in learning prejudice-reduction strategies. The central focus of the book is on developing critical-thinking skills that are prerequisites to reduce prejudice through cognitive sophistication. This book contains valuable and practical "how-to" type information for counselors and teachers. Strategies for identification of discrimination, specification of thinking processes, and emphasis upon valuing those processes that contribute to positive attitudes are highly relevant to reducing prejudice. This handbook is highly recommended for high school counselors and teachers.

Hamm, M. S. (1993). *American skinheads: The criminology and control of hate crime*. Westport: CT: Praeger.

This is an outstanding book that describes the psychological, social, and political dynamics that contribute to the movement of the skinheads. Diverse sociological theories

are woven into an eclectic theory to explain the underlying reasons for the crime and violence committed by skinheads out of sheer hatred. The author believes that Nazism
has its own universal character that prompts its adherents
to engage violently against democratic ideals.

Healey, J. F. (1995). *Race, ethnicity, gender, and class: The sociology of
group conflict and change*. Thousand Oaks, CA: Pine Forge.

Written as a textbook for students interested in the sociology of minority and dominant group relations, this book
discusses discrimination, prejudice, and racial inequalities
as the most daunting, urgent, and challenging issues in the
United States. To enhance intercultural relations, multiple
perspectives, diversity of experiences within different minority groups, and sources of inequalities and injustices are
presented. The contributions of the minority groups to the
success of American society are highlighted.

Helms, J. E. (Ed.). (1990). *Black and White racial identity: Theory,
research, and practice*. Westport, CT: Praeger.

In this edited book, issues relating to theory, research, and
practical applications of racial identity development are
discussed at length. The central focus of this book is on the
development of Black identity and White identity. The role
of racism that contributes to two separate processes of
Black and White identities is underscored. The authors assert that because racism is a part of the cultural milieu, it
can easily become part of a person's racial identity or consciousness.

Hong, M. (Ed.). (1993). *Growing up Asian American: An anthology*.
New York: Morrow.

A number of contributors who are Asian Indians, Chinese,
Japanese, Koreans, and Philippinos present their personal
life experiences as Asian Americans. In the context of ethnicity, the common bond among these writers is self-evi-
dent. The autobiographical accounts of writers include hor-

rifying experiences of interethnic hostilities and hatred. Different perspectives of growing up as Asian Americans are presented. This book is a collection of personal stories enriched with eloquence and passion.

Jackman, M. R. (1994). *The velvet grove: Paternalism and conflict in gender, class, and race relations*. Berkeley, CA: University of California.

This book is a scholarly analysis of the coercive tactics and persuasions that create, maintain, and sustain inequalities in intergroup relations. The author argues that inequality among races, genders, and various social groups can be attributed to the distribution of limited resources. Prejudice and discrimination are explained from another angle in which expropriation of resources from one group to another causes racial, gender, and class conflicts. This book is also an excellent study of the psychodynamics between unequal groups as they engage in the psychological interplay of dominance and subordination.

Kochman, T. (1981). *Black and White: Styles in conflict*. Chicago, IL: University of Chicago.

This book illuminates the potentials for conflict and misunderstandings in interethnic communications. The major theme of this book centers around the idea that cultural differences among African Americans and European Americans play a covert role in communications that are of great social significance. The understanding of stylistic conflicts in Blacks and Whites are also of paramount importance in counseling and psychotherapy. Problems arise in therapeutic alliances when different Black cultural values and communication styles are perceived as deviant from those of the majority European American culture.

Monk, R. C. (Ed.). (1996). *Taking sides: Clashing views on controversial issues in race and ethnicity* (2nd ed.). Guilford, CT: Dushkin.

Designed to enhance critical thinking about controversial issues relating to race and ethnicity, this book is written in the style of a debate. Both pro and con views are presented on 20 major issues from the perspectives of leading sociologists, political pundits, and prominent historians. This book covers some major themes that are representative of the burning issues in the field of race and ethnic relations.

Paniagua, F. A. (1994). *Assessing and treating culturally diverse clients*. Thousand Oaks, CA: Sage.

This is an excellent book for counselors and other mental health practitioners interested in culturally fair assessment of their culturally diverse clients. The main focus of this book is on the identification of cultural variables that may have negative or detrimental effects on counseling practices. This book is a valuable guide to conducting cross-cultural assessments.

Pedersen, P. B., & Ivey, A. (1994). *Culture-centered counseling and interviwing skills*. Westport, CT: Praeger.

Written as a practical guide, this skill-based book emphasizes the importance of intercultural similarities and differences in counseling. Based on data from 55 countries, a model of four synthetic cultures is proposed. This culture-based framework is useful for counselors to understand their clients from different cultures without prejudice and unintentional biases.

Perlmutter, P. (1992). *Divided we fall: A history of ethnic, religious, and racial prejudice in America*. Ames, IA: Iowa State University.

This is a provocative book drenched with historical information about bigotry, racism, and hatred in America and all around the world. Bigotry as a process that does injustices to others is the central theme of this book. The author argues vehemently for ensuring equal opportunities for all and is very concerned about preferential treatment for a few selected groups. He also sounds an alarm that unchecked group rights would make America a nation that is disunited and divided. This author apparently is against the percepts of multiculturalism, but the book is interesting to read for different perspectives.

Pluhar, E. B. (1995). *Beyond prejudice: The moral significance of human and nonhuman animals*. Durham, NC: Duke University.

This book consists of a number of philosophical moral precepts that extend beyond the personal concerns of humans. Pluhar's arguments against human "superiority" have long-range ramifications concerning animal cruelty. The author posits that exploitation of nonhumans by humans is an act of unforgivable prejudice and discrimination and cannot be justified. This book is a scholarly analysis of a plethora of moral questions relating to animal interests that have been historically ignored by humans.

Ponterotto, J. G., & Pedersen, P. B. (1993). *Preventing prejudice: A guide for counselors and educators*. Newbury Park, CA: Sage.

The authors highlight the significance of the indispensable role educators and counselors can play in preventing prejudice. *Preventing Prejudice* is a practical model that delineates various strategies and mechanisms to improve interracial and intercultural relations. In addition to covering the psychodynamics that contribute to the development, continuation, and prevalence of prejudice, the authors offer practical solutions to prevent, combat, and eliminate prejudice. This book is highly recommended for counselors and educators who are interested in improving race relations.

Reardon, B. A. (1995). *Educating for human dignity: Learning about rights and responsibilities*. Philadelphia, PA: University of Pennsylvania.

Human dignity and integrity are presented as the two core and symbiotic concepts that lie at the center of ethical and social values systems. The author maintains that these two values are the heart and soul of the move to combat racism and sexism. An extensive and detailed human rights curricula is proposed to cultivate abilities in students grades K–12 to take principled positions on issues relating to human dignity and human rights.

Ridley, C. R. (1995). *Overcoming unintentional racism in counseling and therapy: A practitioner's guide*. Thousand Oaks, CA: Sage.

This is an excellent book for counselors and psychotherapists concerned about the insidiousness of their unintentional prejudice and racism. The book is replete with clinical examples to caution practitioners against the unintended discriminatory practices that could render their counseling efforts inadvertently ineffective. This practical guide not only provides a scholarly analysis of the problems of racism, but also equips mental health professionals with concrete and practical solutions.

Simpson, G. E., & Yinger, J. M. (1985). *Racial and cultural minorities: An analysis of prejudice and discrimination* (5th ed.). New York: Plenum.

This is one of the classic textbooks on the subject of prejudice and discrimination. It provides some guiding principles and concepts that are indispensable to conducting intensive study of minority-majority relations at all levels. The authors have also tried to present intercultural and interethnic relations within a much broader scope of sciences that explain human behaviors. This book is highly recommended for those interested in prejudice reduction plans and strategies.

Smith, M. P., & Feagin, J. R. (Eds.). (1995). *The bubbling cauldron: Race, ethnicity, and urban crisis*. Minneapolis, MN: The University of Minnesota.

This edited book is a collection of 16 articles contributed by 19 authors. The major focus of the book is on the significance of "race" in U.S. society. The authors postulate that racial differences have historically played a major role in the power structures of American society. This power structure is evident in state politics, which generally represent a racialized legalized order of ethnic domination of the majority group over minority ethnic groups. The authors argue that White majority shape public opinions that determine state policies that could be detrimental to the interests and welfare of other racial groups.

Sniderman, P. M., Tetlock, P. E., & Carmines, E. G. (Eds.). (1993). *Prejudice, politics, and the American dilemma.* Stanford, CA: Stanford University.

This book is a fresh attempt to understand prejudice, politics, and the American racial dilemma from new angles. There is a deliberate attempt to study race issues by focusing on Whites and as well as Blacks. The contributors assert that race is not only a White man's problem. To understand the difficulty and poignancy of these issues, it is imperative that they are viewed from perspectives of both Whites and Blacks.

Glossary

ACCULTURATION: This is the process by which one group (generally a minority or immigrant group) learns and acquires the cultural patterns of another group (generally the dominant group; Healey, 1995).

AFFIRMATIVE ACTION: The term *affirmative action* first appeared in the 1964 Civil Rights Act, and in 1965 President Johnson incorporated it into Executive Order 11246. It embodies two major concepts: (a) nondiscrimination requires the elimination of all existing discriminatory conditions, whether purposeful or inadvertent; and (b) affirmative action requires that employers make additional efforts to recruit, employ, and promote qualified members of groups formerly excluded. It rests on the conviction that the long-range goal of equal opportunity cannot be realized without color-sensitive and gender-sensitive policies in the present (Berry, 1984).

AFROCENTRICITY: The Afrocentric frame of reference is a view of phenomenon from the perspective of the African person. In every situation, the Afrocentric approach seeks the appropriate centrality of the African person (Asante, 1991b).

AFROCENTRIC MOVEMENT: This is a renewed emphasis on Black culture and Black consciousness. This emphasis has taken many forms, which have included an African identity with traditional African names, African clothing, a demand for the institutionalization of African American holidays and celebrations, a renewed interest in Malcolm X and his political philosophy, and Black power. The Afrocentric Movement calls for Afrocentric rather than Eurocentric curriculum in higher education and more African American faculty and administrators (Tryman, 1992).

AGEISM: Ageism represents a significant barrier to empowerment for older adults. According to Whitbourne and Hulicka (1990), ageism is characterized by a combination of stereotypes, prejudice, myths, negative attitudes, various forms of outright discrimination, and attempts to avoid contact with aging and elderly persons.

AMERICAN DILEMMA: Myrdal defined this first in 1944 as a disparity between American ideals of egalitarianism and lofty national standards on one hand and economic, cultural, political forces and personal and societal double standards on the other hand, which contribute to prejudicial and discriminatory practices in real life. Liberty and justice for all is preached, but justice does become blind to the ability of the "almighty dollar" to protect the elite. The real dilemma is between "shoulds" and "woulds"—when at the cognitive plane one thinks idealistically, but in real-life situations one acts at the affective level.

ANTIRACISM ASSERTION: This term refers to the process of dealing with racism without aggression and without yielding to it passively.

ANTI-SEMITISM: refers to prejudiced attitudes or ideological racism directed specifically at Jewish persons. (Healey, 1995).

AMERICANIZATION OR ANGLOCONFORMITY: This kind of assimilation was designed to maintain the predominance of the British-type institutional patterns created during the early years of American society. Under Angloconformity there is relatively little sharing of cultural traits, and immigrant and minority groups are expected to adapt to Anglo-American culture as quickly as possible.

ANTIRACISM: This can be defined as a conscious rejection of the belief in any one race's inferiority or superiority. This in turn leads to a rejection of the necessity for institutional reinforcement of racism for personal acts of prejudice and discrimination needed to affirm racial superiority (Aptheker, 1993).

APARTHEID: Apartheid was a policy of extreme racial segregation formerly followed in South Africa (Healey, 1995).

ASSIMILATION: This is a process in which formerly distinct and separate groups merge. As a society undergoes assimilation, differences between groups begin to decrease. Greater participation in the society's political, economic, and social institutions is observed as minority groups become socially and culturally fused with the dominant group.

AUTHORITARIAN PERSONALITY: An authoritarian personality is often motivated by biased, inappropriate, hasty conclusions that are not based on adequate reality testing. Traits of the authoritarian personality include inflexibility, contempt for weakness, aggressive tendencies, and a lack of self-awareness (Axelson, 1993).

BIPHOBIA: This term is defined as an illogical fear and discomfort with people who are or are thought to be bisexual. Biphobia often leads to intolerance, bigotry, and violence against anyone not acting within heterosexual norms (Schreier, 1995).

BIGOTRY: Bigotry describes the intolerance of one who cannot or refuses to accept others who are different in appearance, hold different beliefs, or possess some other trait(s) that conflicts with the person's own strongly held beliefs. (Kleg, 1993).

THE BLACK NATIONALIST MOVEMENT: Founded in Detroit in 1930 by Wali Farad, this is a completely American brand of Islam. The members identify themselves with the ancient lost tribe of Shabazz.

COERCIVE ACCULTURATION: This phenomenom occurs when a group's culture (i.e., an immigrant or minority group) is attacked, their languages and religions are forbidden, and their institutions are undermined by the majority group. In the late 19th century, immigrants from Europe arriving at the U.S. ports of entry and Native Americans on the reservations were subjected to a policy of coercive acculturation, or forced Americanization. A prime example was the Dawes Allotment Act of 1887, an attempt to transform Native Americans into independent farmers and impose Western notions of private property and land ownership on the tribes. The legislation sought to circumvent the broader kinship, clan, and tribal social structures and replace them with more Western or Americanized systems featuring individualistic, profit-oriented systems (Cornell, 1988).

CULTURE: Culture is what has been learned from experiences in the enviornment and is reflected, shared, and transmitted by the members of a particular society.

CULTURAL AMBIVALENCE: Culturally ambivalent counselors are preoccupied with their own issues about race. As a result, they are less attuned to the psychological conflicts and unresolved issues of their clients.

CULTURAL COUNTERTRANSFERENCE: Cultural countertransference involves the projection of emotional reactions from the therapist of one race onto the client of another race (Ridley, 1995). The mere presence of the client may spark intense emotions in the therapist.

CULTURAL DISCONTINUITY HYPOTHESIS: The cultural discontinuity hypothesis assumes that culturally based differences in the communication styles found in the homes of minority students and in the Anglo culture of the school will lead to conflicts, misunderstandings, and ultimately failure for those students (Monk, 1996).

CULTURAL EMPATHY: Cultural empathy is the ability of counselors to understand and communicate the concerns of clients from their cultural perspective.

CULTURAL ENCAPSULATION: Wrenn (1985) described the dangers of cultural encapsulation among counselors seeking absolutist solutions to ethical problems. Culturally encapsulated counselors tend to be insensitive to cultural variations, define everyone's reality according to their own cultural assumptions, minimize cultural differences, and embrace cultural biases and stereotypes.

CULTURAL LAG: This term refers to the period of time it takes a culture to approximate a goal that is valued by the society.

CULTURAL MISOGYNY: This refers to the devaluation of feminine traits and the hatred of women that is learned and internalized by both men and women (Saakvitne & Pearlman, 1993).

CULTURAL RACISM: Cultural racism describes the beliefs, feelings, and behaviors of the members of a cultural group that assert the categorical superiority of the accomplishments, achievements, possessions, methods, and members of their own group over those of other groups based on the differences in the racial composition of the groups (Jones, 1981).

CULTURAL RELATIVISM: Cultural relativity is the idea that to eliminate cultural biases a behavior must be judged first in relation to the context of the culture in which it occurs (Axelson, 1993, Hall, 1976). This concept makes any comparative appraisal or cross-cultural analysis more difficult, if not impossible.

CULTURAL TRANSFERENCE: Cultural transference involves the emotional reactions of a client of one race transferred to the therapist of another race (Ridley, 1995).

CULTURAL UNIVERSALS: The idea of cultural universals implies a fundamental uniformity behind the seemingly endless diversity of cultural patterns (Axelson, 1993, p. 161).

CULTURE SHOCK: Culture shock is a condition in which an individual who has formerly been exposed to another culture may find situations in a new culture exceedingly uncomfortable. The individual may become somewhat dysfunctional in a number of social aspects (Kleg, 1993).

DE FACTO SEGREGATION: The pattern of racial separation and inequality outside the South is often called de facto segregation: segregation resulting from the apparently voluntary choices of both the dominant and minority groups. Theoretically, no person, law, policy, or specific group is responsible for de facto segregation; it "just happens" as people and groups make decisions about where to live and work. Regardless of who or what was responsible for these patterns, African American communities outside the South have faced more poverty, higher rates of unemployment, and lower quality housing and schools than have the White communities (Healey, 1995).

DEFAMATION: Defamation involves denigration of a group by communication. This may be verbal or written. Among the acts of defamation are jokes, labeling, name-calling, and accusations. Defamation may occur at either the intrasocial or intersocial levels.

DE JURE SEGREGATION: This describes the system of rigid competitive race relations that followed reconstruction in the South. The system lasted from the 1880s until the 1960s and was characterized by laws that mandated racial separation and inequality (Healey, 1995).

DISCRIMINATION: Discrimination is unequal and unfavorable treatment or actions that, when directed toward a target group or its members, limit the economic, social, and political opportunities of that group.

EMPOWERMENT: This term refers in most cases to self-direction and self-determination. Solomon (1976) described empowerment as the process of assisting persons who belong to a stigmatized or marginalized social category to develop and increase skills in the exercise of interpersonal influence and the performance of valued social roles. For the marginalized or powerless group, this process includes becoming aware of the power dynamics in their lives, developing and exercising the skills needed to gain some reasonable control over their lives (without infringing on the rights of others), and supporting the empowerment of others within their community (McWhirter, 1994).

EQUAL STATUS CONTACT HYPOTHESIS: This hypothesis asserts that to reduce prejudice, equal status and cooperative contacts between groups needs to occur (Healey, 1995).

EQUITY IN EDUCATION: This does not mean stifling some voices so that others may be heard; it does not demand the compromising academic standards in the name of egalitarianism. It is a process meant to create new standards that accommodate and nurture differences (Gerlach & Hart, 1992, p. 50).

ETHNIC GROUP: An ethnic group or "ethnos" consists of individuals who share a distinct social and cultural heritage and are united by ties of cultural homogeneity that result in a common way of perceiving, thinking, feeling, and interacting with reality (Kleg, 1993). Yinger (1976) defined an ethnic group as a segment of a larger society whose members are thought, by themselves and/or others, to have a common origin that is passed on from one generation to the next, share important segments of a common culture, and participate in shared activities in which the common origin and culture are significant ingredients.

ETHNIC PREJUDICE: Ethnic prejudice is a negative belief or generalization about a group or a member of that group that is justified on the basis of physical characteristics, such as skin color, or on behaviors or beliefs common to a group that set it apart (Bryant, 1994).

ETHNOCENTRISM: This is a term used by anthropolgists and sociologists to denote a belief that the culture of one's own group is the center of everything—the standard by which all other societies, groups, and life styles are judged or rated (Axelson, 1993).

ETHNOCIDE: In contrast to genocide, ethnocide refers to the suppression of a religion, language, culture and so on, which causes a group to disappear without mass killing (Chalk & Jonassohn, 1990).

GENOCIDE: Genocide is a deliberate and one-sided mass killing committed by a state or other authority with the intent to destroy a group, as that group and membership in it are defined by the perpetrator (Chalk & Jonassohn, 1990). This also refers to acts committed with the intent to destroy, in whole or in part, a national, ethnical, racial, or religious group. Such acts include killing members of the group, preventing births from occurring within the group, and imposing life conditions on the group designed to bring about the physical destruction of the group (United Nations, 1966/1948).

HATE CRIMES: Herek (1988) described hate crimes as actions or words, motivated by prejudice, which are intended to harm or intimidate an individual because of his or her membership in a minority group. Hate crimes include violent assaults, murder, rape, property crimes, and verbal and physical threats of violence and/or other acts of intimidation.

HATE GROUPS: A hate group is any organization with policies and programs based primarily on hostility and hatred toward one or more minority groups.

HATRED: Hatred is a deep-rooted negative feeling that makes a person constantly desire the extinction of the object of hate.

HETEROSEXISM: Heterosexism is a belief in the inherent superiority of demonstrating love only toward members of the opposite sex, and therefore the idea that heterosexuality is, and should be, the normal, healthy, dominant societal norm for sexual orientation. Heterosexism presumes that all people are heterosexual, and those persons who are homosexual are viewed as abnormal, deviant, or pathological (Dworkin & Gutierrez, 1992; Schreier, 1995).

HOMOPHOBIA: This is a term used to describe the excessive irrational fear of contact with people who are, or who are presumed to be, gay or lesbian (Weinberg, 1972; Dworkin and Gutierrez, 1992).

IDEOLOGICAL RACISM: This describes a belief system that asserts that a particular group is inferior.

INDIVIDUAL RACISM: Individual racism includes individual thoughts, feelings, and behaviors often motivated by inflexible attitudes of inherent superiority assumed by a person in relation to others who are consequently viewed as inferior. Axelson (1993) provided some examples of individual racism: the belief in White supremacy, the belief that Blacks or other minority groups are genetically inferior, and the belief that Native Americans are primitive and savage or that most are alcoholic.

INSTITUTIONAL RACISM: This term describes the function, form, and practices followed by many "educational, economic, social, and political institutions or structures [that] intentionally or unintentionally perpetuate inequality based on racial preconceptions). The Kerner Report is a prime example, with at least 12 deeply held grievances and three levels of intensity: (a) police practices, (b) unemployment and underemployment, and (c) inadequate housing (Axelson, 1993, 174).

Institutional racism refers to a pattern of unequal treatment based on group membership, race, and racial preconceptions that is built into the daily operations of many educational, economic, social and political institutions in society. The various forms, functions, and practices of institutional racism, whether intentional or unintentional, perpetuate inequality. It also represents a social system in which race is the major criterion of role assignment, role rewards, and socialization on a positive or negative basis, depending upon the structure of the racial caste hierarchy (Kinloch, 1974, p, 214).

Institutional racism actually has two meanings. First, it is the institutional extension of individual racist beliefs; this consists primarily of using and manipulating duly constituted institutions to maintain a racist advantage over others. Second, it is the byproduct of certain institutional practices that operate to restrict on a racial basis the choices, rights, mobility, and access of groups of individuals.

INTERCULTURAL SENSITIVITY: This refers to the practice of being sensitive to the importance of cultural differences and to the points of view held by people in other cultures (Bhawuk & Brislin, 1992).

INTOLERANCE: Intolerance refers to a generalized tendency to respond negatively to the behaviors, thoughts, customs, and beliefs of outgroups (Duckitt, 1992).

KWANZA: Kwanza is a movement that seeks to establish, express, and celebrate aspects of African American cultural identity. Although not considered a religion, the followers of Kwanza are expected to live by principles of self-determination, collective work and responsibility, collective sharing, purpose, creativity, and faith. Some of the ritualistic aspects were first created in 1966 by activist Maulana Karenga. Kwanza is derived from the Swahili word *kwanza,* which means first (Axelson, 1993).

MINORITY: Wirth (1945) provided a classic definition of a minority:

A group of people who, because of physical or cultural characteristics, are singled out from others in the society in which they live for differential and unequal treatment, and who therefore regard themselves as objects of collective discrimination.... Minority status carries with it the exclusion from full participation in the life of the society. (p. 347)

Axelson (1993) has identified three types of minorities. A racial minority refers to members of those groups who are readily identified by distinctive physical characteristics perceived as different from members of the dominant group in a society. Skin color, hair type, body structure, shape of head or nose or eyes, and color of eyes are often singled out as "different."

Ethnic minorities are usually identified by cultural practices such as language, accent, religion, customs, beliefs, and styles of living.

Although the term *minority* literally means numbering less than half, it does not customarily refer to numerical size when it is used to describe groups of people. For example, when women are described as a minority, the term refers to their political, economic, and social status and freedom in relation to men in the society. Minority status has more to do with the distribution of resources and power than with simple numbers: (a) economic inequality based on ownership or control of property, wealth, and income (class); (b) differences in prestige between groups, or the amount of honor, esteem, or respect given to us by others; or (c) inequality of power, ability to influence others, have decision-making power in the society.

MULTICULTURALISM: This is an umbrella term for a variety of programs and ideas that stress mutual respect for all groups and for the multiple heritages that shaped the United States.

THE NOEL HYPOTHESIS: Sociologist Donald Noel (1968) postulated that some form of racial or ethnic stratification will result if two or more groups come together in a contact situation characterized by ethnocentrism, competition, and a differential in power.

POGROMS: This is the term for government-sponsored attacks or riots aimed at Jews in Eastern Europe and Russia (Healey, 1995).

POLITICAL CORRECTNESS: Political correctness is a political/ideological movement on college campuses and elsewhere in the 1990s that seeks expanded pluralistic diversity in American society, often by government mandate and often by pervading educational curricula, on behalf of disadvantaged groups. The term *political correctness* is used to refer to a liberal orthodoxy that includes, for example, supporting affirmative action programs and quota systems, outlawing hate speech, viewing Black crime solely as a byproduct of a racist system, favoring minority persons over majority persons, requiring multicultural education, requiring instruction in feminist beliefs as part of general education, downplaying European and male influences on Western civilization, and teaching students to think critically about European culture but not about non-European culture (Axelson, 1993, p 167).

POWERLESS: To be powerless is to be unable to take charge and direct the course of one's life due to societal conditions, power dynamics, lack of skills, and/or a disbelief that one can change one's life (McWhirter, 1994).

PREJUDICE: *Prejudice* is a Latin word meaning prejudging without knowing the facts. In his classic book, *The Nature of Prejudice*, Allport (1954) defined prejudice as "an antipathy based on a faulty and inflexible generalization. It may be felt or expressed. It may be directed toward a group as a whole, or toward an individual because he is a member of that group" (p. 9). Axelson

(1993) proposed that prejudice represents the emotional aspect of racism.

PSYCHOLOGICAL VIOLENCE: Psychological violence exits when power is used to dehumanize a person or to willfully destroy or impair a person's self-esteem, happiness, competence, respect, or dignity as a human being (O'Neil, 1993).

RACISM: This concept involves a belief system largely based on stereotypes that holds that some races are inherently superior to others, thus defending certain social advantages by systematically denying access to opportunities or privileges to members of racial groups deemed inferior (Axelson, 1993; Ridley, 1995).

Kinloch (1974) wrote: "Racism thus becomes a societal tradition, reinforced by stereotypes and cultural norms" (p. 5).

SCAPEGOAT HYPOTHESIS: This theory of prejudice promotes the idea that under certain conditions people will use substitute groups as the targets of aggression (Healey, 1995).

SEXISM: According to Lorde (1984), sexism is the belief that one sex is inherently superior to the other and by virtue of this superiority has the right to dominance.

SEGREGATION: Segregation inscribes racism in space; it leaves its mark on the geopolitical organization of a country or the more limited organization of a town (Wieviorka, 1995, p. 55).

SEGREGATION: Segregation is the policy or practice of socially separating people, usually based on race or class.

SEXUAL HARASSMENT: Sexual harassment refers to unwanted sexually oriented behaviors such as sexual comments or jokes, offensive touching, or attempts to coerce compliance with or punish rejection of sexual advances. It is the most recent form of victimization of women to be redefined as a social rather than a personal problem, following rape and wife abuse. A sizable proportion of women surveyed in a wide variety of work settings reported being subject to circumstances characteristic of sexual harassment (Riger, 1991).

SOCIAL DISTANCE: Generally speaking, social distance refers to the grades and degrees of understanding and intimacy that characterize personal and social relations. More specifically, it refers to the degree of intimacy to which a person is willing to admit members of other classes (Healey, 1995).

SYMBOLIC RACISM: Symbolic racism is a more subtle, complex, and indirect way to express negative feelings toward minority groups and opposition to change in dominant-minority relations (see Bobo, 1988; Kinder & Sears, 1981; McConahy, 1986; Sears, 1988). Symbolic racism consists of three primary beliefs: (a) There is no longer any serious or important discrimination in American society; (b) continuing patterns of racial or ethnic inequality are the fault of the minority group themselves (if they would just work harder and apply themselves to jobs and school more diligently, inequality would soon disappear); and (c) since discrimination has largely ended, minority groups are the cause of their own problems with their demands for preferential treatment or special programs, which are unfair and unjustified.

STEREOTYPING: Stereotyping may be broadly defined as rigid preconceptions or overgeneralizations applied to a group of people or to an individual over a period of time, regardless of individual variations (Atkinson, Morten, & Sue, 1979).

WORLDVIEW: A worldview refers to the way a cultural group perceives people and events. It may be broadly defined as how a person perceives his or her relationship to the world (nature, institutions, other people, and things). Worldviews are highly correlated with a person's cultural upbringing and life experiences. Not only are they composed of our attitudes, values, opinions, and concepts, but they may affect how we think, make decisions, behave, and define events (Sue, 1978, p. 419).

XENOPHOBIA: Xenophobia is a fear of strangers. It may account, at least in part, for the process of culture shock (Kleg, 1993, p. 153).

Index